Palgrave Global Media Policy and Business

Series Editors

Petros Iosifidis
City University
London, United Kingdom

Jeanette Steemers
University of Westminster
London, United Kingdom

Gerald Sussman
Portland State University
Portland, Oregon, USA

This innovative series examines the wider social, political, economic and technological changes arising from the globalization of the media and communications industries and assesses their impact on matters of business practice, regulation and policy. Considering media convergence, industry concentration, and new communications practices, the series makes reference to the paradigmatic shift from a system based on national decision-making and the traditions of public service in broadcast and telecommunications delivery to one that is demarcated by commercialization, privatization and monopolization. Bearing in mind this shift, and based on a multi-disciplinary approach, the series tackles three key questions: To what extent do new media developments require changes in regulatory philosophy and objectives? To what extent do new technologies and changing media consumption require changes in business practices and models? And to what extent does privatization alter the creative freedom and public accountability of media enterprises?

More information about this series at
http://www.springer.com/series/14699

Petros Iosifidis • Mark Wheeler

Public Spheres and Mediated Social Networks in the Western Context and Beyond

palgrave
macmillan

Petros Iosifidis
Department of Sociology
City University, London
United Kingdom

Mark Wheeler
Politics and International Relations
London Metropolitan University
London, United Kingdom

Palgrave Global Media Policy and Business
ISBN 978-1-137-41029-0   ISBN 978-1-137-41030-6   (eBook)
DOI 10.1057/978-1-137-41030-6

Library of Congress Control Number: 2016939280

Printed on acid-free paper

This Palgrave Macmillan imprint is published by Springer Nature
The registered company is Macmillan Publishers Ltd. London

FOREWORD

Over the past two decades since the emergence and spread of the Internet, a consensus of sorts has emerged: while there were at first some dismissive voices who contended that it would have little impact on the political world, today most observers concur that, especially in regard to social media, modern communication technologies have impacted profoundly on politics and participation. The problem is that there is still no overarching agreement in terms of how and to what extent this impact takes place, and what significance it has for democratic politics. It has become commonplace to identify 'optimists' and 'pessimists' among the participants in these debates, and while such labels are to some extent valid, they do not, per se, provide us with much analytic insight. All too often in the past, the questions themselves were formulated in a totalising way: *either* the web, with its social media and many affordances, is good for the democracy and the public sphere, *or* it is detrimental—with expectations set on a once-and-for-all answer.

In recent years we have happily seen more nuanced approaches to the web and democracy. These underscore the variegated character of democratic systems and politics; for example, the issue of governance is increasingly added to the more familiar question of the inclusion/exclusion of citizens' communicative participation. Furthermore, public spheres are highlighted as multiplex and historically specific phenomena. Their contingencies cannot be reduced to media technologies, but rather comprise social and cultural dimensions as well, including of course how citizens—and various institutional actors, such as political and economic elites, professional journalists (and increasingly, citizen journalists)—make use of them. Thus, in terms of normatively evaluating the 'success' of any given public sphere phenomenon, one must look beyond, for instance, the extent to which participants follow suitable forms of online deliberation; while important, it is imperative to also take into account a broad array of societal factors.

A key thematic in this regard, present in Habermas' original formulation—and central to what we might in shorthand call the critical tradition—is the question of power relations in regard to public spheres. With all the possible vectors involved, this is by no means an easily speci- fied dimension, and though it has largely not been ignored, it has often been simplified. Here too, more recent research is widening its perspec- tive: the role of the web in public spheres is seen as shaped by features having to do with its political economy, its technical attributes, its social usages and habitus—and how all of these aspects intersect with broader societal dynamics of power.

This growth of insight into what the analysis of public spheres and media technologies actually entails—this cumulative awareness of what is involved on this terrain—is manifested most impressively in this book by Petros Iosifidis and Mark Wheeler. Using an ambitious and innovative conceptual frame, they ask difficult questions regarding public spheres and social media—about governance, hierarchical power relationships and civic participation. The authors explore wider patterns of political communication among citizens, organisations and institutionalised actors, not least the recent rise in populist discourses. They probe the status of journalism and the capacities of power elites to shape online political communication. On a deeper level, there is an investigation of the communicative dynamics between knowledge and igno- rance, and what they mean for democratic ideals and civic practices.

To answer these questions, Iosifidis and Wheeler take an approach that is both unusual in this research field and highly laudable: after their initial frame-establishing conceptual discussions, they turn to a comparative analysis, examining materials deriving from both Western liberal democra- cies and the so-called BRICS countries—which represent an array of both struggling democracies and authoritarian regimes. The mutually illuminated set of findings and conclusions are highly gratifying. Iosifidis and Wheeler are probably indifferent to whether they are called pessimists or optimists; instead they have provided us with a truly fine contribution, a major leap forward in our knowledge and understanding. I am sure the authors would not claim that it offers once-and-for-all answers, but what they have written will no doubt elicit much appreciation—and considerable agreement.

Lund University

Peter Dahlgren
Lund, Sweden

CONTENTS

LIST OF TABLES

CHAPTER 1

Introduction

There has been widespread discussion about the political and economic potential of online media and social networks, their contribution to changes in working and living practices, and growth rates, alongside their enhancement of democratic practices, public sphere and civic cultures, and citizen responsibility and participation. In particular, Web 2.0—the second generation of the World Wide Web, focused on the public collaboration and sharing of information online—has facilitated computer-mediated tools that allow for the creation and exchange of ideas across virtual communities. This emergence of so-called social media has provided the technological and ideological foundation for the production of user-generated content.

These changes have gone hand in hand with the rise of an era in modern politics which has been described as either post-democracy or late modernity. Several political sociologists have defined the period as one characterised by major transformations in democratic values (Beck 1992; Giddens 1991; Lash 1990). Henrik Bang (2004) has argued a discursive form of political activism in which solidarity exists but is not tied to any notion of the common good or of a particular ideology. Bang contends that new types of representation have emerged outside the mainstream political institutions, as citizens have only minimal interest in party politics. Rather than aspire to the duties of citizenship, these virtuous 'everyday makers' want to feel 'involved' in their communities and are taking part

© The Editor(s) (if applicable) and The Author(s) 2016   1
P. Iosifidis, M. Wheeler, *Public Spheres and Mediated
Social Networks in the Western Context and Beyond*,
DOI 10.1057/978-1-137-41030-6_1

in small local narratives founded on a mutuality of interests. Therefore, as political activity is no longer based on ideology and membership, politicians must engage on a continuing basis with citizens to persuade them to participate, as Bang:

> identifies a shift away from an input–output model of politics, in which citizens via parties etc., were negotiated and aggregated into policy outputs by governments, to a recursive one, in which the demo-elite, operating through the political system acts: "in its own terms and on its own values, thereby shaping and constructing societal interests and identity". (Marsh et al. 2010:329)

Consequently, this reformulated view of participatory practices has witnessed a change in the relationship between the citizen and political classes. This reflexivity demands that politicians engage in a more personalised and less ideological set of political communication. Thus, Bang argues, Obama's 2008 Democratic presidential campaign directly interacted with everyday makers through innovative use of new information and communications technologies (ICTs). He notes that MyBarackObama.com (MyBo) mobilised the democratic input of over two million users, and from the 100,000 profiles available, 35,000 affinity groups were organised at a community level. This commonwealth of local associations comprised grassroots activists drawn from youth and ethnic minority delegates, working in an inclusive and relational manner (Bang 2009). Obama thus defined a political image which was founded on reciprocity and shared meaning, and which encouraged popular scrutiny of his political deliberations (Cogburn and Espinoza-Vasquez 2011:205).

Bang's work concerning the reformulation of democratic relations between the political elites and the public ties in with John Keane's vision of 'monitory democracy' (Keane 2009a). Effectively, Keane argues that since 1945, governmental or parliamentary forms of democratic practice have declined. Therefore, the central grip of elections, parties and representative assemblies has weakened, and behaviour in 'all fields of social and political life [has] come to be scrutinized...by a whole host of non-party, extra-parliamentary and often unelected bodies operating within and underneath and beyond the boundaries of territorial states' (Keane 2009b).

These alternative types of accountability are linked with monitoring mechanisms founded on consumer preference, customer voting and networks of redistributed power. The new monitoring formations have included concepts of 'empowerment', 'high-energy democracy', 'stake-holders', 'participatory governance' and 'communicative democracy'. Keane contends that monitory democracy is closely associated with the rise of the new multimedia and Internet communications technologies. Late modernists suggest that the technological revolution replaces hierarchical power with a distributive form of network governance and a constantly evolving version of contemporary democracy (Marsh et al. 2010:326).

These horizontal forms of information were identified by Manual Castells, who argued that such flow of communication has led to overlapping and interlinked devices through which multiple ideas and scrutiny may occur (Castells 2012). For instance, the older mechanisms of media accountability have been replaced by myriad citizen-generated discussion groups. In turn, Castells contends, the networked society facilitates new types of political solidarity through alternative forms of social capital and the construction of grassroots engagement. Clay Shirky maintains that it has become easy to dismantle the barriers to collective action (Shirky 2009). The social media enable a self-directed open source to mobilise against repression, special interests and hermetically sealed ideologies. Such dispersal of power means that cyberspace will create a public sphere which circumvents dominant interests, enabling grassroots organisations to propagate their values (Castells 2012:11).

Moreover, Internet content has witnessed a move away from journalistic 'objectivity', to the 'subjectivity' of bloggers, social networking and citizen journalism. In this context, the malleability of 'hype' has been viewed as a profundity in which everyone's opinions are of equal worth. Thus, one may contend that these power-scrutinising innovations enfranchise citizens through the formation of 'bully pulpits' in which there exists 'one person, many interests, many voices, multiple votes and multiple representatives' (Keane 2009a).

Such arguments have focused on the relative value of voice and output against the requirements of aggregated input and agency to define a normative position of post-democratic behaviour. Marsh et al. (2010:330), however, question the political validity of such activities. First, to what extent have the politics of late modernity actually witnessed a rise of network governance and a decline in hierarchical relations? Second, does such a reliance on 'voice' to garner support from laypersons ignore traditional sources of information? Third, and most important, to what degree do these contentions ignore the structured inequalities, as political elites market themselves through the traditional media and social media to the public?

Similarly, the desirability of consumer-led forms of scrutiny may be seen to underestimate the divisions which exist in modern democracies. In failing to address the nature of power in post-democratic societies, the focus on output does not deal with matters of inequality and may be seen to reinforce fears concerning the democratic deficit. In particular, practices of late modernity may be suggested to favour the voices of the ill-informed over the enlightened. Thus populist attitudes define a distorted version of the common good, and these reconfigured forms of behaviour may operate akin to what Alexis de Tocqueville termed 'soft tyranny' (de Tocqueville 1830). In effect, normative democratic ideals have been undermined by the vagaries of public opinion, conformity to material security, the absence of intellectual freedom and the prejudices of the ignorant.

Consequently, such approaches provide only a partial analysis of the true worth of Internet politics. If the normative expectations of the politics of social media are limited to the measurement of voice and output alone, we can posit that such activity has no greater merit than in relaying the values of the demo-elite to the public or allowing disaffected oppositional groups the means through which to articulate their interests to the public. And as Shirky has noted, the dangers of overabundance have led to varied and uneven levels of participation (Shirky 2011).

Therefore, for Web 2.0 politics to have appropriate value, it must enhance civic virtues through the mechanisms of input and agency as much as illustrating the openings for voice and output. For the online political classes to have democratic worth, they need to demonstrate ideological substance and provide clarity to a fixed range of meanings such that people achieve a real sense of connection with a cause. To this end, social media should provide the representational basis upon which citizens can participate in terms of their own political efficacy to define in a wider sense the common good.

In effect, the Internet holds the potential for a fuller realisation of a democratic set of public spheres in which a true level of engagement and fulfilment will occur (Habermas 1989 [1962]). Social media can facilitate citizenship through the provision of free and accurate information in three important ways. First, individuals will achieve the widest access to information and knowledge to allow them to pursue their rights. Second, citizens will enjoy the broadest range of information, interpretation and debate regarding their political choices, and thus can employ these communication facilities to register criticism and propose alternative courses of action. Finally, individuals will recognise themselves among the multitude of representations offered across a decentralised communications environment wherein they can evolve and extend their levels of representation.

Consequently, social media provide the possibility for radical change in the ways in which public communication takes place, as information diffuses in a faster and wider manner to reach a larger number of people. The interactive nature of the Internet has been a driving force in the technological revolution, allowing for personalised forms of direct communication between the parties and the public. This realisation has inspired the political classes to take to social media to develop political communications strategies in modern election campaigns. These effects have been most notable in Western democracies such as the USA and UK, but have also become apparent in southern states such as India and South Africa. In the summer of 2015, Jeremy Corbyn, the left-wing outsider vying for UK Labour Party leadership, took to Twitter (#JezWeCan) to mobilise youthful political supporters, much to the chagrin of the party grandees and managers (Heritage 2015).

The online networks in turn can empower people to compete against the traditional political classes or media establishment. Totalitarian or despotic regimes in particular have found that it has become nigh impossible to censor or control the social media platforms associated with populist movements in a variety of states, including China, Russian, Iran and Turkey. The rise of the Internet and social media offers the possibility of effective political action, though the democratising power of ICTs varies widely across countries, resulting in different degrees of political and media openness. Conventional economic and political wisdom has been challenged online in southern European countries such as Greece and Spain. Videos like *Kony 2012*, the short film denouncing child abuse in Uganda, garnering more than 30 million views within the first week of its release, or the wave of protests associated with the Arab Spring and the global Occupy movement (an international protest campaign against social and economic inequality), offer illustrative examples of how online communication networks facilitate rapid diffusion of information.

Yet, does this online process actually trigger or reflect a more deep-seated change in public behaviour, from policymaking to political protest and regime change? Can we assume that the online media channel social influence in much the same way as the offline networks—by creating a structure of interactions that facilitates the creation of a new online public sphere and articulates independent decision-making? Moreover, can this political discourse degenerate into personal abuse, ignorance and intolerance? Notably, the social media have been seen to provide the means for extremist and terrorist organisations to engage in the politics of fear at national, regional and global levels. In particular, the Islamic State of Iraq and the Levant (ISIS) successfully utilised computer-mediated tools to propagate its message of a worldwide caliphate and to recruit international sympathisers.

This book critically examines the relevance of the social networks as a public sphere wherein a range of political and sociocultural imperatives may be realised. The central themes of the book address the following questions: Are online and social networks an unstoppable democratising and mobilising force? Is there a need for policy and intervention to ensure the development of comprehensive and inclusive social networking frameworks? The Internet is viewed as both a tool that allows citizens to influence policymaking and an object of new policies and panoptic state regulations, such as data retention, privacy and copyright laws, around which citizens are mobilising.

This volume develops its analysis upon Daniel Hallin and Paulo Mancini's comparative model of media systems with reference to these matters of economic, political and societal development (Hallin and Mancini 2004). A comparative approach is necessary to identify the generic principles that drive the diffusion of online information and set the specificities that different technologies or sociocultural contexts afford. Therefore, examples and cases are drawn from the mature markets of the USA and western Europe, as well as emerging markets from among Brazil, Russia, India, China and South Africa (BRICS) and within other Asian states. As waves of protest sweep both liberal democracies and authoritarian regimes, we delve into a more detailed examination of this rapidly developing field. Through such focus on both mature and emerging markets, our purpose is to draw out the comparative aspects and to strengthen the international character of the project.

To achieve these aims, the book is organised in a tripartite structure:

- Theory and practice
- Western liberal democratic traditions, grassroots politics and the social media
- The rise of the BRICS and online interest

The first section consists of three chapters which examine the evolving online public sphere under the prism of political economy, public policy and democratic participatory values of social media. It asks the questions: Why have the underlying political and capitalist power structures constructed a narrative that has presented marketisation as natural, inevitable and desirable? Can social media contribute to democracy, revolution and expansion of the public sphere, or are they instruments of control and commerce? It also attempts to articulate the public interest framework within a regime of social media governance, and in this context tackles issues such as access, freedom of expression, privacy and intellectual property rights.

The second section of the book focuses on the ostensible political 'content' within the social media, considering issues associated with the representation of mainstream political actors, electoral politics, grassroots or social movements, and traditional and new forms of public diplomacy. It outlines the democratic purposes of social media, while addressing the resonant forms of propaganda and censorship that continue to exist. It includes a discussion of the questions of state or political power against the public interest. This analysis considers the comparative nature of the hybrid forms of traditional and online media systems in modern election campaigns. Another chapter discusses the nature of social movements and the role of the state in disseminating information services. There is also a discussion of the international context concerning the rise of 'public diplomacy 2.0', in which the social media have been used to propagate 'soft power' messages by the US State Department and UK Foreign Office, alongside the international non-government organisations (INGOs), to effect new types of nation branding and diplomatic channels.

The third and final section of the book shifts the focus from mature, liberal democracies to those of non-Western developing countries, as well as authoritarian regimes, and explores the relationship between online mobilisation and policy change in these parts of the world. The proliferation of new technologies and new forms of network action are challenging traditional notions of civil society, and civic action is becoming increasingly flexible in the BRICS and other southern states. The vastly increased access to information which has accompanied the higher rates of digital penetration and the ability to communicate easily and quickly can empower citizens and contribute to democracy in the non-Western world. Conversely, other voices argue that these expectations have been confounded, illuminating the limitations of social media activism, as authoritarian rule has survived or been reconfigured by the Internet to bend the technology to its own purposes. This section considers the role of social networking tools in the creation of an online public sphere, election and political communication strategies, and the initiation of mass protests, uprisings and nationalistic or religious fundamentalist responses in the authoritarian regimes of China and Russia, the Middle East and North African countries, and the post-colonial powers of India and South Africa.

This volume is intended to fill a growing need for research addressing the democratic potential of the Internet and social media. The international nature of innovations in the field of ICTs has necessitated the development of a comparative approach among liberal democracies and non-Western territories, with local variation. The text is addressed to scholars, practitioners and students in social and digital media, and seeks to promote discussion and stimulate thinking in the field.

BIBLIOGRAPHY

Bang H.P. 2004. "Cultural Governance: Governing Reflexive Modernity". *Public Administration* 82(1): 159–190.

Bang H.P. 2009. "'Yes we can': Identity Politics and Project Politics for a Late-modern World". *Urban Research & Practice* 2(2): 117–137.

Beck U. 1992. *Risk Society.* London: Sage Publications.

Castells M. 2012. *Networks of Outrage and Hope: Social Movements in the Internet Age.* Cambridge: Polity.

Cogburn D.L., and F.K. Espinoza-Vasquez. 2011. "From Networked Nominee to Networked Nation: Examining the Impact of Web 2.0 and Social Media on Political Participation and Civic Engagement in the 2008 Obama Campaign". *Journal of Political Marketing* 10(1–2): 189–213.

de Tocqueville A. 1830. *Democracy in America.* Cambridge: Sever and Francis. 1863 reprint Translated by Henry Reeve home page. http://www.books.google.co.uk/books/ democracy in America (accessed September 12, 2010).

Giddens A. 1991. *The Consequence of Modernity.* Stanford, CA: Stanford University Press.

Habermas J. 1989. The Structural Transformation of the Public Sphere: An Inquiry into a Category of Bourgeois Society. Cambridge: Polity Press. Original Work Published 1962.

Hallin D.C., and P. Mancini. 2004. *Comparing Media Systems: Three Models of Media and Politics.* Cambridge: Cambridge University Press.

Heritage S. 2015. "#JezWeCan: Why Jeremy Corbyn gets the Social Media Vote", *The Guardian.* August 4.

Keane J. 2009a. *The Life and Death of Democracy.* New York: Simon and Schuster.

Keane, J. 2009b. "Monitory Democracy and Media-saturated Societies". *Griffith Review*, *Edition 24: Participation Society*. http://www.griffithreview.com/edition-24-participation-society/222-essay/657.html (accessed November 20, 2013).

Lash S. 1990. *The Sociology of Postmodernism*. London: Routledge.

Marsh D., P. 't Hart, and K. Tindall. 2010. "Celebrity Politics: The Politics of the Late Modernity?". *Political Studies Review* 8(3): 322–340.

Shirky C. 2009. *Here Comes Everybody: The Power of Organising without Organisations*. London: Penguin.

Shirky, C. 2011. The Political Power of Social Media: Technology, the Public Sphere, and Political Change, *Foreign Affairs*, January/February issue. http://www.foreignaffairs.com/articles/67038/clay-shirky/the-political-power-of-social-media (accessed March 21, 2014).

PART I

Theory and Practice

CHAPTER 2

Social Media, Public Sphere and Democracy

INTRODUCTION

This chapter provides working definitions of the terms 'network society', 'digital democracy' and 'mediated citizenship', and takes a critical stance as to whether these have acted to shift social dynamics. In the academic writing about democracy, especially with regard to the media, a collective ambivalence emerges, with some writers expressing more optimism and others taking a dimmer view. The questions about democracy become still more complex, not least as modes of citizenship evolve; the gradual shift to what is often dubbed 'mediated citizenship' raises various issues, alongside positive and negative forecasts. Here we explore the literature and academic debate concerning the socio-politics of social media, with particular emphasis on the political value of Web 2.0 technologies. We also analyse the exercise and devolution of power with regard to vertical communication between citizens and government (e.g., with their representatives or agencies). Some efforts in such forms of 'electronic governance' are laudable and facilitate democratic communication. However, others easily fall prey to a power stance that thwarts communication. Recent treatment of power specifically in relation to the media has been addressed by authors such as Coleman and Blumler (2009), who argue that democracy fails to engender relationships of accountability, and advocate an online media commons as a policy course to enhance the democratic character of the role of cyberspace in the public sphere,

P. Iosifidis, M. Wheeler, *Public Spheres and Mediated Social Networks in the Western Context and Beyond*, DOI 10.1057/978-1-137-41030-6_2 a direction similar to the calls for a public service media model in the online world (see, e.g., Iosifidis 2010).

We also address related issues, such as 'reformulated participation', 'consumption' and 'prosumerism', and examine whether these lead to new politics, the reduced role of the state and the increasing empowerment of citizens in the era of electronic governance. One vital issue to be discussed is whether democracy is in fact in serious trouble, and for this assessment, much credence will be given to sceptics such as Putnam (1993, 2000) and Morozov (2012). Putnam has expressed concerns that a 'democratic deficit' has occurred in the form of a collapse of virtue and citizenship, and that this has led to a profound 'thinning' of the political community and the formation of the atomised citizen who is 'bowling alone'. Putnam has argued that new forms of social capital are necessary to reconnect citizens with their societies. Consideration is also given to factors that are conducive to citizen engagement and an inclusive public sphere, and in this context, we refer to Evgeny Morozov's *Net Delusion*. In this volume, Morozov contends that the Internet is a tool that both revolutionaries and authoritarian governments can use, and thus in the latter case, social media sites have been used to entrench dictators and threaten dissidents, making it more difficult to promote democracy. John Keane's cautious view with regard to social media and the public sphere will be explored, as will Henrik Bang's theory of 'everyday makers' in relation to political participation in late modernity.[1] We will also consider the counterarguments, such as Pippa Norris' thesis that democratic engagement has been reinvented for modern times rather than simply atrophied. We look at social media and democracy with a normative eye, but also empirically, and so throughout the book we list a number of examples and cases to validate theoretical points, such as the Arab uprisings and the recent revelations of the extent of US government surveillance of its own citizens and those abroad.

---

[1] Chapter 4 discusses in more detail whether the new communications techniques can overcome the perception of a democratic deficit that has affected modern politics, and contends that Bang's and Keane's approaches provide a partial analysis of the true worth of Internet politics. It demonstrates how Obama's 2008 Democratic presidential campaign directly interacted with everyday makers through the innovative use of new information communication technologies. Similarly, it looks into how Keane's 'monitory democracy' occurred in the UK 2010 general election prime ministerial debates, which brought a heightened level of consumer-led scrutiny to the election, as they placed a focus on political leadership.

The Traditional Public Sphere and the Mass Media

The Traditional Paradigm: The Public Sphere and the Media as the 'Fourth Estate'

In modern democracies, there are typically three branches of government: the legislative branch to make the laws, the executive branch to enforce the laws, and the judicial branch to interpret the laws. However, the rise of mass media has enabled the development of another independent institution, the 'fourth estate', which is central to pluralist democratic processes. The view of the press as the fourth branch of government (or 'fourth estate') is based on the assumption that the media's role is to act as a watchdog of the actions of government. Liberal theorists contend that the existence of an independent press is essential in the process of democratisation and the right of freedom of expression, by strengthening the responsiveness and accountability of governments to all citizens, and by providing a pluralist platform and channel of political expression for a multiplicity of groups and interests (Sen 1999). Under this prism, the media are described as the fourth branch of the government, as they serve a crucial 'checking function', playing a key role in the fortunes of political candidates by ensuring that elected representatives uphold their oath of office and carry out the wishes of the electorate. In this regard, the media act as the custodian of the 'public interest', widening public access to mass media, which in turn promotes democracy and freedom of expression. The widening access to modern technologies—landline telephones, the print and broadcast media, and the new social media—has laid the foundation for an informed citizenry capable of effectively participating in political affairs.

The term 'public communication' in relation to mass media was suggested by Ferguson (1986:ix) to describe 'those processes of information and cultural exchange between media institutions, products and publics which are socially shared, widely available and communal in character'. The context in which these transactions take place is the so-called public sphere, which the political theorist Habermas (1989 [1962]) has articulated as a space for rational and universalistic politics distinct from both the state and the economy, a scene of activity in which people are addressed as citizens, as rational political beings, and not merely as consumers. The concept of the public sphere is a central analytical tool for helping us to make sense of the relationship between the media and democracy (civic engagement). Habermas explained that in the late eighteenth century, a new political class (the bourgeoisie) came to the fore, most notably in Britain, and formed a public body which—in sharp contrast to the old authorities, notably the state and the church—provided the conditions for reason-based public opinion. The creation of a network of institutions within civil society by the bourgeoisie, and the launch of a number of newspapers more specifically, provided the means through which private thoughts could become public. Libraries and universities became places for public debate, while publishing enterprises formed the means by which government was criticised. In principle, that new public sphere was open to all and was protected from the power of both the church and the state.

The Decline of the Traditional Public Sphere

However, as Habermas pointed out, this space for rational and universalistic politics created by the capitalist market was historically damaged by both the extension of the state and the evolution of monopoly capitalism. The formation of large private institutions (advertising agencies, public relations firms) and the deals they made with each other and with the state, while excluding the public, led to the replacement of rational public discourse with power politics. The role of the media was central to the replacement of what Habermas called the 'ideal speech situation' by conditions of 'distorted communication'. Whereas an independent press at the turn of the nineteenth century had led to the formation of rational public debate and public decision-making on political and judicial matters, it later functioned as a manipulative agency controlling public opinion. The media's role in the public debate shifted from the dissemination of rational and independent information, to the shaping of public opinion. Following the changing communications ecology, the public sphere has been discovered as a platform for advertising and public relations. Control of the news media is used to reinforce the power of autocratic regimes and to deter criticism of the government by independent journalists, through official government censorship, state ownership of the main radio and television channels, legal restrictions on freedom of expression and publication (such as stringent libel laws and restrictive official secrets acts), limited competition through oligopolies in commercial ownership, and the use of outright violence and intimidation against journalists and broadcasters (Sussman 2001). As will be shown below, the Internet can be used either way: to empower citizens and enhance the public sphere, or as a means of manipulation and control.

The Structural Transformation of the Public Sphere: The Fifth Estate

The debate surrounding the notion of the public sphere has garnered renewed interest with the emergence of the Internet and other new online media and social networks[2], providing new communication spaces where debate can take place. It should be emphasised from the outset that this material is really at the centre of the study and will shape our approach and analysis of the social media. While Habermas' original work was published well before the digital revolution, computer-mediated communication has taken the place of coffeehouse discourse (Boeder 2005). The diffusion of the Internet since it was first deployed in 1969, along with mobile communications, digital media and a wide range of social software tools, has driven the development of interactive communication (Castells 2007:246). As was once the case with radio, television and print media, the Internet terrain has produced new spaces for information, debate and participation—as well as new possibilities for manipulation and social control. But as Curran, Fenton and Freedman (2012) argued, we need to understand the Internet in its social, economic and political context and avoid a technologically deterministic view. While the rise of traditional news media such as newspapers, radio and television enabled the development of the fourth estate (e.g., the investigative coverage by the *Washington Post*, *Time* and *The New York Times* of the Watergate political scandal in the USA in the 1970s),[3] the growing use of the Internet and related digital technologies is creating a space for networking individuals in ways that, according to Dutton (2009), enable a new source of accountability in government, politics and other sectors. Dutton explains how this emerging 'fifth estate' is being established and why this could challenge the influence of other, more established bases of institutional authority. The author discusses approaches to the governance of this new

[2] A social network can be described as a set of actors (individuals, organisations, families, neighbourhoods, etc.) and relations that hold the actors together (maintain a tie) (Haythornthwaite 2002). The study of social networks can be perceived as a disciplinary enquiry into patterning of relations between social actors. The core premise of the study of social networks is that network structure and position have important behavioural, perceptual and attitudinal implications for the individuals and the social system (Emirbayer 1997).

[3] This and other '-gate' scandals show that, even in an era when print and limited-spectrum audiovisual media were much more closely aligned with political parties, investigative journalism exposed and brought into public scrutiny dirty political actions and controversies regarding secret power.

social and political phenomenon that could nurture the potential of the fifth estate to support the vitality of liberal democratic societies.

The new mantra of media terminology is already characterised by terms such as 'electronic commons', 'virtual democracy', 'electronic agora', 'blogosphere' and 'Twittersphere'. These online forums or social spaces of the Web 2.0 (a nascent movement towards a more interactive and collaborative web, as it provides a platform for online social participation in communities of interest) differ substantially from traditional forms such as public service broadcasting. First, they attract a much larger audience than the traditional media. In 2015, nearly 740 million people—48 % of its 1.4 billion users—logged into Facebook each day (see Chap. 3 for additional statistics). Twitter and Google+, with roughly 600 million users each, see more and more activity every day. These numbers are out of reach for traditional media such as radio and television. In fact, if Facebook were a country, it would now be as populous as China and India, the largest countries on earth in terms of population. But it is not only numbers that matter; social networks allow greater interactivity and many-to-many communication on a global scale, rather than one-to-many as is the case with traditional broadcast media. The democratic potential of the Internet can be realised through the ever-larger amount of debate that can take place on a global scale, in contrast to the limited capacity of traditional media confined within national borders.

The Globalisation of the Public Sphere

In this context, the emergence of the Internet and social media calls for a globalisation of the public sphere and public opinion. Public discourse and the formation of public opinion increasingly occur in a transnational context that crosses national boundaries. Whereas the traditional media in the form of newspapers and public television have been an integral part of the creation of a national public sphere, it is widely assumed that new spheres of communication networks can provide the basis for shared concerns, common tastes and political and cultural turns at a global level. In fact, citizens are taking to the streets in cities across the world to demand greater accountability from their leaders, in numbers not seen since the end of World War I. The issues differ from country to country— austerity measures, violations of privacy, exploitation of the environment or the abuse of electronic surveillance—but they all demonstrate a quest for good governance and the power of the new digital and social media.

These citizen uprisings represent a new force on the world stage that serves as a counterweight to the excesses of the current political order, whether democratic or authoritarian. As the news media have long played an essential role as watchdog over government, a fourth estate that guards against the abuse of power, today's exposure of the surveillance activities of the US National Security Agency, or police brutality in the case of the Taksim Square demonstrations in Turkey in June 2013, show the ability of the new social media to shed light on the workings of government and to provide a public forum for the debate of laws and policies.

As the new media disrupt the industrial model of information, citizens now have the power to oversee the actions of their elected representatives, thereby enabling a more direct form of democracy to emerge. The availability of information via social media like Facebook and Twitter and the rise of user-generated content such as personal blogs have enhanced citizens' ability to communicate and self-organise. The emerging 'citizens movement', or to mimic Castells (2012), the 'social movements in the Internet age', is a worldwide phenomenon and serves as a check and balance on government prerogatives. Millions of citizens have taken to the streets of São Paulo, Tel Aviv, Manila, Madrid and Bangkok, demanding good governance and an end to corruption. Demonstrators have swept away autocratic governments in many Arab countries, including Tunisia, Egypt and Libya. Citizens in southern Europe have called for an end to austerity measures that lead to economic exploitation and hopeless poverty. India demands protection from rape. In China, tens of millions of bloggers have become a virtual citizens lobby pushing for environmental change, blocking the construction of huge new dams and petrochemical plants. It is fair to say, then, that the new social media enhance traditional journalism in defending the public trust. Citizen journalists have expanded the reach and scope of established mass media outlets like the British Broadcasting Corporation (BBC) and Al Jazeera, and have brought an unprecedented degree of transparency to governments. Now that access to mobile phones, news reports, images and opinions are almost universally available, people have become empowered to demand accountability from their governments. As Hoffman (2013) put it, 'Citizens are the new Fourth Estate.' While there are certainly risks that these newly empowered citizens could become pawns of populist demagogues, this is far more likely to happen when the media are controlled by the few than when there are multiple and independent sources of information (Hoffman 2013).

In today's network society, power is multidimensional and is organised around digital, interactive and self-expanding networks whose participants have very diverse interests and values. In direct contrast to power relations embedded in the institutions of society, and especially the state, social movements exercise counter-power by establishing themselves initially through a process of autonomous communication, free from the control of those holding institutional power. As Castells (2012:9) argues, 'Because mass media are largely controlled by governments and media corporations, in the network society communicative autonomy is primarily constructed in the Internet networks and in the platforms of wireless communication.' These social networks carve out a new public space for deliberation, distinct from the constitutionally designated space which is occupied by the dominant political and economic elite. But do these new media enhance democracy and contribute to political participation?

The Democratisation of the Public Sphere

A democratic social system can be defined as one in which the supreme power is vested in the people and exercised by them, directly or indirectly, through a system of representation typically involving periodic free elections. The origins of democracy can be traced to Athens about 2500 years ago. In the sixth century BC, the 'Ancient Agora' was the centre of public life in Athens, and can also be considered the centre of democracy, as Athenian citizens were gathering to listen to speeches by philosophers of the likes of Demosthenes, Plato and Socrates. The Ancient Agora was a place of direct democracy, with people making important political decisions and voting by raising their hands. Nowadays, most democracies around the world are of a representative nature, as citizens typically choose leaders to represent them through general elections. However, the Internet seems to challenge this system, as it offers a powerful means for direct citizen involvement in public life and politics. It satisfies the need for a new form of democracy, a type of post-electoral democracy, whose spirit and institutions have been infused with a commitment to casting out the devils of arbitrary, publicly unaccountable power.

The Internet's democratic potential has been highlighted in such works as those of Rheingold (1993) and Kellner (1997), whose central thesis contends that cyberspace provides an ideal basis for the transnational exchange of dialogue. Similarly optimistic is the view that the Internet tends to democratise access to information and to undermine hierarchies.

For example, de Sola Pool (1983) viewed computer-based communication networks like the Internet as inherently democratic 'technologies of freedom'. In response to this debate around freedom versus control, Danziger et al. (1982) noted that the Internet can support and reinforce many different forms of networks. These connect in the traditional one-to-many pattern of the mass media, but in the new world also provide for patterns such as one-to-one, many-to-one or many-to-many. Therefore, the Internet can be shaped by developers, users and regulators to support the 'communicative power' of both institutions and individuals in many ways.

The Internet can facilitate the spread of debate and deliberation across many parts of the population that may be spatially dispersed. In this sense, the democratic potential of the Internet can be realised through an ever-larger quantity of rational critical debate that can take place within this space, compared to the limited capacity of traditional media that are confined within national borders. Viewed in this way, the emergence of the Internet (and other new online and international media) calls for a globalisation of the public sphere and public opinion. Public discourse and the formation of public opinion increasingly take place in a transnational context that crosses national boundaries. It has been suggested that the new technologies have enabled the formation of such transnational or global public spheres as a forum for political discussion. While the traditional media in the form of newspapers and public television have been an integral component in the creation of a national public sphere, it is widely assumed that new spheres of communication networks can provide the basis for shared concerns, common tastes, and political and cultural turns at a global level. The power of media is increasing with the spread of 24-hour cable news networks, the Internet, the seeming omnipresence of personal audio and video devices, and the proliferation of social networking sites. As such, the influence of the media on enhancing public dialogue and political debate—the so-called political socialisation—has become ubiquitous. But has it?

DEMOCRATIC DEFICIT: PUTNAM'S CONCEPT OF SOCIAL CAPITAL

There have been growing concerns that a 'democratic deficit' has occurred with regard to a collapse of virtue and citizenship. The concept of a democratic deficit, or democratic gap, is the idea that the governance in a country or region in some ways lacks democratic legitimacy. This has led to a profound 'thinning' of the political community and the formation of the atomised citizen who is 'bowling alone' (Putnam 1993). US scholar Robert Putnam considered the theory of social capital as a governance mechanism that provides 'closeness' and 'trustworthiness' among people. Putnam's thesis must incorporate his definition of social capital, and therefore must take into account both structural and cultural dimensions, that is, the strength of social networks (measured in terms of belonging to a wide range of associational groups and social movements) and the cultural norms (measured by feelings of social trust). His use of the term 'social capital' refers to features of social life—networks, norms and trust—that enable participants to act together more effectively to pursue shared objectives (Putnam 1993). Coleman (1988:96) defined social capital according to its function. It is not a single entity, but a variety of entities, with two elements in common: they all consist of some aspect of social structure, and they facilitate certain actions by actors (individuals or corporate) within that structure.

A similar notion was provided by Bourdieu and Wacquant (1992:119) who defined social capital as 'the sum of the resources, actual or virtual, that accrue to an individual or a group by virtue of possessing a durable network of more or less institutionalised relationships of mutual acquaintance and recognition'. Social capital, then, comprises a network, a cluster of norms, values and expectations, which are shared by members of a group (Halpern 2005). To return to Putnam, he argued that new forms of social capital are necessary to reconnect citizens with their societies (Putnam 2000). The fears of inequality have been heightened by the decline of civic virtues, the dismantling of democratic associations and the disengagement of the public with the political classes. Putnam observed that agreement on what constitutes the common good has dissolved as trust has been eroded. To fill the accompanying void, he called for the extension of voluntary organisations to create 'virtuous circles' to accumulate social capital so that enabled citizens may agree on a set of shared aims for collective activity (Putnam 2000). Shing and Chung (2011), however, seem to put their faith in new technology to encourage citizen participation and contribution to the public sphere. With technological advances like the tools of Web 2.0 media, the authors argue, online social network platforms could promote civic engagement that allows for bridging of social capital across geographical, organisational, hierarchical, temporal and spatial barriers.

The argument that citizen engagement and contribution within the public sphere has been eroded can be seen in the case of the European Union (EU), where a democratic deficit is said to exist. The term was initially used to challenge the transfer of legislative powers from national governments to the EU Council of Ministers, and it is most common in traditionally 'Eurosceptic' countries such as the UK. A growing number of politicians and academics have proposed that there is a political communication deficit in the EU, with long-term consequences of apathy, political ignorance and an alarming dissatisfaction among European citizens with the state of politics in Europe. Kaitatzi-Whitlock (2005) investigated the relationship between political communication, politics and policymaking in the EU over a 20-year period, and correlated the political communication deficit with the communication strategies and policies that have been pursued by the EU since the early 1980s, and that have resulted in de-politicising and diminishing the EU's legitimacy as a supranational political entity. The author argued that despite the possibilities for empowerment offered by technology today, European citizens have been deprived of their most fundamental right and need for political information and means of political participation. The Euro crisis has worsened the problem and exacerbated political apathy. This is evidenced by the low European Parliament election turnout in May 2014 of around 43 %, matching the 2009 election turnout, but well below the 1979 election (62 %) or even the 1994 election turnout (57 %).

Pippa Norris is among the commentators disputing the arguments raising concern about citizen disengagement from the traditional channels of political participation, anti-party sentiment and the decay of civil organisations. In her trilogy considering related facets of these phenomena, she maintains that these concerns are not justified. The first volume, *A Virtuous Circle* (Norris 2000), developed a critique of the mass media malaise thesis, demonstrating that attention to the news media was positively, not negatively, linked to civic engagement. The second volume, *Digital Divide* (Norris 2001), explored the potential of the Internet for civic engagement, and the ways in which new online opportunities have affected the availability of resources for political competition, facilitating a more level playing field for smaller challengers and opposition movements with technical skills and know-how. Building upon this foundation, the third volume of the trilogy, *Democratic Phoenix* (Norris 2002), compares systematic evidence for electoral turnout, party membership and civic activism in countries around the world, and suggests good reasons to question popular assumptions of pervasive decline. Norris observes that multiple forms of civic engagement have emerged within modern societies to supplement traditional modes of political activism, and that political participation appears to have evolved and diversified over the years in terms of the agencies (collective organisations), repertoires (the actions commonly used for political expression) and targets (the political actors that participants seek to influence). These developments have been largely driven by the process of societal modernisation and rising levels of human capital, although patterns of participation are also explained by the structure of the state, the role of mobilising agencies, and social inequalities in resources and attitudes. As a result, according to Norris, democratic engagement has not atrophied, but has been reinvented for modern times. Thus we can see that the findings are mixed with regard to the presumed declining confidence of citizens in the capacity of the formal political system to deal with contemporary issues.

SOCIAL MEDIA AND THE PUBLIC SPHERE: JOHN KEANE'S CAUTIOUS VIEW

Much has been written about the implications of democratisation and empowerment associated with the rise of the Internet and the new social media, and much of it can be deemed idealistic and representative of technological determinism (see Nieminen 2009:40). Not surprisingly, attempts to provide for a theoretical and empirical grounding of the 'ideal speech situation'—at least as formulated by Habermas—on the web has been met with scepticism. Coleman (1999) suggests that much online discussion is characterised as bad-tempered, perhaps as a result of the decline in public debate in physical spaces such as open meetings and street corners, where people first learned to argue effectively. Wilhelm (1999) also alludes to the dangers of poor dialogue and a skewed distribution of contributors in cyberspace. As Boeder (2005) argues, it is often the case that major decisions and actions concerning transnational matters occur without intense public scrutiny. In this section, we attempt to identify the basic contours of the notion of the public sphere that is taking shape in the realm of social media and, for this purpose, will refer to John Keane's work on monitoring democracy.

According to Keane (2008), strong caution is counselled in the face of such utopian extravagance, not least because the new age of 'communicative abundance' is unstable, even self-contradictory—for instance, in the widening power gaps between the communication-rich and communication-poor, the latter of whom seem almost unneeded as communicators or consumers. He claims that our world is now living through an historic sea change, one that is taking us away from the old world of representative democracy, towards a form of democracy with entirely different contours and dynamics, workings and political implications, namely 'monitory democracy'. Keane (2008) argues that the growth of monitory democracy is closely tied to the growth of media-saturated societies—societies in which all institutions operate within fields of media defined by communicative abundance. This monitory democracy and its powerful mechanisms of handling and moderating conflict must take into account the mediation of power and conflict by the institutions of communication. In the age of monitory democracy, the old utopia of shedding light on power—pushing, for instance, towards freedom of information, 'government in the sunshine' and greater transparency—strongly motivates journalists, citizens, lawyers, judges, NGOs and others (Keane 2008).

Thus monitory democracy has been aided by the end of the age of scarcity and the emergence of communicative abundance (and the wide availability of computerised media networks). Citizens nowadays have at their discretion multiple means to scrutinise, criticise and resist their government, not just through parliaments, but also through watchdogs, audits, local assemblies and civil society monitors. Keane's central example of monitory democracy in action is India, as this vast emerging country has a distinctive combination of almost limitless political variety. One could also argue that countries like Britain lived through a monitory democratic moment in 2011–2013, as the expense scandal (in which public figures were claiming money for personal expenses like mortgages and swimming pools) showed how much more difficult it has become for politicians to keep things hidden. Silvio Berlusconi's government in Italy also collapsed following sex scandals made known by the new social media. As one commentator (Runciman 2009) put it, monitoring democracy is an essentially negative idea of politics—it is, as Keane argues, the idea of a form of politics in which 'nobody should rule'. As such, it is only a partial description of what democracy is and what it needs to be.

The Internet's Contribution to Politics: Bang's Theory

The Internet's contribution to politics is evidenced by the fact that since the mid-1990s, most general elections in democratic countries have had official websites, and the major political parties across the globe are trying to improve their online activities. Pippa Norris' comparative analysis discussed above also provides evidence of democratic engagement and growing political participation in the modern era. But can the Internet and social media undermine democratic institutions and erode traditional institutions of representative, deliberative democracy by providing the means for citizens to directly participate in public policymaking? To answer this question, we refer to Bang's concept of everyday makers.

Bang argues that the nature of politics and political participation has changed in the era of late modernity.[4] In his view, tensions exist between engagement norms and duty norms. This distinction revolves around, on the one hand, whether people get involved out of a sense of duty or because they want to make a difference, and on the other, the difference between having a project identity and having a legitimating or oppositional identity. For Bang, people have engagement norms and a project identity, rather than duty norms and a legitimating and/or oppositional identity. Citizens have thus reacted in innovative ways to the increased change and complexity associated with late modernity: they have engagement norms and a project identity, so they certainly are not apathetic, but they reject duty norms and have no legitimating (or indeed oppositional) identity. Rather, they are increasingly reflexive, drawing on their own experience and engaging on their own terms. Some have become what Bang terms 'expert citizens', those who use their skills not for listening to but for speaking on behalf of ordinary citizens. In many ways, the emergence of the everyday maker is a response to the expert citizen (see Marsh and Vromen 2013).

Bang identifies five key characteristics of everyday makers: (a) their participation is ad hoc, cause-specific and part-time, and thus not driven by organisational membership; (b) everyday makers have minimal interest in party-based and organised politics, and stay away from state-based participation such as consultation exercises, thereby distinguishing themselves from expert citizens, who operate in partnership and collaboration with the state; (c) everyday makers' participation is grounded in their lived experiences and is thus immediate and local, certainly non-ideological,

---

[4]Polish-British sociologist Zygmunt Bauman argued that late modernity (or 'liquid modernity' as he terms it) is marked by the global capitalist economies, the process of increasing privatisation of services and the information revolution. In his *Liquid Modernity*, Bauman (2000) investigates how we have moved away from a 'heavy' and 'solid' hardware-focused modernity to a 'light' and 'liquid' software-based modernity.

but driven by a project identity; (d) they are not interested in idea-driven social and political change, but rather in issue- or cause-driven projects; (e) finally, they are involved in politics for fun and to express themselves. For this reason, creative forms of action, expression and multimedia use are often at the core of participation for everyday makers.

Marsh and Vromen (2013) viewed the concept of everyday makers as one of the most interesting developments in recent conceptual work on political participation, but looked at it critically, drawing on a series of empirical examples. In their view, one must acknowledge that there are many participating citizens who demonstrate some, but not all, of the characteristics of everyday makers. While Bang does not discuss variation among everyday makers along this dimension, Marsh and Vromen consider them to be very important, and as such, one must either distinguish between different types of everyday makers or, alternatively, recognise the need for more categories. The authors illustrate this point by applying Bang's model to six contemporary case studies of participation: three from the UK (Marsh, O'Toole and Jones' work on young people and politics in Birmingham; Taylor's study of feminist activists in Manchester; and the case of UK Uncut), one transnational (Halupka's research on the group Anonymous), and two from Australia (Vromen and Coleman's work on GetUp! in Australia; Jackson and Chen's research on Occupy Sydney). Furlong and Cartmel (2012) appear to share their view, referring to the UK case, and in particular to the social change and political engagement among young people in 2009/2010.

The Public Interest and Media Governance

Regulatory issues associated with social media will be examined in detail in Chap. 4, which identifies key policy variables within national governments (UK and USA) and at a supranational level (EU). Here, it suffices to note that the articulation of a public interest framework in a regime of social media governance must take into account both traditional concerns (such as access, media plurality and freedom of expression) and emerging concerns. These new concerns include privacy and intellectual property rights, transparency surrounding data processing and the protection of users from harmful content (violence, sexually explicit content, hate speech and harassment). Some of these concerns have been with us for some time, but specific points of focus in the Internet era include issues of access to and use of user data by social media platforms, typically for advertising and marketing purposes, and/or by insurance companies.

So, what can we do to protect ourselves from these threats? Most countries have adopted content regulation (especially *negative* content regulation—restricting the propagation of certain types of information, text, sounds and images, and imposing advertising restrictions) and have expanded it to cover the online world. However, the restriction or suppression of harmful and politically or socially undesirable content is at odds with the principle of freedom of speech in democratic societies, and therefore, the application of contemporary policy to content rules is not a straightforward task. Also, the non-interventionist approach in matters of speech and communications as an inherent principle among liberal democracies is incompatible with the imposition of negative media content policies. Thus it has been put forth that the online digital era brings with it an increased responsibility to the individual media users, and that social media platforms should enable individual responsibility and autonomy. Commentators such as Singer (2014) claim that users should now play a more prominent role in social media governance, as they are increasingly involved in the production and dissemination of online content through their functions as citizen journalists. Certainly, the public is to bear more responsibility and, indeed, to be more accountable in using the Internet and social media. At the same time, social media platforms must comply with guidelines regarding acceptable levels of transparency and accountability set by governments or international bodies, for these are crucial if the public is to bear more responsibility and, indeed, to be more accountable in the use of the Internet and social media. The complex issue of whether citizens can actually become custodians of the emergent model of public interest is further elaborated in Chap. 4.

Social Media and Democracy

The key question here is whether the social media play a contributory role in democracy, revolution and expansion of the public sphere, or whether they are, first and foremost, instruments of control and commerce. To answer this question, we now engage with social media sceptics and discuss various concerns that have arisen regarding the contribution of electronic networks to democracy.

Unstructured Participation

First, the open participatory nature of the Internet and social media can give rise to chaos, to a scenario in which there are no model rules of behaviour, thereby allowing no structured conversation. Gladwell (2010) stressed that successful activism requires strategic hierarchies, with a careful and precise allocation of tasks. The social media, conversely, create loose and essentially leaderless networks, incapable of organising revolution. As networks typically have no centralised leadership structure or clear lines of authority, they cannot reach consensus and cannot set strategic goals. Social sites also have the tendency to distract people from important issues. Morozov (2012) contends that few people use the Internet and social media for political activism, whereas huge numbers use it to view pornography, play games, watch movies or share pictures. This frivolous use of the Internet and social media is well known in Western societies, and is now spreading to authoritarian regimes. Furthermore, Morozov notes the danger that the sheer volume of information available through social media—coupled with its increased general availability via the Internet and 24/7 news cycles—may lead to shorter attention spans, in which important news is quickly supplanted by new developments elsewhere. For example, the 'Twitterverse' flocked to read and retweet news of the ultimately unsuccessful Iranian uprising of June 2009, yet the story was swiftly cast aside upon the death of pop megastar Michael Jackson. While social media may create more immediate and louder conversations, those conversations may tend to be shallow, short and easily displaced by the newest 'big thing' (Joseph 2012).

Unreliable Information

A related issue is that a good deal of Internet content is unreliable. As a widespread information source, the Internet should provide reliable, authentic and up-to-date information, but user-generated content—and blogs in particular—are often deemed unreliable sources, containing personal and one-sided opinion. While it is fair to say that common sense (house rules) and common decency should be the rule or acceptable practice when posting material on the Internet, as this is largely a self-regulated area, reaction comes only when someone complains. There is clearly a need for a better balance in enforcing appropriate online behaviour, assigning liability and protecting freedom of speech. Indeed, providing an informed, and safe, online experience is important for both consumers and businesses. Dahlberg (2007) found online debate to be polarising, with a general lack of listening between people. He noted that the Internet and social media fail to adequately consider the asymmetries of power through which deliberation and consensus are achieved, the intersubjective basis of meaning, a centrality of respect for difference in democracy, and the democratic role of 'like-minded' deliberative groups. What is often absent in online deliberations is a consensus-based, justified and rational decision, let alone the inclusion of everyone affected by that decision. But it is fair to say that very little online content is legally actionable, and an even smaller proportion is actually subjected to any kind of legal action. Exceptions to this are cases like the famous Sally Bercow tweet case that took place in the UK. In November 2012, Bercow used her Twitter account to imply that Lord McAlpine, a Conservative peer, was the unnamed politician alleged by the BBC to be a paedophile. The allegations proved to be unfounded, and the peer took legal action against Bercow and others. In May 2013, the High Court found that Sally Bercow's tweet was libellous, and Bercow agreed to pay damages. However, most content that people publish is not defamatory. At the EU level, the Electronic Commerce Directive (EU 2002) establishes clear rules and protections that online retailers and service providers must comply with when dealing with consumers in EU member countries, and which cover platforms that allow other persons to publish user-generated content.

Censorship

Third, censorship can be an issue. The extent of Internet censorship varies on a country-by-country basis. While most democratic countries have moderate Internet censorship, other countries go so far as to limit the access of news or other information and to suppress discussion among citizens. The governments of China, North Korea and Cuba, for example, restrict their citizens' Internet access by blocking specific websites. Amnesty International, an NGO dealing with human rights, notes that China has the largest recorded number of imprisoned journalists and cyber-dissidents in the world. Facebook, Twitter and YouTube are all explicitly blocked in China, and in March 2010, Google withdrew from China owing to an ever-stronger censorship of its searches. Domestic Chinese equivalents of these sites, such as Baidu, Taobao, Renren and QQ, have been launched, and these can be more readily controlled by the state. Likewise, the Cuban Internet is among the most tightly controlled in the world, while Internet access in North Korea is permitted only with special authorisation, and is primarily used for government purposes.

In Turkey, on 20 March 2014, after tweets began spreading linking the prime minister to a corruption scandal, the Erdogan government imposed a block on Twitter, only to be lifted a few days later thanks to a Turkish court order. Douglas Frantz, a US State Department official, likened the move to '21st century book burning' (see http://blogs.state.gov/stories/2014/03/21/21st-century-book-burning, accessed 28 March 2014). The USA has not always lived up to its values concerning freedom of expression; despite the country's strong democratic tradition, the post 9/11 era gave rise to concerns over privacy and freedom, as evidenced by the passing of the 2001 Patriot Act, which expanded law enforcement's surveillance and investigative powers. In Europe, in the immediate aftermath of the British riots in August 2011, which resulted in widespread looting and property damage, British Prime Minister David Cameron blamed social media in part for the unrest, and raised the possibility of banning individuals suspected of using social media to organise criminal activity, and otherwise censoring social networks.

Corporate Online Activity and Privacy Concerns

Fourth, the Internet has become a major arena for corporate activity, similar to other branches of the cultural industries. Individualisation of consumption has been accompanied by consolidation of media ownership, producing global multimedia corporations, intent on redeveloping cyberspace as retail real estate (Murdock 2004). Fuchs (2011a) argues that the Internet and social media today are stratified, non-participatory spaces, and that an alternative, non-corporate Internet is needed. Giant corporations colonise social media and dominate their attention economy. In a more recent work, Fuchs (2014) takes a further step, and contends that large corporate (and to a lesser extent, political) actors dominate and therefore centralise the formation of speech, association, assembly and opinion on social media.

> Liberal freedoms turn on capitalist social media into their opposite. The concept of social media participation is an ideology...it seems both necessary and feasible to theorize 'Web 2.0' not as a participatory system, but by employing more negative, critical terms such as class, exploitation and surplus value (Fuchs 2014:102).

Corporate social media gather data on users by continuously monitoring and recording online activities. Collected data are then stored, merged and analysed in order to create detailed user profiles containing information about personal interests and online behaviours. This, in turn, enables targeted advertising, with the objective of luring consumers into buying products and services. The mechanism of targeted advertising on social media has been termed 'panoptic sorting' (see Gandy 1993a, b), as the social media are able to obtain a comprehensive, detailed picture of the interests and activities of their users. According to Fuchs (2014:110), corporate social media sell users' data commodity to advertising clients at a price that is greater than the invested constant and variable capital. In another work, Fuchs (2013) argues that social media 'prosumers' are double objects of commodification: they are commodities themselves, and through this commodification, their consciousness while online is permanently exposed to commodity logic in the form of advertisements.

> With the rise of user-generated content, free access social networking platforms, and other free access platforms that yield profit by online advertisement—a development subsumed under categories such as web 2.0, social software, and social networking sites—the web seems to come close to accumulation strategies employed by the capital on traditional mass media like TV or radio. The users who upload photos, and images, write wall posting and comments, send mail to their contacts, accumulate friends or browse other profiles on Facebook, constitute an audience commodity that is sold to advertisers. The difference between the audience commodity on traditional mass media and on the Internet is that in the latter case the users are also content producers; there is user-generated content, the users engage in permanent creative activity, communication, community building, and content-production (Fuchs 2013).

There is considerable debate concerning the privacy of people's correspondence when they are using online services such as email, text messaging and social media. Put simply, in the past, people created content with the expectation that it would remain private, but with the advent of social media, with text messages and tweets, this content now resides in the public space. Do large social media sites, then, take steps to protect user privacy? This is dealt with in Chap. 3.

Absence of Critical Discussion

Fifth, extensive dialogue and critical discussion (the very essence of the public sphere) is often absent on the Net. There seems to be a gap between 'access to information' and an 'ability for conversation and dialogue', as meaningful debate is typically lacking on social networking sites, which are dominated by trivial exchanges. In the case of Twitter, for example, dialogue is constrained by the very fact that it is limited to the exchange of swift, short messages (up to 140 characters). While this allows for a greater number of active participants in the communication process, it leaves little space for substantive social and political dialogue involving groups and individuals. Shirky (2011) argues that 'political freedom has to be accompanied by a civil society literate enough and densely connected enough to discuss the issues presented to the public'. He endorses the theory of sociologists Elihu Katz and Paul Lazarsfeld (1970), that the formation of well-considered political opinions is a two-step process. The first step requires access to information; the second, the use of that information in conversation and debate. Within this framework, Shirky argues, social media sites have revolutionised how people form political opinions and have made information so widely accessible that more people than ever before are able to develop considered points of view.

Lastly, despite its increasing prominence as a place where people access news and advertisers spend money, the Internet remains a distribution medium, not a source of original news content. Although Internet companies invest in this medium, the investment has tended to be in technology and not in journalists. Internet sites unaffiliated with traditional media typically collect stories from various newspapers and wire services, or comment on the news, but do little original local news coverage or investigative reporting. So, is the ability of the Internet to contribute to democracy by creating a healthier public sphere just a myth? Is the creation of new social and political units by social media a cyber-fantasy? Not quite, as was argued in a previous work (Iosifidis 2011). If traditional media such as newspapers helped to create public spaces where people initiated forms of communication within nation-states, new social media can do likewise in the international space in which citizens increasingly invest their time to communicate with one another and to create content. It all depends on how one uses the Internet and social media. As is true for all new media technologies, the Internet and social media can provide a useful tool or the basis for a healthier democracy and an enhanced public space, but they themselves cannot create such a space. And they can be used either as an instrument of empowerment or as a means of domination.

CONCLUSION

In this chapter, we have presented the theoretical framework of the book and have critically investigated the complex interaction between social media and contemporary democratic politics, providing a grounded analysis of the emerging importance of social media within the public sphere and with respect to democracy and civic engagement. While it is widely assumed that social media applications such as Facebook, Twitter and YouTube are empowering people and making political processes more democratic, the evidence is not always there to support such assertions. The literature review examined the salience of the network as a metaphor for understanding our social world, but also the centrality of the Internet in civic and political networks. As Loader and Mercea (2011:x) have argued, on one hand, it is often assumed that 'the widespread use of the Internet for social networking, blogging, video-sharing and tweeting has an elective affinity with participatory democracy'. On the other hand, they suggest that 'such optimistic claims for the political benefit of social networking are in sharp contrast to much of the mainstream academic discourse surrounding the prospects for digital democratic governance'.

In this chapter, we have discussed the central question of whether the social media actually provide new forms of participatory democracy and enhance the public sphere. We have intentionally taken a more circumspect and open-ended approach here, and have offered a balanced view from the perspective of both sceptics and optimists. The two sections of the book that follow are intended to test these concepts against empirical material drawn from the Global North (Sect. 1) and South (Sect. 2). The first section will explore the relationship between online mobilisation and policy change in mature, liberal democracies, while the second section will shift the focus from the Western world to the non-Western developing countries as well as authoritarian regimes.

BIBLIOGRAPHY

Bauman Z. 2000. *Liquid Modernity*. Cambridge: Polity.

Boeder, P. 2005. "'Habermas' Heritage: The Future of the Public Sphere in the Network Society", *First Monday* 10(9), September 5. http://firstmonday.org/htbin/cgiwrap/bin/ojs/index.php/fm/article/view/1280/1200 (accessed June 11, 2014).

Bourdieu P., and J.D. Wacquant. 1992. *An Invitation to Reflexive Sociology*. Chicago: University of Chicago.

Castells M. 2007. "Communication, Power and Counter-power in the Network Society". *International Journal of Communication* 8: 238–266.

Castells M. 2012. *Networks of Outrage and Hope: Social Movements in the Internet Age*. Cambridge: Polity.

Coleman J.S. 1988. "Social Capital in the Creation of Human Capital". *The American Journal of Sociology* 94: S95–S120.

Coleman J.S. 1999. "Cutting Out the Middle Man: From Virtual Representation to Direct Deliberation". In *Digital Democracy: Discourse and Decision-Making in the Information Age*, eds. B.N. Hague, and B.D. Loader, 195–210. London: Routledge.

Coleman S., and J. Blumler. 2009. *The Internet and Democratic Citizenship: Theory, Practice and Policy*. New York: Cambridge University Press.

Curran J., N. Fenton, and D. Freedman. 2012. *Misunderstanding the Internet*. London: Routledge.

Dahlberg L. 2007. "Rethinking the Fragmentation of the Cyberpublic: From Consensus to Contestation". *New Media and Society* 9(5): 827–847.

Danziger, J.N. et al. 1982. *Information Technology Management in Developing Countries* (USA: IRM Press).

De Sola Pool 1983. *Technologies of Freedom* (Belknap Press of Harvard University Press).

Dutton, W.H. 2009. "The Fifth Estate Emerging through the Network of Networks". *Prometheus* 27(1): 1–15. http://papers.ssrn.com/sol3/papers.cfm?abstract_id=1167502 (accessed June 7, 2014).

Emirbayer M. 1997. "Manifesto for a Relational Sociology". *The American Journal of Sociology* 103(2): 281–317.

European Union (EU). 2002. The Electronic Commerce Directive (00/31/EC) and the Electronic Commerce (EC Directive) Regulations 2002 (SI 2002 No. 2013).

Ferguson M., ed. 1986. *New Communication Technologies and the Public Interest*. London: Sage.

Fuchs C. 2011a. *Foundations of Critical Media and Information Studies*. New York: Routledge.

Fuchs C. 2013. "Social Media and Capitalism: In Producing the Internet". In *Critical Perspectives of Social Media*, ed. T. Olsson, 25–44. Göteborg: Nordicom.

Fuchs C. 2014. *Social Media: A Critical Introduction.* London: Sage.

Furlong A., and F. Cartmel. 2012. "Social Change and Political Engagement among Young People: Generation and the 2009/2010 British Election Survey". *Parliamentary Affairs* 65(1): 13–28.

Gandy O.H. 1993a. "Toward a Political Economy of Personal Information". *Critical Studies in Mass Communication* 10(1): 70–97.

Gandy O.H. 1993b. *The Panoptic Sort.* Boulder, CO: Westview Press.

Gladwell, M. 2010. "Small Change", *New Yorker*, October 4. http://www.newyorker.com/reporting/2010/10/04/101004fa_fact_gladwell (accessed March 22, 2014).

Habermas, J. 1989. The Structural Transformation of the Public Sphere: An Inquiry into a Category of Bourgeois Society. Cambridge: Polity Press. Original Work Published 1962.

Halpern D. 2005. *Social Capital.* Cambridge: Policy Press.

Haythornthwaite C. 2002. "Strong, Weak and Latent Ties and the Impact of New Media". *The Information Society* 18(5): 385–401.

Hoffman, D. 2013. *Citizens: The New Forth Estate.* http://www.huffingtonpost.com/david-hoffman/citizens-the-new-fourth-e_b_3894819.html (accessed June 9, 2014).

Iosifidis P. 2010. *Reinventing Public Service Communication: European Broadcasters and Beyond.* Basingstoke: Palgrave Macmillan.

Iosifidis, P. 2011a. *Global Media and Communication Policy* (Basingstoke: Palgrave Macmillan).

Joseph, S. 2012. "Social Media, Political Change, and Human Rights". Boston College International and Comparative Law Review 35(1): 145–188. http://lawdigitalcommons.bc.edu/iclr/vol35/iss1/3 (accessed February 25, 2014).

Kaitatzi-Whitlock, S. 2005. *Europe's Political Communication Deficit* (Arima: Bury St Edmunds).

Katz E., and Paul F. Lazarsfeld. 1970. *Personal Influence: The Part Played by People in the Flow of Mass Communications.* New Brunswick, NJ: Transaction Publishers.

Keane, J. 2008. "Monitoring Democracy?" Paper prepared for the ESRC Seminar Series, 'Emergent Publics', The Open University, Milton Keynes, March. http://www.open.ac.uk/socialsciences/emergentpublics/seminar1/keane_monitory_democracy.pdf (accessed June 12, 2014).

Kellner, D. 1997. Intellectuals, the New Public Spheres, and Techno-politics. http://www.gseis.ucla.edu/faculty/kellner/essays/intellectualsnewpublicspheres.pdf (accessed March 27, 2014).

Loader B., and D. Mercea. 2011. "NETWORKING DEMOCRACY? Social Media Innovations and Participatory Politics". *Information Communication and Society* 14(6): 757–769.

Marsh, D., and A. Vromen. 2013. Everyday Makers with a Difference?: Contemporary Forms of Political Participation. http://www.tasa.org.au/uploads/2012/11/Marsh-David-Vromen-Ariadne.pdf (accessed June 11, 2014).

Murdock, G. 2004. 'Building the Digital Commons: Public Broadcasting in the Age of the Internet', Speech, Spry Memorial Lecture, University of Montreal, 22 November. At https://pantherfile.uwm.edu/type/www/116/Theory_OtherTexts/Theory/Murdock_BuildingDigitalCommons.pdf (accessed 5 March 2016).

Morozov, E. 2012. The Net Delusion: The Dark Side of Internet Freedom. *Public Affairs.*

Nieminen H. 2009. "Media in Crisis? Social, Economic and Epistemic Dimensions". In *Communicative Approaches to Politics and Ethics in Europe*, eds. N. Carpentier et al., 31–43. Estonia: Tartu University Press.

Pippa, N. 2000. *A Virtuous Circle: Political Communications in Post-industrial Societies.* (Cambridge: Cambridge University Press).

Pippa, N. 2001. *Digital Divide: Civil Engagement, Information Poverty, and the Internet Worldwide.* (Cambridge: Cambridge University Press).

Pippa, N. 2002. *Democratic Phoenix: Reinventing Political Activism.* (Cambridge: Cambridge University Press).

Putnam R.D. 1993. *Making Democracy Work: Civil Traditions in Modern Italy.* Princeton, NJ: Princeton University Press.

Putnam R.D. 2000. *Bowling Alone.* New York: Simon and Schuster.

Runciman, D. 2009. What a Way to Run a Country, *The Observer*, June 7. http://www.theguardian.com/books/2009/jun/07/life-death-democracy-john-keane (accessed June 28, 2014).

Sen A. 1999. *Development as Freedom.* New York: Anchor Books.

Shing, K., and K. Chung. 2011. An Empirical Analysis of Online Social Network Structure to Understand Citizen Engagement in Public Policy and Community Building, *International Journal of Electronic Governance*, special issue on (Re) Creating Public Sphere, Civic Culture and Civic Engagement: Public Service Media vs. Online Social Networks.

Shirky, C. 2011. The Political Power of Social Media: Technology, the Public Sphere, and Political Change, *Foreign Affairs*, January/February issue. http://www.foreignaffairs.com/articles/67038/clay-shirky/the-political-power-of-social-media (accessed March 21, 2014).

Singer J.B. 2014. "User-generated Visibility: Secondary Gatekeeping in a Shared Media Space". *New Media & Society* 16(1): 55–73.

Sussman L.R. 2001. *Press Freedom in Our Genes.* Reston, VA: World Press Freedom Committee.

Wilhelm A.G. 1999. "Virtual Sounding Boards: How Deliberative is Online Political Discussion?". In *Digital Democracy: Discourse and Decision-Making in the Information Age*, eds. B.N. Hague, and B.D. Loader, 154–178. London: Routledge.

CHAPTER 3

The Political Economy of Social Media

INTRODUCTION

Online social networks have emerged as the new way in which people connect socially. The current leader is Facebook, with over 1.4 billion members, followed by QQ, WeChat, LinkedIn, Google+ and Twitter, to name but a few (http://www.statista.com/statistics/272014/global-social-networks-ranked-by-number-of-users/, accessed 15 July 2015). Over 60 % of people worldwide use social networks, with the Philippines, Indonesia, Malaysia, Brazil, Russia, India, Singapore, Poland, Mexico, Hong Kong, the USA, Canada and China constituting the most highly engaged countries (see https://www.google.co.uk/webhp?sourceid=chrome-instant&ion=1&espv=2&ie=UTF-8#q=social%20media%20use%20by%20country, accessed 19 July 2015). Every day, there are about 175 million tweets and 2.5 billion items of content shared on Facebook, and 70 % of all Internet navigation is now conducted on a mobile device. At the same time, content communities provide sites where users can share content with other members of their online community, with well-known examples of these including Flickr for photos and YouTube for video. Every second there are more than 50,000 YouTube videos being viewed around the world, with videos embedded in blogs, websites and online stores.

© The Editor(s) (if applicable) and The Author(s) 2016
P. Iosifidis, M. Wheeler, *Public Spheres and Mediated
Social Networks in the Western Context and Beyond,*
DOI 10.1057/978-1-137-41030-6_3

Such user numbers are impressive, given that Web 2.0 environments[1] are young and fairly recent in the new digital economy. These statistics thus illustrate the enormous scope and reach of social media today.

One common characteristic among social media sites is that they are widely accessible free of cost across the corporate sector as well as socio-economic classes. Online social networking sites have often been perceived as revolutionary new media tools: on the one hand, they change the face of business as we know it (e.g., they enable the creation of a brand name, targeted advertising marketing, etc.), and on the other, they allow greater citizen participation in the dissemination of information and creation of content. The networked population is gaining greater access to information, enhanced opportunities to engage in public speech and an ability to undertake collective action. In his techno-future classic book *Being Digital*, Nicholas Negroponte (1995) noted that the information superhighway is about the global movement of weightless bits at the speed of light. Alvin Toffler's (1981) views on what he calls the Third Wave 'prosumer' (the electronic-age producer–consumer) are an example of his optimism, as he declares that the current age of knowledge brings greater freedom and individualisation. We are now in what Forrester calls the 'age of the customer' (see http://blogs.forrester.com/category/age_of_the_customer). Technology gurus like Don Tapscott and Anthony Williams perceive social network sites as technologies of revolution, as they enable consumers to become producers to the extent that there is overlap between production and consumption (often termed 'prosumption').

> You can participate in the economy as an equal, co-creating value with your peers and favourite companies to meet your very personal needs, to engage in fulfilling communities, to change the world or just to have fun! Prosumption comes full circle! (Tapscott and Williams 2006:150).

But perhaps most controversial has been the theory of objectivism developed by Russian-American philosopher Ayn Rand. Briefly, Rand implored man to eschew the edicts of others, reject altruism and embrace a morality

---

[1] Kaplan and Haenlein (2009:61) contend that Web 2.0 is a notion used to illustrate the new ways in which software developers and end-users have started to exploit the World Wide Web as a platform, whereby content and applications are no longer created and published by individuals, but are instead continuously modified by all users in participatory and collaborative fashion.

of self-interest. Her objectivist ideas were popular and influenced groups working in the technology sector of California. The Californian ideology, a techno-utopian belief that computer networks could measure, control and self-stabilise societies, without hierarchical political control, and that people could work only for their own happiness, became widespread in Silicon Valley. However, Adam Curtis' polemic *All Watched Over by Machines of Loving Grace*, first broadcast on the British Broadcasting Corporation's BBC2 channel in May 2011, fiercely criticised Silicon Valley's rather disturbing love of Ayn Rand's fiction and her concepts of self-interested objectivism, which some argue have underpinned cyberspace. The documentary series suggested that man is not liberated—and in fact is enslaved—by computers. It is a premise that is difficult to refute, as we are overloaded with overheated laptops, tablets and 4G mobile phones, constantly exchanging tweets, receiving text messages, experiencing the bleeping and nagging of onscreen emails and Skype, and having our worth dictated by a league table of how many people clicked the link to us or 'Facebooked' it (see also Dent 2011).

Other sceptics like Tom Smith (2009) and Evgeny Morozov (2012) contend that this celebratory rhetoric and techno-futurism is misleading, and that while user-driven technologies such as blogs, social networks and video-sharing platforms have changed the way in which users interact with one another and the Internet, people also leave data trails behind them every time they interact with these media. There is increasing consumer awareness about the value of their data, online identity and 'commodification' of user-generated content, and growing resentment that social interactions are being used as a basis for the advertising business. Facebook's near monopoly of our online identities and model of monetising customers' data has raised concerns regarding privacy. Every time a user searches online for the best restaurant deal, or just shares news with Facebook 'friends' or tweets to their followers, their online presence leaves cyberfootprints that are collected by giant companies like Facebook, Twitter, Google and Microsoft, providing new insight into all aspects of everyday life. This is a key to the mechanisms through which the social media extract surplus profit, and is vital to their financial coordination. As social media users do not actually pay for the service, they are the commodity themselves, and one of the reasons online social platforms exist is that they commercially exploit people who join them and who use them to share information and data. The economics of social media, however, actually contradict the claim that consumers have become producers and that the current age of knowledge brings greater freedom and citizen empowerment.

Privacy concerns are gaining momentum amid growing controversy surrounding the increased merger activity and concentration of power in these technology giants. In the past, media markets and regulations were distinct, based on distribution technology. For example, broadcasting was traditionally subject to content regulation in order to promote diversity of content, whereas the telecommunications sector was subject to economic value, with a focus on supporting investment and affordable access to the network. Technological convergence, however, has meant that previously distinct types of media have merged, with the best and most disruptive actual example of convergence being the Internet (Michalis 2013). With digital convergence a much-discussed tendency, firms have been crossing the lines that once divided the mass media, telecommunications and computer industries (Noam 2013), and forming what Cunningham and Silver (2013) term the 'new King Kongs' of online media distribution, including Google, Apple, Amazon, Facebook and Microsoft. McChesney (2013:130–131) observed that 13 of the 30 largest publicly funded companies in the USA are not Internet-related, and some of these are larger than the major telecommunications firms such as AT&T, Verizon and Comcast. Facebook, for example, has acquired ten companies since its launch, with its largest acquisition being the February 2014 purchase of WhatsApp, a cross-platform instant messaging subscription service for smartphones, at a price of $19 billion, while the photo-sharing app Instagram was acquired in 2012 for $1 billion.

This chapter seeks to provide an understanding of how these contests and debates have been (and are) shaped by a combination of economic, political, sociocultural and technological forces. It deals with structural changes and the processes of convergence in the media and communications field, as well as the related issue of innovation as an economic driver. As such, it will include a discussion of the economics of social media and the rise of knowledge entrepreneurs such as Facebook founder and CEO Mark Zuckerberg. Here we will focus on market and regulatory issues, and thus adopt an analytical approach focused on what is often termed the 'political economy of communications'. In exploring this approach, we consider the transition from old to networked media and the regulatory issues that have emerged in relation to ownership, organisation and licensing of information services.

MEDIA MARKET SHIFTS

Our analysis of social networking sites takes place against a backdrop of two key developments. First, the last three decades or so have witnessed a period of almost constant technological change within the media industries, which have witnessed the development of new broadcast delivery technologies such as satellite and digital television, as well as the growth of new media technologies, chiefly the Internet, mobile phones and social media, which are increasingly the engines driving engagement, interaction, hype and interest. This change has been facilitated by the development of the global Internet infrastructure, the World Wide Web, microprocessors and other digital ICTs. The technological shift is said to enable the development of a 'democratised' or 'many-to-many' communications architecture, in contrast to the earlier 'one-to-many', 'top-down' communication forms of mass society, thus providing for a highly interactive process of communication and content production among media producers and consumers. Technological advances commonly signify a familiar transition from 'old media' to 'new media', where the latter are identified primarily in terms of their digital rather than analogue form, and where the rendering of these media is based on the creation and manipulation of numerical data (computer binary code) (Gane and Beer 2008:6). Analysis and critical inquiry into these new media forms, regardless of their perceived 'democratic' character, are still crucial, as they are developed and function within a market economy frequently at odds with the public interest,[2] just like older mass media communications (Gane and Beer 2008:6). In fact, the emerging system is termed 'digital capitalism'—which, however, is still capitalism, a system that 'turns resources like workers, raw materials, land and information into marketable commodities that earn a profit for those who invest capital into the system. New media deepen and extend tendencies within earlier forms of capitalism by opening new possibilities to turn media and audiences into saleable commodities' (Mosco 2008:54).

Second, and just as important, digital technologies and market developments have also been shaped by a general shift towards the 'marketisation' of broadcasting, particularly in Europe and the USA, but also throughout much of the rest of the world (Murdock 2000; Murdock and

---

[2] The term 'public interest' is broad, vague and loosely constructed. It changes over time and when considered from different perspectives, and thus defining it is notoriously difficult. McQuail (1992:3) defines the public interest as 'informational, cultural and social benefits to the wider society which go beyond the immediate, particular and individual interests'.

Wasko 2007; Freedman 2008:50–52; Hesmondhalgh 2007:105–136). Inspired by neo-liberal ideas, over the last three decades, marketisation has been pursued through four major policy and/or regulatory interventions, employed in various combinations (Evens, Iosifidis and Smith 2013:5–6):

- Privatisation (the sale of public assets to private investors). Whereas in the USA there were relatively few public assets to be sold in the first place, numerous European governments have overseen the complete or partial privatisation of publicly owned broadcasters (e.g., TF1 in France) and telecommunications operators (e.g., Deutsch Telekom in Germany).
- Liberalisation (opening previously restricted markets to new entrants). For example, the 1996 US Telecommunications Act allowed cable and telecommunications companies to enter each other's markets, and relaxed restrictions on cross-media ownership. Similarly, during the late 1980s and 1990s, EU directives facilitated the opening up of both European broadcasting (Television without Frontiers, renamed Audiovisual Media Services) and telecommunications markets to competition.
- Reorientation of regulation (away from the defence of the public interest, to the promotion of 'fair' competition). In Europe, this trend is best illustrated by the increased influence of the European Commission (EC) Directorate for Competition over key areas of media regulation, such as mergers, and the definition of 'state aid' with regard to public service broadcasters (Wheeler 2004). In the USA, the removal of long-standing public interest regulations such as the Fairness Doctrine and Financial Interest and Syndication (Fin-Syn) Rules during the late 1980s and 1990s can also be seen to represent the prioritisation of competition (and free speech) concerns over any wider interpretation of the public interest.
- Corporatisation (urging or obliging publicly financed organisations to seek additional sources of income and to maximise their market value). For example, successive British governments have urged the BBC to pursue commercial opportunities (mostly overseas) via its commercial arm, BBC Worldwide, and to reduce its operating costs (Born 2004). Alongside new developments in broadcasting technology such as encryption and digitalisation, these political initiatives have facilitated the growing commodification of broadcasting. Perhaps most notably, throughout Europe, the universality of

broadcasting traditionally offered by public service broadcasters has been eroded by the growth of pay TV, and even in the USA, the major free-to-air commercial networks face increased competitive pressure from pay TV services available via cable and satellite—all of which means that 'more and more television services are offered for sale at a price and [are] available only to those who can afford to pay' (Murdock and Wasko 2007:43). As we will show below, social media today are also becoming highly corporate.

POLITICAL ECONOMY AND THE ROLE OF THE STATE

Taken together, these technological, market and commercial developments present various media policy challenges that are addressed under the purview of the political economy theory. Broadly speaking, the political economy approach to understanding the media is concerned with the ways in which media organisations' behaviour (and the content they provide) is shaped by the economic and political context in which they operate. The term 'political economy' was originally associated with classical economics (Adam Smith used the term in in 1776 in *The Wealth of Nations*), and later with neo-Marxian forms of thought (Artz, Macek and Cloud 2006), media imperialism (Chakravartty and Zhao 2008), media commercialisation and the decline of public service media (PSM) (Mansell 2002; Sparks 2007; Iosifidis 2007, 2010), but its current emphasis is on the role of the state in the global era and the nature of capitalist economies across nations (international or comparative political economy) (Calabrese and Sparks 2004; Murdock and Wasko 2007; Mosco 2008; Iosifidis 2011a; McChesney 2013; Ho and Fung 2016).

Certainly, what was once a largely national market for media producers and consumers, overseen primarily by the nation-state, is now a global market, characterised by reduced national government power and ability to regulate. This new system is synonymous with the shift from 'government' to 'governance', which denotes a change from a unified policy exercised by the national government, to a more complex system encompassing a number of policy actors, intergovernmental agencies and political institutions (Iosifidis 2011a). Supranational and regional organisations with a predominantly economic focus (but also sociocultural agendas) have played an active role in the area of media and communications policy. The most significant of these include the World Trade Organization (WTO) free trade institution, the International Telecommunication Union (ITU), the Internet Corporation for Assigned Names and Numbers (ICANN) and the United Nations Educational, Scientific and Cultural Organization (UNESCO)—and in particular, the UNESCO Convention on the Protection and Promotion of the Diversity of Cultural Expressions, which came into effect in March 2007. Regional deals such as the EU and the Free Trade Area of the Americas (FTAA) also dictate policy agenda. These bodies tackle various aspects of international systems and simultaneously effect national regulatory regimes. This process of governance and the resulting 'complex interdependence' in the information era brings more activities into an international agreements framework. The governance process is viewed by some as synonymous with reduced state power, for national governments are now but one player among many in the domestic and international arenas. Referring to the UK, Rhodes (1994) suggested that the country's membership in the EU has seen power flow upwards from the central state to a supranational tier of government.

However, another camp of scholars point to the emergence of the 'regulatory state'.[3] In this regard, the role of the state in the national and international arenas remains strong. At a European level, national governments have taken care to avoid restraint of market development, but they still intervene in order to maintain open and fair competition and to protect the interests of the public in ensuring access to a variety of services. For example, governments are responsible for maintaining and promoting public interest goals such as political pluralism and cultural diversity, which are considered to be in the national interest, where the EU has no jurisdiction to intervene. The establishment of super-regulatory bodies like Ofcom in the UK in 2003, replacing five separate broadcast and telecommunications regulators, can be seen as very much a product of the regulatory state. Although at face value this regulatory overhaul might seem to be a fairly straightforward response by UK policymakers to the convergence of television, telecommunications and computing technologies facilitated by digitalisation, 'this motion should not obscure the fact that the establishment of Ofcom was also the institutional culmination of a significant shift in the focus of UK television regulation, away from the allocation of relatively scarce spectrum to achieve public service objectives and towards the control of market power to facilitate free market competition' (Smith 2006). As Harding (2000) noted, one of the government's

---

[3] For an in-depth recent analysis of the role of the state in the era of globalisation see Ho and Fung (2016).

objectives has been to put competition law at the centre of media regulation. Competition law, however, may be incapable of addressing the various regulatory challenges posed by the rise of social media.

THE GROWTH OF SOCIAL MEDIA

The mass media model that characterised most of the previous century was influenced by structural arrangements based primarily on a market economy and minimal state regulation. This model developed within the control of media proprietors, relying upon monetised labour, and was co-opted by institutional arrangements such as class, race and gender. It was subject to only a modicum of constraint by governmental policy operating within the nation-state system (Picard 2014:98). Today, the media landscape is undergoing transformations that change those structural arrangements through the processes of digitalisation and globalisation, and through the appearance of increasingly influential actors other than the state, including intergovernmental agencies, civil society and grass-roots organisations. These intermediaries give the power of speech to people who previously had no effective means of raising their voices. Civil society includes all those who are not part of government, private enterprise or intergovernmental organisations (Raboy 2004:228). Non-state entities such as NGOs are examples of subnational hierarchies existing below the state level (Kumar 2010:157). Transnational movements of civil societies and NGOs have assumed an important role of late in influencing the processes of decision-making in international media and communications policy. UNESCO and other global organisations that represent the non-corporatist perspective on the media have gradually gained momentum, as evidenced by the Convention on the Protection and Promotion of the Diversity of Cultural Expressions, which represents a protectionist alternative to the principles of free trade, and highlights UNESCO's renewed role in the area of global media governance.

But it is mainly technological developments that are changing who can communicate, what is communicated and how it is communicated. Citizen-consumers use contemporary communications technologies for self-expression, participating in self-defined communities and contributing to debate about developments in society. These technologies represent a shift in democratic responsibility from institutional media to amorphous digital communities, and are important to the public as they pursue personhood, identity and culture (Picard 2014:99). The online forums or social spaces of the Web 2.0 differ substantially from the traditional forms such as that of Public Service Broadcasting (PSB), in that they allow more interactivity and many-to-many rather than one-to-many types of communication. They appear to be ideal spaces for initiating public debate and social change. This issue will be dealt with in the next section, especially with reference to political power, but we must first provide some definitions and statistics relating to social media in order to put things into context.

Social media are defined as 'online resources that people use to share content: video, photos, images, text, ideas, insight, humour, opinion, gossip, news' (Drury 2008). In other words, they are a blur of tweets, shares and content. They are global, embedded in every corner of the web, and used by all age groups. Social media have become a ubiquitous part of everyday life. In 2015, nearly 630 million people logged onto Facebook daily—48 % of its 1.4 billion users. Twitter, Google+, Tumblr and Pinterest see more and more activity every day. And it is fair to assume that most users have multiple social networks. Here are some striking statistics regarding the social media (http://www.jeffbullas.com/2014/01/17/20-social-media-facts-and-statistics-you-should-know-in-2014/)

- Seventy-two per cent of all Internet users are now active on social media.
- Usage among the 18–29 age demographic is 89 %.
- The 30–49 bracket sits at 72 %.
- Sixty per cent of the 50–60 group are active on social media.
- In the 65+ bracket, 43 % are using social media.
- Time spent on Facebook per hour spent online differs across countries, but the top three are the USA, Australia and the UK: US citizens are on top, at 16 minutes per hour, followed by the Australians at 14 minutes and the British at 13 minutes.
- Seventy-one per cent of users access social media from a mobile device.

These statistics demonstrate that the paradigm of social media being used only by the younger generation should now be put to rest. Facebook is still the largest social medium, but there are signs that by 2016, Google+ may match Facebook on 'social sharing' if one considers that it has been around for less than three years and is growing at 33 % per annum. Twitter is also now a public company and is among the fastest-growing networks, with 44 % growth from 2012 to 2014, and 288 million monthly active users in 2015. One should also refer to other important social media channels, including Pinterest, Instagram, Tumblr, Vine and SlideShare, among many others. We continue this rather brief section with some of the latest figures concerning leading site Facebook's 1.4 billion users, as well as an analytical description of Facebook's and Twitter's latest corporate developments:

- One million web pages are accessed using the 'Login with Facebook' feature.
- Twenty-three per cent of Facebook users login at least five times per day.
- Forty-seven per cent of Americans say Facebook is their number-one influencer of purchases.
- Seventy per cent of marketers used Facebook to gain new customers.

Meanwhile, Twitter continues to evolve as a microblogging platform. Technologically, the firm has continued to innovate with the launch of Twitter cards, leading to more media rich user experiences. Much of Twitter navigation is now conducted on a mobile device. Research from Nielsen (see https://blog.twitter.com/en-gb/2014/80-of-uk-users-access-twitter-via-their-mobile) has reported that 'mobile is written into the DNA of Twitter', as 80 % of UK users access Twitter via their mobile device. Nielsen found similarly strong results across Europe for everyday mobile use. In Spain, similar to the UK, 80 % of users access Twitter through a mobile device, and this is the primary method for 69 %; in France, the numbers are 68 % and 60 %, respectively, and in the Netherlands, usage is the same for both, at 72 %. The Nielsen research also notes that the tools available to marketers and advertisers using Twitter are becoming more sophisticated, as is the framework that content marketers are using to relate to Twitter as a platform. Lastly, engagement with users seems to be a better metric of success on social media than sheer number of followers. Twitter pays increasing attention to how much content is being shared and read. The effectiveness of Twitter's strategy has increasingly to do with the level of engagement that happens organically and is cultivated.

However, there have been regular controversies around social media's increasingly corporate nature, inappropriate content and model of monetising data. Like many in Silicon Valley, Zuckerberg is famous for running his multibillion-dollar company Facebook with the philosophy 'move fast and break things'. Employees are encouraged to ask forgiveness, not permission. Prototypes are quickly launched, piloted and improved, and then launched again (see http://techcrunch.com/2013/09/19/why-zuckerberg-thinks-government-should-not-move-fast-and-break-things/). This strategy, while avoiding the bureaucracy and legal requirements of painstaking approvals and the inclusion of contract bids of all parties, can also lead to problems. Consumers are becoming increasingly aware of the value of their data and their online identity, and are sceptical of social transactions that are used as the basis for an advertising business. Monetising data, social media advertising and privacy issues will be discussed in some detail below, but social media's (and especially Facebook's) handling of online identities has alerted privacy campaigners. Meanwhile, controversies have arisen regarding inappropriate content. For instance, in April 2013, Facebook refused for more than 7 days to take down two graphic videos of beheadings, while defending the publication of an unexpurgated video of a woman beating a baby. The firm's policy (like other consumer sites of scale) is that it has had to automate content moderation and rely on users to flag content, and yet poor and inconsistent decisions are made by individuals when extreme cases surface in the media.

Political Economy, Social Media and Corporate Activity

It is clear then that the Internet and social networking sites have become a major arena for corporate activity, similar to other branches of the cultural industries. Individualisation of consumption has been accompanied by consolidation of media ownership, producing global multimedia corporations intent on redeveloping cyberspace as retail real estate (Murdock 2004). Fuchs (2011a) argues that the Internet and social media today are stratified, non-participatory spaces, and that an alternative, non-corporate Internet is needed. Giant corporations colonise social media and dominate their attention economy. In a more recent work, Fuchs (2014) takes a further step and contends that large corporate (and to a lesser extent, political) actors dominate, and therefore centralise, the formation of speech, association, assembly and opinion on social media.

> Liberal freedoms turn on capitalist social media into their opposite. The concept of social media participation is an ideology...it seems both necessary

and feasible to theorize "Web 2.0" not as a participatory system, but by employing more negative, critical terms such as class, exploitation and surplus value. (Fuchs 2014:102)

Corporate social media gather data on users by continuously monitoring and recording online activities. Collected data are then stored, merged and analysed in order to create detailed user profiles containing information about personal interests and online behaviours. This in turn enables targeted advertising, with the objective of luring consumers into buying products and services. The mechanism of targeted advertising on social media has been termed 'panoptic sorting' (see Gandy 1993a, b), as the social media are able to obtain a comprehensive, detailed picture of the interests and activities of their users. According to Fuchs (2014:110), corporate social media sell the users' data commodity to advertising clients at a price that is greater than the invested constant and variable capital. In another work, Fuchs (2013) argues that social media 'prosumers' are double objects of commodification: they are commodities themselves, and through this commodification, their consciousness while online is permanently exposed to commodity logic in the form of advertisements.

Political economy investigates the social whole, or the totality of social relations, which make up the economic, political, social and cultural areas of life (Mosco 2008:3–4). The marriage of politics and culture with the processes of resource production, distribution and exchange aids in understanding social processes. The economic analysis of the general laws of production, distribution and circulation of goods blends well with the political focus on social inequalities produced by these processes, tying issues of power and inequality to those of market deficiency or failure in explaining social change. This chapter attempts to map new circuits of accumulation, and to show how these circuits, in part, determine and cement new social relations on the Internet and social media. At the same time, this approach is sceptical of the superiority of free markets. The political economy of social media is nothing more than the political economy of capitalism applied to social media. Looking at the Internet and social media through the lens of capitalism reveals that what makes the online capital accumulation process different from that of established media such as broadcasting is the way in which it acquires the audience commodity.

Television advertisers buy statistics about potential viewer attention to advertisements, a passive audience model. Internet companies instead may offer and refine information collected from an active audience when users spontaneously provide data about their personal tastes, preferences, desires, and pathways through their browsers. Internet advertisers thus can more accurately target the audiences they intend to reach (Bolano and Vieira 2014:5).

Fuchs (2011b, 2014) also refers to the transformation of users as audience and uses the term 'audience commodity' to highlight the fact that any user activity is of interest to the Internet company only as a raw material that, in the process, informational workers produce as audience commodity and sell to advertisers. Fuchs argues that Internet firms use social network site users in two ways. First, they treat user-produced 'free' content as raw material for their search engine cataloguing systems. Second, the surveillance of users' browsing habits is based on users' tacit permission allowing these firms to track, stockpile and manipulate the data derived from usage. In this chapter, we explore policy recommendations to address the perceived asymmetries of the economic social relationship established between social networks and users. We focus on the question of power as it is embedded in social networking sites, and particularly the language of Facebook's and Twitter's privacy policies and terms of use. We concentrate on the production, distribution and exchange of communications resources and commodities, with an eye towards the actors involved in these processes. Thus the discussion centres on questions of media ownership and control, processes of consolidation, diversification strategies (investment), commercialisation and commodification, internationalisation and accumulation of power, the workings of the profit motive (competition), and the consequences of media content and practices (production, consumption, meaning-making) (see also Boyd-Barrett 1995).

The Audience as a Commodity

The audience as a commodity is the new means of virtual production in terms of social media economics. Growing debate has arisen regarding business ethics around the behaviour of Facebook, Twitter and Google in terms of these digital trails. Facebook's policy statement states that 'when we deliver ads, we do not share your information'. This might be true for personally identifying information, but a site that made more than $10 billion in advertising revenue in 2013 does, indeed, collect vast amounts of data of interest to advertisers. We have all had an experience where Facebook seemed to 'know' that we were looking for a piece of furniture or a holiday spot, and offered up the corresponding advert. One case that triggered controversy was the discovery, via the publication of a research paper in the *Proceedings of the National Academy of Sciences* (see http://www.pnas.org/content/111/24/8788.ful, accessed 20 July 2014), that for one week in January 2012, Facebook researchers deliberately skewed what 689,003 Facebook users saw when they logged in. In that experiment, the researchers tested whether emotional contagion occurred outside of in-person interactions between individuals, by reducing the amount of emotional content in the news feed. The study showed that when positive expressions were reduced, people produced fewer positive posts and more negative posts; when negative expressions were reduced, the opposite pattern occurred. The lesson to be learned from this 'emotional contagion' study is the ease with which people allowed themselves to be monitored and manipulated by a giant corporation. In fact, Facebook users are being algorithmically managed (see http://www.theguardian.com/technology/2014/jul/06/we-shouldnt-expect-facebook-to-behave-ethically, accessed 20 July 2014).). The arguments about whether the experiment was unethical also reveal the extent to which big data is changing our regulatory practices. The data protection framework may protect specific types of personal information (see below), but data analytics allows corporations to build information 'mosaics' about individuals by assembling large numbers of the digital traces that we all leave in cyberspace.

PUBLIC SERVICE VERSUS PUBLIC CHOICE PHILOSOPHIES

That the Internet and social networking sites have increasingly become privatised and turned into a business is a cause for concern. This is because these new media—as, indeed, all established private media—are seen as not just another industry. This industry is unique because of the dual nature of the content being produced, which is simultaneously a commodity—a private good, as media outlets use their products for the accumulation of profit—and a public good, as the content constitutes a part of the public sphere. As a result, commercial media institutions on the one hand have a sociocultural function, and on the other they are driven by economic interests. Is that dual character of private media content aligned with their safeguarding of democracy and the public interest? Equally questionable is the assumption that private media mirror public opinion. The political economy approach is based on the premise that the media are powerful, and therefore able not merely to mirror but also to influence public opinion and shape public discourse.

The commercialisation of the Internet and social networking sites prompts one to reconsider the role of public access media in enhancing civic engagement, forming political identities and culture and tackling the 'democratic deficit' in the era of commodification of the communications media. In the USA, public access television has been for some decades now an established venue for alternative democratic communication. In Europe, PSB has traditionally been open to all at affordable prices; households are usually required to pay an annual licence fee in exchange for high-quality content, particularly in news, current affairs, education and the dissemination of culture. Of course, these media are top-down hierarchical institutions, and as Kellner (1997) admits, many will claim that democratic politics involves face-to-face conversation, discussion and consensus-building. But for intelligent debate and consensus to be achieved, individuals must be informed, and PSM, accessible to all, are important sources of information in the present age, helping activist groups and individuals obtain and disseminate information. Apart from universal accessibility, PSM organisations have been proven a credible and trustworthy source of information. During the second Gulf War, and more recently the Ukraine crisis, more people tuned to the BBC and its unrivalled team of correspondents to access news and reaction. The websites of PSM also rank among the most-visited non-commercial portal sites, with the BBC the most trusted and widely used site in Europe (Council of Europe 2008:14). The BBC has achieved this position by exploring ways in which the Internet can extend public broadcasting's core mission of offering cultural resources for 'thick' citizenship (Murdock 2004). The shared commitment of PSM to the public interest and the common good is well established.

In addition, the PSM can make a sociocultural difference and can contribute to the creation of an inclusive public sphere and enhanced civic engagement in at least three broad areas: information (particularly factuality and accuracy of news and public representations), cultural representation (which creates a pluralistic social and cultural community) and universality (as PSM are available to all at the point of reception). They offer a counterbalance to the commodification of media and concentration of power in both established (Disney, News Corp, etc.) and new media titans (e.g., Facebook, Google and Amazon). The functions and the value that PSM provide are not offered in equal volume and quality by online content providers and profit-driven systems (Iosifidis 2010). Their universal coverage and widespread access guarantee a public space that is accessible to mass audiences and can function as a forum for democratic public discourse. An important characteristic of the civic role related to the public sphere is the availability of impartial, accurate, non-market-oriented news and current affairs that are provided by public media. Another is the provision of high-quality (innovative, risky, diverse and home-grown) programming and culture for various minority ethnic and religious groups in a pluralist, multicultural society. These socially beneficial functions support the role of public media in today's deregulated communications marketplace. There is a continued need for strong, well-funded public institutions, capable of delivering socially valuable content that will keep public debate alive. For this to happen, however, regulation must ensure, first, that PSM have the necessary mandate as a core component of their remit, and second, that PSM are held to account for fulfilling their mandate and mission. As the Council of Europe (2008) noted, policy must recognise the role of PSM as a priority within democracy such that citizens are ensured sufficient resources and support.

SOCIAL MEDIA POLICY CHALLENGES: INTELLECTUAL PROPERTY RIGHTS, ELECTRONIC SURVEILLANCE AND PRIVACY ISSUES

The ease of freely downloading music and video, of sharing files containing data, audio and video, and of copying material of all sorts challenges the ability of capitalism to maintain and police its property and market regimes (Mosco 2008:55). New media make it easier to copy and share work under copyright, thereby pushing governments and businesses alike to tighten their control, especially in countries like China, where illegal digital downloading is common practice. Not only does technology represent a challenge to property and market rules, it enables individuals to disrupt the system, as electronic social networking permits social movements to mobilise and coordinate as never before (Mosco 2008:56). This work casts a critical eye with regard to the enthusiasm that accompanies social networking. Certainly, social media can be revolutionary, changing the face of business as we know it, of organisational structures, and then changing the definition of authority as we know it as well, putting consumers at the heart of the conversation. Yet there are various inherent risks for both individuals and businesses. The Internet is overloaded with intellectual property infringement, pirated films and music, and leaked confidential information. Electronic surveillance is among the major issues requiring attention, as the new media have made it possible for companies to monitor people's activities and violate personal privacy rights (Lyon 2003). What regulatory regime is appropriate for dealing with these issues on social media? How can regulators balance the right to free speech with the need to protect people? Whose responsibility is it?

The growth of the Internet and the emergence of low-cost technologies such as computers with large amounts of processing power and storage have made high-quality copying of digital media inexpensive, quick, global and easy to make and distribute. The huge numbers of people on the Internet are all potential copyright infringers. At the same time, the ability to enforce copyright laws to combat this risk has been perceived as difficult for reasons including the distributive nature of this network of networks; the cross-network technological operation of the Internet without regard to national boundaries or jurisdictions; the seeming anonymity of the Internet, which creates difficulty in detecting individual infringers; the ability to quickly set up mirror sites with infringing content; and the 'historical' (in relative terms) culture of the Internet, that information and technologies were shared in building it. In light of all of these concerns in the face of Internet growth and the sophistication of consumer technologies, the content-producing community around the world has pressed for Internet- and digital media-specific reforms to the copyright regime at both the international and national levels. These reforms have largely been concerned with the creation of new rights to fit the distribution of works over the Internet, the protection of technological measures to prevent copying of and access to digital works, and the enhancement of enforcement schemes (Flanagan and Maniatis 2008). The international protection of copyright is governed by the World Intellectual Property Organisation (WIPO), and especially the WIPO Copyright and Performers and Producers Rights Treaties; the WTO, particularly the Agreement on Trade-Related Aspects of Intellectual Property Rights (TRIPS); and UNESCO, through its Universal Copyright Convention. But to many lawmakers, scholars and Internet users, the calls for tougher enforcement of intellectual property rights look like desperate attempts to salvage an outdated copyright system that needs to adapt to the modern world. American academic and political activist Lawrence Lessig, for example, is a proponent of reduced copyright and trademark legal restrictions, particularly in technology applications (see http://p2pfoundation.

net/Lawrence_Lessig:_Five_Proposals_for_Copyright_Reform, accessed 16 July 2015).

Meanwhile, the subject of privacy has risen to the level of public discourse with the revelations of Edward Snowden, who exposed a secret mass surveillance programme by the US National Security Agency. Many voices have claimed that this exposure will be a catalyst in altering policy discourse about privacy in the USA and abroad (see Epstein et al. 2004:144). There has been much attention on Internet surveillance by government agencies, but this chapter focuses primarily on the intense debate concerning the privacy of peoples' correspondence when they are using online services such as email, text messaging and social media. Put simply, in the past, people created content with the expectation that it would remain private, but with the advent of social media, with text messages and tweets, this content now resides in the public space. Once we are logged onto Facebook or Twitter, we are essentially telling everyone where we are, what we are doing, 24 hours a day. This social media world creates an environment of open distribution, and because the technology is indeed pervasive and the amount of data we are creating very large, it is difficult to regulate. But do large social media sites take steps to protect user privacy? Perhaps we should refer to Christian Fuchs' critical discourse analysis of Facebook's privacy policy (2011b) in order to draw a conclusion on social media's treatment of privacy issues. In what Fuchs calls liberal or bourgeois notions of privacy (Fuchs 2011b), he contends that such notions mask socioeconomic inequality and protect capital and the rich from public accountability (Fuchs 2011b:140). He shows the asymmetric relationship between social media providers and social media users, and argues that social media sites like Facebook frame privacy in a way that protects their interests at the expense of their users. His findings are echoed by other critical discourse studies which also demonstrate the continued commodification of user data by Facebook and Twitter. For instance, Butosi's (2012) work on Facebook, Twitter and privacy is an important contribution to political economic research on social networking. His historical analysis of the privacy policies and terms of use documents demonstrates how they have changed over time concurrently with the managerial changes of both Facebook and Twitter, which have led to their reorientation as organisations driven by profit motivations.

Butosi also refers to Mark Zuckerberg, CEO and founder of Facebook, and his views on privacy which, first and foremost, articulate an opinion of privacy that works in his company's interest. Since people's data and profiles are the new valuable commodity for social media sites, privacy must then be relativised and rendered ambiguous in the sense of a double standard that protects companies yet exposes consumers to privacy abuses by them for profitable gain. As Butosi notes, it is no secret that Zuckerberg believes that the age of privacy is over. The term 'privacy', commonly understood here in terms of the degree to which one has control over the distribution of their personal data, is a concept left ill-defined and underdeveloped in social media discourse, thus rendering the term rather vague. This vague and seemingly contradictory usage, however, is precisely how Zuckerberg deploys the term, which allows him to assert that privacy is somehow no longer a 'social norm' (Johnson, Crawford, and Palfrey 2004). In an age of social networking and the proliferation of ICT, to be private seems to commit oneself to a romantic yearning for a bygone era! This understanding of privacy as outmoded is very often criticised by virtue of evidence that demonstrates, to the contrary, the willingness of people to share information with others so openly, to communicate and to be public; these actions are misunderstood as the opposite of being private. The definition of privacy, at least in the confines of public discourse, must remain ambiguous in order for companies like Facebook and Twitter to benefit from corporate privacy protections afforded by law. It is not difficult to see that these social networking sites have a direct economic interest in monetising user activity.

In policy terms, since 2011, advertisements on social media have been covered by the same rules as other advertisements. Policy priorities should perhaps be to ensure that rules are well understood and followed by all interested parties. As the Internet is typically a self-regulated area, what is required is transparency, or making clear that an advertisement is, in fact, an advertisement. People need to know when they are being advertised to, and the responsibility to make it obvious lies with the social media sites. The United Nations Charter (1945) and the Universal Declaration of Human Rights (1948) established rules and norms that countries could not abridge. Specifically on the issue of how companies are collecting data and the way they are using it, here the classic Universal Declaration of Human Rights (Article 12, The Right to Privacy) and the European Convention on Human Rights (Article 8, Right to Respect for Private and Family Life) apply, which is effectively the right to the privacy of our correspondence. In the UK, the Data Protection Act 1998 defines UK law on the processing of data on identifiable living people, and it is the country's major piece of legislation governing the protection of personal data. Although the act itself does not mention privacy, it was enacted to bring UK law into line with the EU Data Protection Directive of 1995, which required member states to protect people's fundamental rights and freedoms, and in particular their right to privacy with respect to the processing of personal data. In practice, it provides a way for individuals to control information about themselves.

Lynsay Taffe, former Director of Communications, Marketing and Public Affairs of the Advertising Standards Authority (ASA), outlines three areas of priority with respect to advertising and marketing on social media. First, there should be transparency, or making clear that an ad is an ad. People must know when they are being advertised to so that they can make an informed decision, and if this is not obvious from the context, firms have a responsibility to make it obvious. When it comes to user-generated content, Taffe admits that this presents a problem for brands, but she is quick to clarify that the ASA does not regulate what members of the public say; they regulate what companies say. Given that social media are about conversation, an interaction can occasionally cause something that a member of the public has said to be considered part of a firm's brand communication. Thus companies must be cautious in situations when, for instance, someone tweets something about a firm's product or says something misleading about the product, and the company endorses it (Taffe 2013). David Cushman (2013), Strategy Partner at the Social Partners, acknowledges that the Internet and social media world is a peer-to-peer environment of open distribution in which anything can be passed on, from a nasty advert to pornography. He suggests that this environment should essentially be self-regulated, in which there must be some sort of social responsibility and trust on the part of both companies and individuals. But can self-regulation protect us from potential risks such as misuse of customer data, theft and leaking of sensitive information, and misleading advertising, to name but a few? The sophistication of the Internet allows only for more, not less, surveillance of individuals and violations of privacy.

CONCLUSION

This chapter has provided a political economy analysis, with a focus on market and regulatory issues, to aid in understanding the implications of social media for power structures in society. When traditional print and broadcast media were the major means of mass communication and information, the process was characterised by slow production and high fixed costs, eventually resulting in high levels of media market concentration and accumulation of power in the hands of a few. The emergence of the Internet and social networking sites has rendered the structure of the 'old' media world obsolete and the amount of content that can travel over online networks virtually infinite.

> Social media is no longer a way of exchanging personal messages with friends. These messages are public, they're global, they're at least semi-permanent, they can be journalistic, they can be news sharing and news gathering and news breaking; they can also be enormously damaging and generally speaking, once the genie is out of the bottle is impossible to put it back in. (Phillips 2013)

The Internet has also been termed highly 'interactive', allowing many-to-many communications, to the point that some contend that the social media create an economy that is more open, more participatory and more democratic—one need only refer to various Internet social movements that have been used as tools of revolutions and democratisation ('Revolution 2.0', 'Facebook/Twitter revolution'). Others, however, maintain that social media are instruments of control and commerce. In fact, the transition of the Internet from an inter-academic network to a commercial communications enterprise has caused old controversies to resurface and has brought about new policy challenges.

Despite the rapidly changing media ecology, many of the basic questions of media and communications studies remain relevant. Concentration of media ownership is still very much an issue, and it is becoming more intense due to media convergence which blurs the boundaries between media sectors even further, thereby allowing companies to accumulate power across sectors. Corporatisation and profit maximisation strategies of private media have intensified as they seek to maximise their market value. But this leaves little space for accountable, publicly funded institutions. In some cases, PSM have been encouraged to undertake commercial strategies, as evidenced by the successive British governments that have urged the BBC to pursue commercial opportunities (mostly overseas) via its commercial arm. Public interest tests in relation to changes in ownership and control must be maintained and strengthened. At another level, the contention that the social media play a supportive role in social change by strengthening the public sphere echoes the historical role of the printing press, although new media's contribution to democracy is still questionable. Internet freedom and accessibility may be a reality in most countries, but one should remember that 'access to information' does not necessarily result in 'access to conversation' and enhancement of the public sphere.

Finally, community expectations concerning privacy, fairness, accuracy and transparency in the Internet and social media's reporting of news and information remains crucial and requires policing. For example, the European Court of Justice (ECJ), the EU's highest court, has confirmed that existing EU law includes something, albeit in limited form, that privacy advocates and the EC have long sought: the right to be digitally forgotten. The court boosted this cause in a landmark case in which a Spanish lawyer, Mario Costeja Gonzalez, sued Google because its search results linked his name to a newspaper article from 1998 about a now-resolved lawsuit. The court ruled that Google had not displayed links to information that was 'inadequate, irrelevant or excessive', given the purpose for which they were processed and the time elapsed. The 'right to be forgotten', however, is difficult to implement. Even while Google is made to censor its search results in Europe, in the USA the free speech provisions of the First Amendment usually trump privacy concerns. The ECJ ruling makes an allowance for a 'public interest' defence, but Europe will hardly want to build a Chinese-style firewall to prevent that (The Economist 2014b).

Lastly, this chapter shares the concerns of the 'cyber-sceptics' regarding the democratic value of social networks, but given that these online movements are new, it suggests that it is too early to evaluate their ultimate contribution to democracy and cultural change. The political and economic power traditionally associated with the established media is being diverted to online social networks. These are much cheaper to create and expand, and therefore much more accessible for most people. The new ways to communicate offer greater interactivity and greater connectivity, both essential to the development of the public space. The rise of the social media, however, has been associated with the concentration of power, corporatism and commercialism, censorship, electronic surveillance and data protection and privacy concerns. Above all, there seems to be a gap between social media's ability to mobilise people and the ability to initiate and maintain meaningful debate. Commercialisation and the digital revolution have made some of the most cherished institutions of democracy more relevant than ever: strong, accountable and independent PSM can serve the public interest and the common good by enhancing public deliberation.

BIBLIOGRAPHY

Artz L., S. Macek, and D.L. Cloud, eds. 2006. *Marxism and Communication Studies: The Point is to Change It*. New York: Peter Lang.

Bolano Cesar R.S., and Eloy S. Vieira. 2014. "The Political Economy of the Internet: Social Networking Sites and a Reply to Fuchs". *Television & New Media* 15(3): 1–10.

Born G. 2004. *Uncertain Vision: Birt, Dyke and the Reinvention of the BBC*. London: Secker & Warburg.

Boyd-Barrett O. 1995. "The Political Economy Approach". In *Conceptualising the Public Sphere Approaches to Media: A Reader*, eds. O. Boyd-Barrett, and C. Newbold. London: Arnold.

Butosi, C. 2012. *Social Net-Working: Exploring the Political Economy of the Online Social Network Industry*, Thesis submitted in partial fulfilment of the requirements for the degree of Master of Arts, Western University. http://ir.lib.uwo.ca/cgi/viewcontent.cgi?article=1692&context=etd (accessed March 26, 2014).

Calabrese A., and C. Sparks, eds. 2004. *Towards a Political Economy of Culture: Capitalism and Communication in the Twenty-First Century*. Landman: Rowman and Littlefield.

Chakravartty P., and Y. Zhao, eds. 2008. *Global Communication: Toward a Transcultural Political Economy*. Landman, MD: Rowman and Littlefield.

Cunningham S., and J. Silver. 2013. *Screen Distribution and the New King Kongs of the Online World*. Basingstoke: Palgrave Macmillan.

Cushman D. 2013. *Advertising and Marketing on Social Media, Westminster Forum*. July: Policy Priorities for Social Media.

Council of Europe 2008. 'Strategies of Public Service Media as regards Promoting a Wider Democratic Participation of Individuals – Compilation of Good Practices', Report prepared by the Group of Specialists on Public Service Media in the Information Society (MC-S-PSM), November. Available at: http://www.coe.int/t/dghl/standardsetting/media/Doc/H-Inf(2009)6_en.pdf (accessed 5 March 2016).

Dent, G. 2011. Computers are the Boss of Us All? We Don't Know What You Mean Curtis, *The Guardian*, May 21. http://www.theguardian.com/tv-and-radio/2011/may/21/adam-curtis-all-watched-over (accessed April 22, 2014).

Drury G. 2008. "Social Media: Should Marketers Engage and How Can it be Done Effectively". *Journal of Direct, Data and Digital Marketing Practice* 9: 274–277.

Epstein D. et al. 2014. "It's the Definition Stupid! Framing of Online Privacy in the Internet Governance Forum Debates'". *Journal of Information Policy* 4: 144–172.

Evens T., P. Iosifids, and P. Smith. 2013. *The Political Economy of Television Sports Rights*. Basingstoke: Palgrave Macmillan.

Flanagan, A. and S.M. Maniatis. 2008. *Intellectual Property on the Internet: Section A: Digital copyright.* http://www.londoninternational.ac.uk/sites/default/files/intellectual_property_internet.pdf (accessed April 20, 2014).

Freedman D. 2008. *The Politics of Media Policy.* Cambridge: Polity Press.

Fuchs C. 2011a. *Foundations of Critical Media and Information Studies.* New York: Routledge.

Fuchs C. 2011b. "An Alternative View of Privacy on Facebook". *Information* 2(1): 140–165.

Fuchs C. 2013. "Social Media and Capitalism: In Producing the Internet". In *Critical Perspectives of Social Media*, ed. T. Olsson, 25–44. Göteborg: Nordicom.

Fuchs C. 2014. *Social Media: A Critical Introduction.* London: Sage.

Gandy O.H. 1993a. "Toward a Political Economy of Personal Information". *Critical Studies in Mass Communication* 10(1): 70–97.

Gandy O.H. 1993b. *The Panoptic Sort.* Boulder, CO: Westview Press.

Gane N., and D. Beer. 2008. *New Media: The key Concepts.* Oxford: BERG.

Harding J. 2000. "An Overhaul? Yes, But...,". *Financial Times* 12: 2–3.

Hesmondhalgh D. 2007. *The Cultural Industries.* London: Sage.

Ho V., and A. Fung. 2016. "Cultural Policy, Chinese National Identity and Globalization". In *Global Media and National Policies: The Return of the State,* eds. T. Flew, P. Iosifidis, and J. Steemers. Basingstoke: Palgrave Macmillan.

Iosifidis, P. 2007. *Public Television in the Digital Era: Technological Challenges and New Strategies for Europe* (Basingstoke, UK: Palgrave Macmillan).

Iosifidis P. 2010. *Reinventing Public Service Communication: European Broadcasters and Beyond..* Basingstoke: Palgrave Macmillan.

Iosifidis, P. 2011a. *Global Media and Communication Policy* (Basingstoke: Palgrave Macmillan).

Johnson D.R., S.P. Crawford, and J.G. Palfrey. 2004. "The Accountable Net: Peer Production of Internet Governance". *Virginia Journal of Law and Technology* 9(9).

Kaplan, A.M. and M. Haenlein 2010. 'Users of the World, Unite! The Challenges and Opportunities of Social Media', *Business Horizons* 53(1): 59–68.

Kellner, D. 1997. Intellectuals, the New Public Spheres, and Techno-politics. http://www.gseis.ucla.edu/faculty/kellner/essays/intellectualsnewpublic-spheres.pdf (accessed March 27, 2014).

Kumar S. 2010. "Google Earth and the Nation State: Sovereignty in the Age of New Media". *Global Media and Communication* 6(2): 154–176.

Lyon D. 2003. *Surveillance After September 11.* London: Polity.

Mansell R. 2002. "From Digital Divides to Digital Entitlements in Knowledge Societies". *Current Sociology* 5(3): 407–426.

McChesney R. 2013. *Digital Disconnect: How Capitalism is Turning the Internet Against Democracy.* New York: New Press.

McQuail D. 1992. *Media Performance: Mass Communication and the Public Interest.* London: Sage.

Michalis M. 2013. "Thirty Years of Private Television in Europe—Trends and Key Moments". In *Private Television in Western Europe: Content, Markets, Policies*, eds. K. Donders, C. Pauwela, and J. Loisen, 37–55. Basingstoke: Palgrave Macmillan.

Morozov, E. 2012. The Net Delusion: The Dark Side of Internet Freedom. *Public Affairs.*

Mosco V. 2008. "Current Trends in the Political Economy of Communication". *Global Media Journal—Canadian Edition* 1(1): 45–63.

Murdock G. 2000. "Digital Futures: European Television in the Age of Convergence". In *Television across Europe: A Comparative Introduction*, eds. J. Wieten, G. Murdock, and P. Dahlgren, 35–57. London: Sage.

Murdock, G. 2004. 'Building the Digital Commons: Public Broadcasting in the Age of the Internet', Speech, Spry Memorial Lecture, University of Montreal, 22 November. At https://pantherfile.uwm.edu/type/www/116/Theory_OtherTexts/Theory/Murdock_BuildingDigitalCommons.pdf (accessed 5 March 2016).

Murdock G., and J. Wasko. 2007. "Introduction". In *Media in the Age of Marketization*, eds. G. Murdock, and J. Wasko, 1–7. Cresskill: Hampton Press.

Negroponte N. 1995. *Being Digital.* New York: Hodder & Stoughton.

Noam, E. 2013. Who Owns the World's Media? Columbia Business School. March 31. http://papers.ssrn.com/sol3/papers.cfm?abstract_id=2242670 (accessed April 2, 2014).

Phillips, G. 2013. Defamation and the Regulation of User-generated Content. *Speech, Westminster Forum*, Policy Priorities for Social Media. July 10.

Picard R.G. 2014. "Panel I: The Future of the Political Economy of Press Freedom". *Communication Law and Policy* 19(1): 97–107.

Raboy M. 2004. "The World Summit on the Information Society and its Legacy for Global Governance". *International Communication Gazette* 66(3–4): 225–232.

Rhodes R.A.W. 1994. "The Hollowing Out of the State". *Political Quarterly* 65(2): 138–151.

Smith P. 2006. "The Politics of UK Television Policy: The Making of Ofcom". *Media Culture & Society* 28(6): 929–940.

Smith T. 2009. "The Social Media Revolution". *International Journal of Market Research* 51(4): 559–561.

Sparks C. 2007. *Globalisation, Development and the Mass Media*. London: Sage.

Taffe, L. 2013. Advertising and Marketing on Social Media, *Speech*, Westminster Forum, Policy Priorities for Social Media, July.

Tapscott D., and A.D. Williams. 2006. *Wikinomics: How Mass Collaboration Changes Everything*. New York: Portfolio.

Toffler A. 1981. *The Third Wave.* Toronto, ON: Bantam Books.

The Economist 2014b. 'AT&T Buys DirecTV: Bundles and Bulk', 24 May, pp. 60–1.

Wheeler M. 2004. "Supranational Regulation: Television and the European Union". *European Journal of Communication* 19(3): 349–369.

CHAPTER 4

Western Media Policy Frameworks and Values

INTRODUCTION

In this chapter, we start by providing an analytical framework concerning the regulatory issues associated with the social media. We then move on to identify key policy variables within national governments such as the UK and the USA, and at a supranational level in the EU. Our purpose is to analyse, assess and explain matters of political interest, neo-liberalism and the ideological values of the free market that have shaped the contemporary audiovisual and communications environments. We include a critical discussion on policy frameworks and values linked with the emphasis on neo-liberalism and the ideological values of market mechanisms. Briefly, market liberals see the free market (and unhindered competition) as an instrument with which to achieve certain goals, such as freedom of expression and consumer choice. Critics express moral, political and social objections to market liberalism and the market itself, for the market is not a neutral 'process', but a deliberately imposed structure to implement the objectives of a liberal ideology. Criticism of the market overlaps with general critique of liberalism.[1]

---

[1] Liberalism is a political ideology associated with the work of Adam Smith and his 1776 book *The Wealth of Nations*, referring to policies promoting entrepreneurship by removing government control and intervention. Neo-liberalism is a term that was coined some three decades ago to refer to a process of global economic liberalisation to increase international trade and commerce.

© The Editor(s) (if applicable) and The Author(s) 2016   65
P. Iosifidis, M. Wheeler, *Public Spheres and Mediated Social Networks in the Western Context and Beyond*, DOI 10.1057/978-1-137-41030-6_4

Here, the questions of citizenship and pluralism will be compared and contrasted with the imperatives of consumption, production, and economic scope and scale. Since its inception, the goal of media policy has been to preserve the public interest, but policy has also been a balancing act between the need to promote the public's needs, government interests and the demands of the corporate sector. The oftentimes conflicting missions have resulted in tensions between the civil, commercial and public sectors, which have been exacerbated by the revolutionary nature and intrusion of the new media. The widespread availability of ICTs makes it difficult to preserve the legal regime of private property that has historically limited flows of communication, so new legal and regulatory controls are required to set limits on what people can do, and to address trademark, copyright, pattern law, electronic surveillance and personal privacy in the current era.

We will consider policy developments ranging from the transformative US Telecommunications Act of 1996, which reconfigured ownership within the converging and global communications marketplace, to more recent EU reforms such as the replacement of the Television without Frontiers (TWF) Directive with the Audiovisual Media Services Directive (AVMSD). The chapter will identify how these policy frameworks have facilitated the formation of unitary regulatory agencies, including the US FCC and the UK Office of Communications (Ofcom), and whether they have deregulated carriageway and content provisions. We will also address the fallout within the communications environment from EU-driven competition policy regarding mergers and state aid concerning public service media (PSM).

MEDIA GOVERNANCE AND THE PUBLIC INTEREST

We start our analysis by attempting to articulate the connection between the public interest and media governance, understood as an inherently broader, more inclusive concept than media regulation or media policy. As opposed to a more narrowly defined regime of media policy in which official policymakers are the main players in shaping and implementing public policies and regulations, in a regime of media governance, policymakers coexist and make decisions together with the corporate sector, NGOs and civil society organisations, as well as media audiences (Helberger 2008; Iosifidis 2011a, b, c; Hasebrink 2012). The emergence of the Internet as a social media platform is the main enabler of the development of such multiple stakeholders and actions, for the very origins of the platform and its operational functions reflect a decentralised, collectivist undertaking of governmental, commercial and non-profit stakeholders (Schulz et al. 2011). How, then, can the public interest framework be shaped in the era of social media governance?

As briefly mentioned in Chap. 2, the articulation of a public interest framework in a regime of social media governance must take into account both traditional concerns (such as access, media plurality and freedom of expression) and emerging concerns, which include privacy and intellectual property rights, transparency surrounding data processing and the protection of users from harmful content (vioslence, sexually explicit content, hate speech and harassment). Some of these concerns have been with us for some time, but specific points of focus in the Internet era include issues of access to and usage of user data by social media platforms, typically for advertising and marketing purposes, and/or insurance companies. Content ownership, especially the application of copyright laws to the practices in which social media facilitate the production and dissemination of user-generated content, may also integrate copyright material. The protection of minors has always been high on the agenda of regulators, but this issue has gained renewed interest in the online world in an attempt to define enhanced safeguards for user data, the vulnerability of minors to sexual predators, and their exposure to hate speech and online bullying.

So, what can we do to protect ourselves from these threats? Most countries have adopted content regulation, and have expanded it to cover the online world. Content regulation is country- and culture-specific, and is therefore largely the responsibility of nation-states. Content issues are primarily national in nature, and directly and closely related to the cultural, social and democratic needs of a particular society. National governments have applied both *negative* content regulation—restricting diffusion of certain types of information, text, sound and images, and imposing advertising restrictions—and *positive* content regulation—promoting access to content, guaranteeing quality and safeguarding diversity. However, the restriction or suppression of harmful and politically or socially undesirable content is at odds with the principle of freedom of speech in democratic societies, and therefore, the application of contemporary policy to content rules is not a straightforward task. Also, the non-interventionist approach in matters of speech and communications as an inherent principle among liberal democracies is incompatible with the imposition of negative media content policies. In the USA, the commitment to free speech as guaranteed by the First Amendment does not allow, at least in theory, for controls on the flow of information to citizens. However, the US broadcasting sector is subject to rules limiting content, particularly in the areas of obscenity, indecency and children's programming. For example, the 1990 Children's Television Act provides for limitations in commercial advertising between programmes. There have also been many cases in which the FCC has banned obscene and/or indecent material (see Freedman 2008:126–134).

In the UK, Ofcom ensures that generally accepted standards are applied to the content of broadcasting services, so as to provide adequate protection of the public from the inclusion of harmful and/or offensive material in such services. The relevant legislation in section two of the Ofcom Broadcasting Code, Harm and Offence (http://stakeholders.ofcom. org.uk/broadcasting/broadcast-codes/broadcast-code/harmoffence/, accessed 24 June 2014), stipulates that programmes must not include material which condones or glamorises violent, dangerous or seriously antisocial behaviour and/or leads to suicide attempts. These restrictions have now been extended to social media platforms. The specific priorities of Facebook, Twitter, YouTube and other social media once again include (or should include) protecting users from exposure to indecent or violent content, safeguarding user data and restricting the posting and circulation of copyright material.

We can see, then, that the emergent meaning of the public interest is oriented more around protecting the public with regard to what the social media platforms should *not* do. It has also been suggested, however, that the online digital era brings with it an increased responsibility of the individual media users and that social media platforms should enable individual responsibility and autonomy. Citizen journalists who are producing and disseminating user-generated content are increasingly conducting the filtering, mediating and disclosing that are integral parts of traditional journalism (Goode 2010). In this context, individual media users serve a so-called gatekeeping function for their social network. According to Singer (2014), whenever social media users identify and disseminate news and information, they carry out important journalistic functions, and therefore act as 'secondary gatekeepers'. Singer contends that users now play a more predominant role in social media governance, as they have the ability to make editorial judgments about what is worth reporting and what is trivial. Thus social media sites and blogs are becoming an important tool for news discovery for people across generations.

However, trust and accuracy in the news and information produced and disseminated via social media is open to question. Research carried out by the Media Insight Project (2014) found that Americans view news from social media with varied levels of scepticism. More specifically, US citizens are nearly three times as likely to express high levels of trust about what they learn from a news organisation (43 % say they trust it mostly or completely) as they are to trust what they discover through social media (only 15 % of those who have used it to get news say they had high levels of trust in what they learned). The research also found that those numbers vary little by generation. Such lack of trust may be attributable to information overload: when everyone is tweeting and posting their opinions, it is difficult for consumers to know which 'voices' to trust. This leads us to a wider issue: is 'viewer empowerment' a utopia? It is true that, thanks to new technology, individual media users now have the tools required to take on more responsibility, but can they actually become custodians of the emergent model of the public interest? There are a number of complexities in how media platforms operate that might prevent this model of the public interest from materialising. For example, social media platforms may not comply with acceptable levels of transparency and accountability that have been set by governments or international bodies. Yet this is crucial if the public is to bear more responsibility and, indeed, to be more accountable in using the Internet and social media. Is there such a thing as 'public service Internet'?

Media and Communications Policy in the USA

The US media landscape has been dramatically transformed over the past three decades or so. The digital switchover from analogue to digital broadcasting was completed in 2009, much earlier than in most parts of the world, and certainly earlier than many EU countries. The proliferation and consumer embrace of pay TV services including cable, satellite and Internet Protocol television (IPTV) has affected terrestrial over-the-air television, and the digitisation of content has challenged traditional models of media and journalism. Broadcast network news from the established networks ABC, CBS and NBC that once commanded an overwhelming share of the television audience have each lost between one and two million viewers over the past 5 years, as part of an overall decline in audience size of almost 20 % since 2005 (Mapping Digital Media: United States 2011). Meanwhile, the Internet has disrupted various industries: news, music, photography, movies, retailing and financial services. It has altered existing patterns of communications and offered entirely new ways to connect. Many more voices are heard today in political and policy discourse thanks to new digital platforms, although media concentration in traditional media sectors remains a problem in many countries (Noam 2013). Social media sites have come to play an important role in political organising, fundraising and mobilisation. Facebook technology is now embedded in many major platforms, and new platforms such as the Huffington Post and Townhall.com have achieved considerable reach. Activists are now embedding digital processes more deeply within the methods of community organising, not just in election campaigns, but in mobilising volunteer efforts after natural disasters and for social causes (Mapping Digital Media: United States 2011).

The growth of digital media and the Internet are bringing about a major reconsideration of the ways in which the communications industry is regulated. Traditionally, communications regulation has been divided into two broad categories: first, regulation of broadcast media (radio, television, cable and satellite), which distribute primarily professionally produced, advertising-supported entertainment and information output to a mass audience; and second, regulation of telecommunications (telegraphy, wireline telephony and mobile telephony), which provide two-way communications for individuals and businesses. The question is whether these separate 'silos' of regulation still make sense in light of the new information and communications ecosystems that are reshaping the media environment. In particular, what type of regulation (if any) is most appropriate for the broadband Internet, whether delivered over a wire or wirelessly? To explore these questions, the 27th Annual Aspen Institute Conference on Communications Policy met in August 2012 to rethink the government's role in communications regulation. The meeting brought together a group of experts with extensive experience in the field, not least because nearly half of the participants were either currently serving or had served on the regulatory agency FCC, while others were actively involved as scholars of or advocates for regulatory actions in the field. Despite differences in views among participants, there was a notable degree of overlap in their conclusions. There was strong consensus that the current regulatory system was not working well and was likely to become even more dysfunctional as technology continued to evolve. The rationale for maintaining separate regulatory silos for different media grows increasingly tenuous as these sectors become part of an increasingly pervasive broadband Internet infrastructure (The Aspen Institute 2013).

One of the problems, identified by Stefaan Verhulst, Chief of Research at the Markle Foundation, was this disconnect between media-specific regulation and the realities of digital media. The traditional regulatory model is based not only on assumed distinctions among different media—for example, technical characteristics, types of function, economic structure and audience—but also on legislative decisions that have established different regulatory mechanisms for different media enshrined in different titles in the communications act. The result has been the creation of separate 'silos' of regulation that have become increasingly anachronistic as technology has blurred the lines between media. Legal scholars and others have proposed substituting a horizontal 'layers' model for these vertical silos. The layers-based policy framework is based on a multi-level protocol stack that network engineers use to describe the various components that make up the Internet. It starts at the 'bottom' with the *physical layer* (telephone line, coaxial cable, fibre, wireless, etc.), and then a *logical layer* consisting of transport protocols (TCP/IP, HTTP) that define how messages are encoded and transported online. Above this is the *application layer* that defines how the network is used (e.g., search, social networks, websites), and at the top of the stack is the *content layer* (text, speech, image, video, music, telemetry), which is the actual information that is conveyed by the Internet. Proponents of this approach argue that in a converged world, such an approach provides a more logical, consistent means to identify issues that may need regulatory attention.

FEDERAL COMMUNICATIONS COMMISSION

The FCC regulatory agency was established with the passage of the Communications Act of 1934, which could be said to have begun the modern era of communications regulation (The Communications Act 1934). Despite many far-reaching changes in technology and in the political and economic climate, the FCC has survived and continues to operate much as it has since it was created over 80 years ago. The FCC comprises five commissioners, nominated by the president and confirmed by the Senate for 5-year terms, no more than three of whom may be associated with the same political party. In fact, the political party that controls the White House will populate the FCC with three commissioners (including the chairman), and members of the other party occupy the two remaining positions. Not surprisingly, when votes are split at the FCC, they almost always break along party lines. This is consistent with the overall picture of US media regulation over the past few decades, which has been defined by increasing politicisation in terms of both digital and non-digital platforms (Mapping Digital Media: United States 2011).

The FCC, Media Ownership Rules and Media Mergers

By and large, competition issues and corporate interests prevail in the regulatory decisions of the FCC. Despite its long existence, strength and unified structure, it has often been seen as a classic example of a regulatory body that has been 'captured' by the industries it regulates (see Dunbar 2005; Brown and Blevins 2008; Freedman 2008). Over time, the FCC has adopted an economic perspective to please business interests and has tended to ignore alternative perspectives that might have given greater consideration to sociocultural matters (Blevins and Brown 2006). Unlike what has taken place in Europe, regulatory actions directed at promoting diversity and pluralism, and free and independent news production in the digital epoch have yet to emerge in any meaningful sense. This is evidenced by the deregulatory philosophy of the 1996 communications act, which paved the way for media mergers and acquisitions by allowing for media cross-ownership (ownership of multiple media businesses by a physical person or corporation). It is also evidenced by the FCC's July 2003 decision to relax media ownership rules, and in particular the decision to raise the cap on the proportion of TV households a single corporation could reach nationally from 35 % to 45 %. The review and ultimate relaxation of ownership rules was prompted in part by a decision of the US Court of Appeals for the District of Columbia in the case *FCC v. Fox Television Stations, Inc.* (2002), which had questioned the justification for the regulation limiting the number of TV stations a single entity could control.

Despite opposition from a number of members of Congress and public media advocacy organisations, then FCC Chairman Powell was determined to move ahead with the revised ownership rules. Following growing resistance from Congress, the public and the courts (the Third Circuit Court of Appeals in the city of Philadelphia had ruled in favour of the case *Prometheus Radio Project vs. FCC* (2004) and eventually prevented the regulatory agency from implementing the new rules), the final outcome was a 'compromise' of raising the cap to 39 %. Commentators have argued that this was not really a compromise, since 39 % allowed News Corporation (owner of the Fox network) and Viacom (owner of CBS network) to retain all of their television stations (Brown and Blevins 2008; Freedman 2008). For Brown and Blevins (2008:453–454), the Fox case reveals, among other issues, the special power of media corporations, the FCC's long history of ignoring the public and the dominance of neo-liberal thinking in Washington, D.C. The prevailing logic within the FCC has been that, given the increasing penetration of the Internet and other new media, it makes increasingly less sense to restrict ownership concentration in traditional media such as radio, TV and newspapers. As a result, ownership diversity in these media sectors has decreased and many mergers have been allowed, enabled by the deregulatory philosophy of the Telecommunications Act of 1996.

One such event that stands out is the 2010 megamerger between a content company (NBCUniversal), which was the country's oldest and largest news and entertainment provider, and a telecommunications provider, the largest US cable and Internet company (Comcast), to create Comcast-NBCUniversal. In January 2011, the FCC approved the deal by a four-to-one vote, with the Justice Department's antitrust division giving its blessing the same day, despite opposing voices arguing that consumers lose when the same company owns the content and the pipes that deliver that content. The merger wave in the telecommunications and television industries rolls on. In May 2014, AT&T, the second largest US supplier of both mobile phone and fixed-line broadband services, agreed to buy DirecTV, the country's leading satellite TV distributor, for $48.5 billion. The logic behind the merger is that telecommunications and television firms, not only in the USA but everywhere, prefer to sell customers bundles of mobile telephony, fixed lines, broadband and TV rather than individualised services, in order to keep up with competition. AT&T was already streaming TV programming over the Internet, but in only 22 US states and to merely 5.7 subscribers, whereas DirecTV brought another 20.3 customers and national coverage (which AT&T had in mobile services).

DirecTV had valuable content too: a lucrative contract with the National Football League to show Sunday afternoon games. A similar logic underlies a proposed $45 billion tie-up between the two largest US cable TV firms, Comcast and Time Warner Cable (which also rank first and third in broadband, respectively) (*The Economist* 2014). US regulators are widely expected to approve these mergers, although in a rare decision in 2011, the Department of Justice rejected AT&T's proposed $39 billion purchase of T-Mobile USA on the grounds that the US telecommunications giant had not made concessions (for instance, expanding high-speed broadband access in rural areas). It is clear that the business of supplying pay TV, Internet connections and phone service is narrowing to a handful of giant firms. However, such mergers raise issues of cost, diversity of content and ownership, editorial bias and concerns over censorship. This should be an era when choices are multiplying for customers shopping for an Internet connection, pay TV service or smartphone plan. Instead, major companies are allowed to bundle this 'triple play' and reduce choices, buy up rivals, and limit options with offerings billed as simplified packages.

The merger mania is also likely to even further reduce the offering of minority output, which currently exists only thanks to (marginalised) public broadcasting. In direct contrast to the European situation, where PSM play an essential role in safeguarding a pluralist society and meeting its cultural and social needs, the USA presents a unique case, in that commercial broadcasting was permitted before the development of public broadcasting. The latter was to serve as a 'forum for debate and controversy', providing a 'voice for groups in the community that may otherwise be unheard' so that we could 'see America whole, in all its diversity' (Starr 2004). However, some observers suggest that it has become increasingly integrated into the commercial broadcasting industry. Hoynes (1994) argued that the public TV system had turned mainly to business, talk, news and wildlife formats in its programme offerings, owing to an inadequate funding structure. In any case, the overall impact of public television on cultural, social and political life is negligible, and in 2011, it claimed less than 2 % of the average daily audience share. Despite signs of recovery (according to Nielsen NPOWER, the Public Broadcasting Service had an average primetime rating of 1.43 during the 2013–2014 season, an increase of 7 % over the previous season; see http://www.pbs.org/about/background/), US public TV is consigned to a position as a 'niche' broadcaster, out of reach for the vast majority of Americans.

The FCC and Convergence Policies

In an attempt to address the rise of digital computing and digital communications, and the convergence of the two in particular, the FCC launched three so-called Computer Inquiries, intended to explore the interrelationships of computing and communications and their implications for regulatory policies. In the first, Computer I, which concluded in 1971, the

FCC attempted to distinguish between 'communication' services, which involved the use of computers only to control the switching of messages but not to alter the content of those messages, and 'data processing' services, which involved acting on the content of messages through functions such as storing, sorting, retrieving or calculating. The FCC decided that the former type of service should continue to be regulated, while the latter should remain unregulated except for restrictions on the ability of incumbents such as AT&T to offer them. However, the commission soon found that many services were 'hybrids', combining elements of the two types of functions, thereby complicating its effort to distinguish between them. The commission's second inquiry, Computer II, concluding in 1980, attempted to restore order by proposing a distinction between 'basic' services that only involve message transmission, and 'enhanced services' that include some degree of computer processing, and establishing different regulatory requirements for each type of service. The third and final inquiry, Computer III, conducted in the mid-1980s, focused on creating a set of provisions that would allow local exchange carriers (the newly created 'Baby Bells') to provide enhanced services, without competing unfairly with other entities that did not own similar network facilities.

The 1996 telecommunications act enshrined a version of the FCC's 'basic/enhanced' dichotomy into law by distinguishing between 'telecommunications' and 'information services', with only the former subject to regulation. As the Internet began to grow in the 1990s, the FCC generally refrained from attempting to regulate the new medium. When companies like AOL began offering dial-up Internet access over the telephone network, it was treated as an unregulated information service. Furthermore, incumbent telephone companies were required to provide capacity on a common carrier basis to Internet service providers (ISPs) and were prevented from imposing per-minute access charges on them, which allowed ISPs to offer flat-rate pricing. With the rise over the past decade of broadband Internet access provided directly by telephone companies and cable television operators, the FCC was forced to determine the status of a service that integrated pure transmission and computer processing functions. In 2002, the agency classified 'broadband Internet access' as an information service, freeing telephone and cable providers from legacy regulatory obligations in its provision (The Aspen Institute 2013).

However, the market for broadband Internet access is not very competitive in most markets in the USA, which creates the potential for dominant telecommunications to discriminate against competing services that use their networks, such as web-based applications, streaming video and Internet telephony. Recognising this danger, the FCC's Open Internet Order in December 2010 attempted to establish a 'level playing field' for such offerings. The order laid down three rules for broadband providers: disclosure of how they manipulated network traffic, if at all; unfettered use by consumers of all 'lawful' websites, services and software, specifically including voice and video streaming; and a prohibition on throttling the speed of outside companies and services compared to its own or with any favouritism. Yet the appeals court judges found that the order attempted to impose common carrier-style rules on an unregulated market:

> Given that the Commission has chosen to classify broadband providers in a manner that exempts them from treatment as common carriers, the Communications Act expressly prohibits the Commission from nonetheless regulating them as such. Because the Commission has failed to establish that the anti-discrimination and anti-blocking rules do not impose per se common carrier obligations, we vacate those portions of the Open Internet Order.

Clearly, the court left intact only the requirement for transparency. Its decision, however, excludes Verizon, Google, Netflix and other broadband providers from the FCC's net neutrality rules, and at the same time is likely to encourage their attempts to establish another new pricing scheme.

MEDIA AND COMMUNICATIONS POLICY IN THE UK

The British public has been well served by the mixed economy of a public broadcaster, a regulated private sector and the arrival of satellite and cable broadcasters. The UK has had one of the highest levels of digital television take-up in Europe, completing the digital switchover conversion in 2012. Freeview, a British Broadcasting Corporation (BBC)-backed digital terrestrial venture launched in 2002, has been the main driver of digital television take-up. At the same time, the use of Internet at home has increased significantly, reaching about 85 % of all households in 2013, driven by the rise in PC and laptop ownership, as well as broadband rollout, which now accounts for almost 100 % of home Internet connections. As has been the case elsewhere, these advancements have affected news production and consumption, and although television is still the most widely accessed and trusted news platform, young people and ethnic minorities are increasingly tuning out of terrestrial television news. Print news is also in decline, as readers and advertisers migrate to the Internet. User-generated content (UGC), the blogosphere and social networking have become the most popular new media activities in the UK. Online news provision is dominated by an emerging oligopoly of online content providers and aggregators including the BBC, the *Daily Mail, The Guardian*, Google, Yahoo!, AOL and MSN (Iosifidis 2015; Mapping Digital Media: United States 2011).

In Britain, there has traditionally been political consensus on the positive contribution of television to society, and this has resulted in unprecedented support for the concept of public service in broadcasting. Despite the progressive move away from a highly regulated commercial sector towards market deregulation (reflected in the Communications Act 2003, which seeks to liberalise), the country is determined to retain the public service principles that have shaped the TV market. This is evidenced by the establishment of a content board, a committee of the main Ofcom board, which serves as Ofcom's primary forum for the regulation of content-related aspects of the broadcasting industry, particularly quality and standards. It is also evidenced by the government's endorsement and support of the BBC in an increasingly crowded marketplace. Critics argue, however, that technological and regulatory changes have altered the emphasis and character of the programming of both public and private terrestrial channels, which now provide less pluralistic, distinctive and diverse output (see Iosifidis 2007, 2012).

THE SETTING UP OF OFCOM

In terms of policymaking in the digital environment, the key step in the UK was the establishment of Ofcom in 2003 as a response to converging media markets and to the need for a coordinated regulatory framework. The British government, originally through its 2000 communications white paper, and later through its communications bill on 13 July 2001, which resulted in the Communications Act 2003, expressed the view that convergence of communications services makes it increasingly difficult to designate an infrastructure as specific to a particular service, and thus leads to the arbitrary designation of individual operators and services into one category or another. The communications white paper acknowledged that 'the communications revolution has arrived', thus demanding a new framework for communications regulation in the twenty-first century. As such, the white paper made a case for merging telecommunications and broadcasting regulators into a super body, Ofcom, along the lines of the FCC in the USA. Searching for possible solutions to the current convergence problems, policymakers in Britain considered it necessary to propose institutional integration of telecommunications and media regulations, at both an organisational level (regulator) and a normative level (laws).

The establishment of a single regulator was met with mixed feelings. Some argued that this would ensure the adoption of consistent and relevant rules across all converged sectors. After all, if all communications are just zeros and ones, it then becomes impossible to sustain a regulatory system based on the application of different sets of rules for different forms of communication, such as broadcasting and telecommunications (Smith 2006). Others raised concerns over the attempt to put economic and social issues under the same roof. Up to that point, regulatory bodies had overseen the broadcasting and telecommunications sectors under different statutes and had different roles and functions. The Independent Television Commission (ITC) put emphasis on content regulation, whereas the Office of Telecommunications (Oftel) was concerned with structural regulation. Critics of merging those bodies claimed that there was bound to be a clash between the two. Another fear was that the better-resourced telecommunications sector might dominate the smaller broadcasting sector under a converged regulator. Andrew Graham (2000) argued that the new era required effective regulation, but not a single regulator combining economic regulation with issues of political voice or quality of content, which are different in kind. As there are no objective ways of measuring the latter, a separate regulatory body is required to deal with these separate matters of public interest.

Now, over a decade later, the risk painted by many at the time—that one regulatory tradition (telecommunications) would dominate the other (broadcasting)—has materialised. Ofcom has been set up as a converged regulator with responsibility both for carriage regulation and content, products and services, either public or commercial. The expected advantages were effectiveness and efficiency gains, greater synergy and lower transaction costs. As Livingstone et al. (2007:613) put it, 'Ofcom was conceived as a powerful sector-wide regulator that could flexibly respond to new challenges while being "future proofed" against changes that could otherwise destabilise or impede technological innovation and market expansion.' While some of these efficiencies might have been achieved, we will show below that Ofcom has been dominated by one regulatory tradition (telecommunications—economic imperative), with sociocultural objectives (broadcasting—social imperative) taking a back seat (Vick 2006).

In addition, one of the key objectives of the regulatory agency has been to put competition law at the centre of media regulation. Competition law can be described as a set of regulatory mechanisms used to tackle market failures, typically arising from high market share, dominant positions, firm expansion and barriers to entry. The 2000 white paper that paved the way for the new regulator revealed the then New Labour government's intention to 're-base broadcasting regulation upon modern Competition Act principles and give the regulator [Ofcom] concurrent powers with the OFT [Office of Fair Trading], which the ITC currently lacks' (DCMS and DTI 2000:para. 8.9.1). Ofcom has a statutory duty to deal with competition issues in communications markets, especially as they are frequently raised as regulatory disputes (in which Ofcom intervenes to resolve). Most disputes are in relation to pricing issues alleging abusive/unfair pricing or refusal to supply. As was stated by the chief executive of the regulator at the time, Ofcom's powers include requiring supply, setting pricing and other terms going forward, and—crucially—the discretion to award repayment (Richards 2010).

Another reason put forward to justify the positioning of Ofcom primarily as an economic regulator is the subordination of the *citizen interest* (the citizen rationale is concentrated on the long-term social benefits broadcasting brings to society, democracy, culture, identity and civic engagement) to the *consumer interest* (short-term benefits to individuals expressed through viewing choices, pay TV services, online and web services, etc.) (see Harvey 2006; Livingstone et al. 2007). In recent years, Ofcom has chosen to deal with consumer issues online and has encouraged openness in practices, processes and charges for those it regulates. In an era dominated by the debate on 'network neutrality' or 'Internet traffic management' (at the heart of this debate is the concern that traffic management could be used as a form of anticompetitive behaviour, e.g., a provider limiting its subscribers' access to particular services), the prevailing regulatory language is to protect 'consumer interest' or 'consumer transparency' rather than 'citizen interest' or 'citizen rights'. Consumer policy (focusing on demand-side market failures like transaction costs) goes hand in hand with competition policy (seeking to address the supply side) in a complex, converged communications industry. The bottom line is that the broader agenda of establishing a new converged regulatory framework in the UK foregrounds competition as the primary instrument to deal with communication matters.

Further evidence of Ofcom's intention to accommodate commercial concerns is provided in the regulatory agency's ability to shape the behaviour of the public broadcaster BBC. While the regulator's primary responsibility is to facilitate a thriving communications industry, its approach to the BBC seems to suggest a different set of political priorities (Freedman 2008:149). Despite the agency's continued backing of the idea of an independent, publicly funded public broadcaster, it has increased the financial stringency of the corporation, and has continually asked it to justify the need for non-commercial output and to scale down its commercial enterprises. The BBC has been asked to reform its governance structure and set up a new governing body, the BBC Trust, as 'the custodian of its purposes'.

Any new services are now subject to a test that measures the 'public value' of the proposed services based on 'objectivity, rigor and transparency' against their impact on the market. This reflects, then, the New Labour government's determination to ensure that the BBC does not unfairly distort the market. Meanwhile, the BBC has been instructed to act as a key driver of the digital revolution and facilitator of the digital switchover (Iosifidis 2006, 2011a). It must be noted that the BBC has been given the huge task of digital conversion (now complete), while at the same time its licence fee has been frozen until 2017. As one commentator put it, borrowing heavily from Ofcom's recommendations, '[Ofcom] sees the BBC not as an autonomous proponent of public service values but as an organisation that is part of an increasingly competitive, marketised environment and needs regulating according to that logic' (Freedman 2008:169). More recently, it was suggested that the BBC close certain TV broadcasting activities and instead deliver them online. For instance, this is the plan for the BBC3 channel targeting the 16–34 demographic.

Media and Communications Policy in the EU

Media and communications policy in the EU has been conducted at a national level, with each member state developing a specific regulatory regime to oversee communications issues in its territory. Europe-wide (and even international) cooperation has been largely confined to technical issues, such as radio spectrum and international tariffs. There have been notable differences concerning the type and intensity of regulation between different media. While the print media have traditionally enjoyed a great degree of autonomy and self-regulation (Hutchinson 2007), broadcasting has been subject to state intervention because of technical matters (spectrum scarcity), but also because of its capacity to influence listeners and viewers in their choices. Content in broadcasting has been regulated for political and social reasons, with governments and political parties using broadcasting as a means to promote their ideas and policies. In contrast, regulation of telecommunications has been based on economic principles, notably on 'natural monopoly and network externalities arguments' (Garnham 1990), with emphasis on increasing penetration and promotion of universal service, whereas content has been left unregulated.

A common theme of national communications regulatory regimes has been to promote social cohesion and solidarity, and to create an informed citizenry by ensuring that the media offer a wide range of content that supports particular social, civil and political values. But media policy and regulation has typically been influenced by national variables and has largely considered national historical experience, culture and values. National political and social conditions determine the regulation of content available through the media, either by ensuring universality of reception or by guaranteeing that certain programming genres are made available to the public. The national focus also characterises structural regulation of media sectors (regulation of 'who owns what' that intends to limit media owners' ability to influence citizens). Governments have adopted a wide range of different tools (media and cross-media ownership rules, licencing regimes, competition law) to facilitate a plurality in the provision of information.

Over time, these differences blur as the EU emerges as a supranational organisation seeking to harmonise national media policies. In fact, the EU has progressively become a major player in national communications policy and regulation. European institutions such as the EC, the European Parliament (EP), the ECJ and the Council of Europe (CoE) play a significant role in shaping and directing national communications practices, mainly in the areas of media ownership, pluralism, public service broadcasting and digital switchover. Although these institutions have different objectives and varying degrees of influence (e.g., the EC as the executive body has more clout than the EP, whose role in communications is mainly consultative), there is a distinctive pattern of policy convergence emerging within the EU, aimed at two goals. The first is the completion and efficient functioning of the internal market, which is characterised as an area without internal frontiers in which the free movement of goods, persons, services and capital is ensured. The second goal concerns pursuing reregulation, soft governance initiatives and an industrial policy as the main incentive of audiovisual policy, especially with regard to the new online media. This goes hand in hand with the 'new paradigm' of media policy prioritising economic goals over social and political welfare (Van Guilenburg and McQuail 2003). It also reflects the broad political and ideological endorsement of market-based solutions—or as some have succinctly commented (Wheeler 2004; Michalis 2007), the EU has sought to enhance expansion of media services through the principles of liberalisation and harmonisation.

Despite this, it is clear that the EU's regulatory competence in the arena of public interest goals and cultural matters is limited in comparison to its direct powers to intervene in the economic field, principally on the basis of economic instruments (competition law, merger regulation). For instance, member states are still responsible for establishing media ownership rules 'for considerations of public interest' (see below).

Furthermore, the EU has become involved with several state aid procedures concerning the funding and licensing of public service broadcasters (PSBs) and has hardened its stance against PSBs and their anticompetitive effect in terms of market distortion. While the EU recognises the right of member states to determine the organisation and funding of their PSBs in accordance with the protocol of the 1997 Treaty of Amsterdam (which strikes a balance between the realisation of the public service remit entrusted upon PSBs and the achievement of the common supranational interest in the undistorted functioning of the internal market), the criteria of market distortion and unfair competitive practice have come to define the EU's monitoring approach.

Ongoing Transformations of the European Media Landscape

The EU is characterised by cultural and linguistic diversity, which is a potential competitive advantage on the world market, but has also posed a challenge in an environmental portrait by network effects. Network effects in the media and Internet environment may lend a significant comparative advantage to operators and providers active in a borderless market, enabling them to raise sizeable budgets and take advantage of economies of scale. Entrants who offer audiovisual content online without territorial access restrictions can turn the over 400 million EU Internet users (see http://www.internetworldstats.com/stats9.htm, accessed 20

July 2015) into potential viewers and thus challenge the position of traditional players.

There has been a steady move towards the convergence of media services and the way in which these services are consumed and delivered. As in the USA and elsewhere, the move towards an increasingly connected society challenges and changes audiovisual business models, public policy and consumer behaviour. Policymakers are struggling to find a regulatory framework that will support and enable the creation and availability of digital content and promote effective competition, while ensuring appropriate levels of protection from illegal and harmful content. Lines are blurring between the familiar twentieth-century consumption patterns of linear broadcasting received by TV sets versus on-demand services delivered to computers. While linear general viewing times are still around 4 hours per day across the EU (Yearbook of the European Audiovisual Observatory, Vol. II, p. 171), the converged experience gradually becomes a reality, and market players develop and adapt business models. Technology already allows the user to create, distribute and access all types of content irrespective of time, place or device. Furthermore, with every smartphone enabling converged production and consumption, one would expect a future shift from 'lean-back' consumption to active participation.

The EU's framework directive classified electronic communications into 'electronic communications networks' (ECNs) and 'electronic communications services' (ECS). Its AVMSD (EU 2010) divides the media into linear (television broadcasts) and nonlinear (on-demand) services that are often utilised in response to content regulations under convergence. This division was seen by some Internet advocates as a violation of free speech and a means to bring content regulation in through the back door. In any case, the directive may not be sufficient, as it is not applicable for some newly emerged media. Eventually, in April 2013, the EU released the green paper, 'Preparing for a Fully Converged Audiovisual World: Growth, Creation and Values', to seek public consultation on the implications of the ongoing transformation of the audiovisual media landscape, characterised by a steady increase in the convergence of media services and the way these services are consumed and delivered. The commission's vision is to seize the opportunity of this changing technological environment to ensure the widest possible access to European diversified content for all Europeans and the widest possible choice of high-quality offerings (EC 2013a, b). As convergence will become gradually more tangible over the next decade, the green paper acknowledges that it might have an impact on a number of legal instruments, including the AVMSD, the E-Commerce Directive (EC 2000) and the electronic communications framework (e.g., Universal Services Directive Article 31, spectrum policy, Article 6 Access Directive).

Similar to previous green papers, the consultation does not presuppose any specific outcome. However, it paves the way towards possible regulatory and policy responses in the longer term, in particular linking up commission initiatives such as the Better Internet for Kids Coalition (see http://ec.europa.eu/digital-agenda/en/creating-better-internet-kids) and possible activities to follow up the report of the High Level Group on Media Freedom and Pluralism (see http://ec.europa.eu/information_society/media_taskforce/doc/pluralism/hlg/hlg_final_report.pdf), as well as work on self-regulatory initiatives. These latter initiatives gain momentum as the EU is committed to reducing the regulatory burden on industry to encourage innovation and boost productivity across the economy and therefore increasingly rely on self-regulation, especially when it comes to new services.

Self- and Co-regulation

Self-regulation and co-regulation are explicitly encouraged by the EC in the AVMSD, which replaced the TWF Directive in 2007. Self-regulation is a situation in which the industry regulates itself, while co-regulation involves a combination of state and non-state regulation. The text of the AVMSD is the first legislative proposal by the commission related to the media sector where such an explicit reference to self- and co-regulation is made. More specifically, the new rules of the AVMSD require governments to encourage self-regulation in certain fields, sometimes combined with government intervention (co-regulation)—where their legal systems allow (Article 4[7]). Such regimes must be broadly accepted by the main stakeholders and provide for effective enforcement. As a result, various EU countries have implemented or expanded already existing self-regulatory mechanisms in the communications field. In Britain, the Advertising Standards Authority (ASA), traditionally a self-regulatory body overseeing non-broadcast advertising such as press, cinema and posters, has since 2004 been contracted out the regulation of broadcast advertising content. By delegating broadcast advertising to the ASA, the regulator, Ofcom, ensures procedures of public accountability that can include the monitoring of its effectiveness.

Ofcom encourages self-regulation of the various media, such as by a code of practice for the labelling of the content of products like films, DVDs, CDs, computer games and television programmes. 'As technological convergence of the various forms of media continues so lightly regulated new forms will clash with more heavily regulated old forms. A code of practice for all forms of media is therefore becoming more and more important' (Bartle and Vass 2007:71). The Internet has provided momentum for the imposition of self- and co-regulatory mechanisms, as it is a media platform that is not straightforwardly subject to existing regulatory provisions. Today, ISPs, online content producers and advertisers are calling for such mechanisms in order to stimulate innovation and creativity and to promote diversity in the online and on-demand terrain. An interesting issue to explore would be to seek to hold Internet users more accountable through the development of innovative mechanisms. Some scholars (Johnson et al. 2004) argue that problems of online life—spam, informational privacy and network security—lend themselves to what is described as 'peer production of governance'. According to Dutton (2007), these are typified by self-governing processes developed for successful novel online applications, such as Wikipedia and the eBay online auction service, where users participate in setting up and monitoring governance rules.

Prioritising the Economic Imperative

The EU broadcasting policy has not been static, but evolving. The balance of interests and values has varied over the decades, from cultural and democratic objectives in the early 1980s, to economic and industrial goals increasingly since the early 1990s. The EC policies focus mainly on internal market perspective (or the 'digital single market', as the new fashionable mantra) and differ strikingly from those of the CoE and the EP, which through various resolutions and declarations have paid more attention to the cultural dimension. As Michalis (2010) notes, the EC stance towards broadcasting has been more about negative than positive integration, for competition and economic objectives have been prioritised at the expense of sociocultural objectives. The EC has shaped the broadcasting scene in Europe through the creation of an audiovisual internal market and through its strong competition powers, where it enjoys autonomy for action. This has been achieved despite fierce member state opposition in areas such as broadcasting content and ownership. The EC has been able to regulate more effectively in the adjacent sector of telecommunications, which is free of content and subject only to structural regulation. Still, European broadcasting policy has been developed through competition considerations, economically oriented policy and ECJ decisions.

The evolution of the EC's policy reveals that the primary rationale for such policy is the economic imperative, developing three axes of regulation: regulation of networks (fixed and mobile telecommunications networks, Internet Protocol networks; broadcasting networks, cable and satellite networks); regulation of service provision (with broadcasting being the most heavily regulated domain); and regulation of content (Kalimo and Pauwels 2009; Casarosa 2009). The 2007 AVMSD confirms that cultural concerns are overshadowed by the more pressing need to break down market barriers to facilitate transborder broadcasting. The AVMSD was certainly a victory for liberal economic forces, but it contains cultural considerations such as 'quotas' requiring broadcasters to devote the majority of their programming to European works. According to Michalis (2010:42) the quota provision (itself a cultural policy tool) stands out from the overwhelmingly liberalising provisions of the directive, although various elements minimise its significance, most notably the provision requiring member states to fulfil the quotas 'where practicable and by appropriate means', making it a symbolic rather than substantial provision, and by the fact that it is a political agreement and thus not legally binding.

The objectives of an EU interventionist and monitoring role have been twofold: the completion and effective functioning of the internal market for media services, and steering the course of the debate over reregulation at the national level. The above analysis shows that the EU has progressively acquired a more effective role in media and communication policy matters. The EC, in particular, has deeply influenced national media policies by acting as a policy entrepreneur and by influencing national policy change through the recommendation of best practices, models and sanctions, employing a 'soft law' approach, which includes the publication of reports, communications, green papers and other legislative documents. The various legislative documents addressing media and communications issues have provided member states with a useful tool, in particular the benchmarking capable of indirectly steering the political choices of national governments (Casarosa 2009:23).

Meanwhile, as stated above, member states maintain much of their sovereignty rights. The failed attempt to launch a harmonisation directive on pluralism and media ownership in the mid-1990s demonstrated the political sensitivities surrounding the subject and the need for a balanced and realistic approach that would take into account the specificities of media markets in the various member states. The failure of the EC to secure sufficient political compromise to enact a directive on the concentration of media ownership demonstrates the difficulties that European institutions face in overriding the resistance of national governments, especially the most powerful governments of Germany and the UK (Humphreys 2009:197). The EC came back to the issue of pluralism by commissioning an Independent Study (2009) with the aim of developing a neutral and objective monitoring mechanism that could enhance the auditability of media pluralism. This instrument would equip policymakers and regulatory authorities with the tools to detect and manage societal risks in this area, and would provide them with a stronger evidentiary basis from which to define priorities and actions for improving media pluralism within the EU. Instead of imposing measures on member states, this mechanism would ensure a uniform approach in dealing with pluralism issues and would provide a more objective basis for the often heated political and economic arguments.

In the case of setting a Europe-wide deadline for digital switchover by the year 2012, the EC was careful to emphasise that this is an indicative and not an absolute deadline. The commission's pressure for member states to hurry towards digitalisation in order to create a workable internal market may lead some countries to an ill-timed and insufficiently planned introduction of digital terrestrial TV services in efforts to catch up with other, more advanced territories. It is increasingly believed that member states, especially those with low digital TV take-up, should be left with some flexibility to set a later date for analogue switch-off. Furthermore, under the new rules of the AVMSD, member states have maintained their right to restrict broadcast of unsuitable content (Article 2[4]-[6]), including the retransmission of unsuitable on-demand audiovisual content that may not be banned in its country of origin. To sum up, while the EU has deeply influenced the choices of national governments in their media and communications policies, member states keep much of their regulatory power over issues such as the organisation and funding of PSBs, the implementation of media ownership rules, the protection of media pluralism, and the decision of when to switch off the analogue frequency for terrestrial television services.

Therefore, member states have managed to keep their competence in politically sensitive areas—such as safeguards for media pluralism, ownership and PSBs—but the EC's increasing monitoring role in sociocultural and democratic functions of broadcasting is evident. As was discussed, the EC intends to assume a monitoring role of media pluralism in the EU member states rather than one of initiating regulation (e.g., a directive) that would lack a legal basis upon which the regulation could be based. Another example of the EC's interventionist and monitoring role is the state aid for broadcasting. It should be noted that the commission's policy impinges on the broadcasters' public service activities through the general content regulation of the audiovisual sector, the main legislative document of which is the AVMSD, laying down rules for advertising, European programme quotas and so on. But a more implicit means of control is via general competition law, the most relevant part of which is the state aid rules that set out to harmonise market conditions in order to create a 'level playing field' for commercial and public businesses. As a general principle, the EC recognises the crucial role of PSBs in light of their contribution to the quality of public discourse, the promotion of societal integration and national culture, and their emphasis on news and education. Yet the 2009 Broadcasting Communication shows that the commission has tightened control of state aid in the area of public service broadcasting. Although this does not necessarily mean the end of the 'State aid saga', future practice will reveal whether the aim of the new communication—to ensure a level playing field between PSBs and private operators—can ultimately be achieved.

CONCLUSION

This chapter examined the discrepancies and challenges resulting from the development of new digital media and the Internet, as well as convergence in policymaking, and assessed the reforms adopted in reaction to these advances. It highlighted the prominent role of competition policy and the economic imperative that has dominated the regulatory tradition at the UK, US and EU levels, and offered examples of converged regulatory actions in the respective communications industries. In the USA, competition issues and business interests have prevailed in the regulatory decisions of the FCC, as evidenced by the regulatory agency's 2003 decision to relax media ownership rules. There is a tendency to ignore alternative perspectives that might have given greater consideration to sociocultural matters, and this is further reinforced by the deregulatory philosophy of the Communications Act of 1996, which paved the way for media mergers and acquisitions by allowing for media cross-ownership. As the Internet began to grow in the 1990s, the FCC generally refrained from attempting to regulate this new medium, to allow it to flourish, and yet the market for broadband Internet access is not highly competitive in most markets in the USA—which creates the possibility for dominant telecommunications entities to discriminate against competing services.

In the UK, the establishment of Ofcom in 2003—which was the merger of five regulatory agencies—was a response to converging media markets and to the need for a coordinated regulatory framework. The converged super-regulator has been given the responsibility for both carriage regulation and content. At any one time, Ofcom seemed to be working on a bewildering range of technically and financially complex telecommunications issues and on a wide range of politically and financially complex cable, satellite, television, radio, advertising, Internet and mobile communications issues (Tunstall 2010). Ofcom can be considered primarily an economic regulator, since it puts the interests of the consumer before the interests of the citizen. In fact, in the current digital era, the prevailing language within the regulatory agency is to protect 'consumer interest' or 'consumer transparency', rather than 'citizen interest' or 'citizen rights'. Ofcom's intention to accommodate commercial concerns provides the regulatory agency the ability to shape the behaviour of the public broadcaster BBC. Despite continued backing of the idea of an independent, publicly funded public broadcaster, it has increased the financial stringency of the corporation, and has continually asked it to justify the need for non-commercial output and to scale down its commercial enterprises. Any new BBC services are now subject to a test to measure the 'public value' of the proposed services based on 'objectivity, rigour and transparency' against their impact on the market. Ofcom's numerous reports are packed with data and statistical tables. In the Ofcom era, 'public service broadcasting' has been quantified.

Given that the EC provides a good example of communications market integration on a political-strategic level, we have devoted a large space in this work to reviewing the EC policy for regulatory convergence, and have concluded that such a policy has had the following objectives: acceleration of market liberalisation, acceleration of the decision-making process and simplification of regulation, and a growing reliance on competition law rather than sector-specific regulation. Matters of derogation and subsidiarity, however, are being contested with reference to digital switchover and the take-up of social media services, which exacerbates the divisions within the EU narrative of political integration and national sovereignty. The evolution of the European communications policy reveals that the primary rationale for such policy is the economic imperative. The 2007 AVMSD confirms that cultural concerns are overshadowed by the more pressing need to break down market barriers to facilitate transborder broadcasting.

The AVMSD was certainly a victory for liberal economic forces, but it contains cultural considerations such as 'quotas' requiring broadcasters to devote the majority of their programming to European works.

BIBLIOGRAPHY

Barbrook R., and A. Cameron. 1996. "The Californian Ideology". *Science as Culture* 6(1): 44–72.

Bhaduri A. 2010. "India Unwired—Why New Media is Not (yet) the Message for Political Communication". In *Social Media and Politics: Online Social Networking and Political Communication in Asia*, ed. P. Behnke. Singapore: Konrad-Adenauer-Stiftung Media Programme Asia.

Boyd-Barrett O. 1995. "The Political Economy Approach". In *Conceptualising the Public Sphere Approaches to Media: A Reader*, eds. O. Boyd-Barrett, and C. Newbold. London: Arnold.

Castells M. 2007. "Communication, Power and Counter-power in the Network Society". *International Journal of Communication* 8: 238–266.

DCMS (Departments of Culture, Media and Sport) and DTI (Department of Trade and Industry). 2000. *A New Future of Communications (Cm 5010)*. London: TSO.

Dewaal, A. 2012. Don't Elevate Kony, *World Peace Foundation*, March 10. http://sites.tufts.edu/reinventingpeace/2012/03/10/dont-elevate-kony/ (accessed June 18, 2014).

The Communications Act. 1934. Public Law Number 416, 48 Stat. 1064. http://transition.fcc.gov/Reports/1934new.pdf.

Dunbar J. 2005. "Who is Watching the Watchdog?". In *The Future of Media: Resistance and Reform in the 21st Century*, eds. R.W. McChesney, R. Newman, and B. Scott, 127–140. New York: Seven Stories Press.

Dutton, W.H. 2007. Through the Network (of networks)—the Fifth Estate. Inaugural Lecture, University of Oxford. October 15. http://people.oii.ox.ac.uk/dutton/wp-content/uploads/2007/10/5th-estate-lecture-text.pdf (accessed May 28, 2014).

EC (European Commission). 2000. "Directive 2000/31/EC of the European Parliament and of the Council of 8 June 2000 on certain legal aspects of information society services, in particular electronic commerce, in the Internal Market (Directive on electronic commerce)", Official Journal L 178, 17/07/2000.

EC (European Commission). 2010a. *Brussels Wants to Delve Deep into the Running of National Economies—It Should Beware of Digging Too Far*, October 2, p. 52.

European Union (EU) Directive. 2010. 2010/13/EU of the European Parliament and of the Council of 10 March 2010 on the Coordination of Certain Provisions Laid Down by Law, Regulation or Administrative Action in Member States Concerning the Provision of Audiovisual Media Services (AVMSD), OJ L 95, 15 Apr 2010.

Fox Television Stations Inc. vs. FCC, 280F.3d 1027. 2002.
Freedman D. 2008. *The Politics of Media Policy*. Cambridge: Polity Press.
Garnham N. 1990. *Capitalism and Communication*. London: Sage.
Graham A. 2000. "Public Policy Issues for UK Broadcasting". In *E-Britannia: The Communications Revolution*, eds. S. Barnett et al., 93–108. Luton: University of Luton Press.
Goode L. 2010. "Social News, Citizen Journalism and Democracy". *New Media & Society* 11(8): 1287–1305.
Harvey S. 2006. "Ofcom's First Year and Neo-liberalism's Blind Spot: Attacking the Culture of Production". *Screen* 47(1): 91–105.
Hasebrink U. 2012. "The Role of the Audience within Media Governance: The Neglected Dimension of Media Literacy". *Media Studies* 3(6): 58–73.
Helberger N. 2008. "From Eyeball to Creator: Toying with Audience Empowerment in the Audiovisual Media Services Directive". *Entertainment Law Review* 6: 128–137.
Hoynes W. 1994. *Public Television for Sale. Media, the Market, and the Public Sphere*. Boulder, CO: Westview.
Humphreys P. 2009. "EU Audiovisual Policy, Cultural Diversity and the Future of Public Service Broadcasting". In *Mediating Europe. New Media, Mass Communications and the European Public Sphere*, eds. J. Harrison, and B. Wessels, 183–212. New York: Berghahn.
Hutchinson, D. 2007. "The EU and the Press: Policy or Non-policy?" In *Media and Cultural Policy in the European Union*, ed. K. Sarikakis, 24 European Media studies.
Independent Study. 2009. "Indicators for Media Pluralism in the Member States—Towards a Risk-Based Approach." Prepared for the European Commission DG Information Society and Media by K.U. Leuven—ICRI, Jönköping International Business School—MMTC and Ernst & Young Consultancy, April Preliminary Final Report. Leuven, Belgium.
Iosifidis P. 2006. "Digital Switchover in Europe". *International Communication Gazette* 68(3): 249–268.
Iosifidis P. 2011a. *Global Media and Communication Policy*. Basingstoke: Palgrave Macmillan.
Iosifidis P. 2011b. "The Public Sphere, Social Networks and Public Service Media". *Information, Communication & Society* 14(5): 619–637.
Iosifidis P. 2011c. "Growing Pains? The Transition to Digital Television in Europe". *European Journal of Communication* 26(1): 1–15.
Johnson D.R., S.P. Crawford, and J.G. Palfrey. 2004. "The Accountable Net: Peer Production of Internet Governance". *Virginia Journal of Law and Technology* 9(9).
Kalimo, H. and C. Pauwels. 2009. "The converging media and communications environment". In *Rethinking European Media and Communications Policy*, ed. C. Pauwels et al. Institute for European Studies, Brussels University Press: VUBPRESS.

Livingstone S., P. Lunt, and L. Miller. 2007. "Citizens and Consumers: Discursive Debates During and After the Communications Act 2003". *Media Culture & Society* 29(4): 613–638.

Mapping Digital Media: United States. 2011. A Report by the Open Society Foundations. http://www.opensocietyfoundations.org/sites/default/files/mapping-digital-media-united-states-20111123.pdf (accessed May 17, 2014).

Media Insight Project. 2014. An Initiative of the American Press Institute and the Associated Press-NORC Centre for Public Affairs Research, www.americanpressinstitute.org/publications/reports/survey-research/personal-news-cycle/ (accessed June 25, 2014).

Michalis M. 2007. *Governing European Communications*. Lanham, MD: Lexington.

Michalis M. 2010. "EU Broadcasting Governance and PSB: Between a Rock and a Hard Place". In *Reinventing Public Service Communication: European Broadcasters and Beyond*, ed. P. Iosifidis, 36–48. Basingstoke, UK: Palgrave Macmillan.

Noam, E. 2013. Who Owns the World's Media? Columbia Business School. March 31. http://papers.ssrn.com/sol3/papers.cfm?abstract_id=2242670 (accessed April 2, 2014).

Richards M., Ed. 2010. The Complex Regulatory Environment in the Communications Sector. Speech to the UCL Javons Institute for Competition Law and Economics Annual Colloquium, July 13. https://www.competitionpolicyinternational.com/the-complex-regulatory-environment-in-the-communications-sector (accessed May 23, 2014).

Schulz, W. et al. 2011. Mapping the Frontiers of Governance in Social Media. Paper prepared for the 1st Berlin Symposium on Internet and Society, October 25–27, http://berlinsymposium.org/sites/berlinsymposium.org/files/social_media_governance_0.pdf (accessed June 24, 2014).

Singer J.B. 2014. "User-generated Visibility: Secondary Gatekeeping in a Shared Media Space". *New Media & Society* 16(1): 55–73.

Smith P. 2006. "The Politics of UK Television Policy: The Making of Ofcom". *Media Culture & Society* 28(6): 929–940.

Starr, J.M. 2004. *An Alternative View of the Future of Public Television*. Chicago, IL: University of Chicago Cultural Policy Centre. December 1.

Tunstall J. 2010. "The BBC and UK Public Service Broadcasting". In *Reinventing Public Service Communication: European Broadcasters and Beyond*, ed. P. Iosifidis, 145–157. Basingstoke: Palgrave Macmillan.

Van Guilenburg J., and D. McQuail. 2003. "Media Policy Paradigm Shifts: Towards a New Communications Policy Paradigm". *European Journal of Communication* 18(2): 181–207.

Vick D.W. 2006. "Regulatory Convergence?". *Legal Studies* 26(1): 26–64.

Wheeler M. 2004. "Supranational Regulation: Television and the European Union". *European Journal of Communication* 19(3): 349–369.

PART II

Western Liberal Democratic Traditions, Grassroots Politics and the Social Media

Modern Political Communication and Web 2.0 in Representative Democracies: The United States and the British Experience

INTRODUCTION

Within modern election campaigns, there has been an exponential take-up of online forms of campaigning and employment of social media. During the 1990s and the first two decades of the twenty-first century, this use of the Internet emerged from its use as an add-on to the television-based presidential campaigns in the USA—and to a lesser degree, the general elections in the UK—to its role as an essential component within the wider communication of candidate and party messages. In some respects, the traditional forms of political advertising have been enhanced through the employment of party websites and candidate blogs and the incorporation of social networks such as Facebook, YouTube and Twitter. However, the social media have more profoundly facilitated interactive communication between the political elites and public, to encourage new forms of participation (Bang 2009; Keane 2009).

Our analysis will employ Andrew Chadwick's concept of the 'hybrid media system' to consider how the social media have been incorporated into mainstream political communication strategies:

> The hybrid media system is built upon interactions among older and new media logics—where logics are defined as technologies, genres norms, behaviours and organisational forms—in the reflexively connected fields of media and politics. (Chadwick 2013:12)

© The Editor(s) (if applicable) and The Author(s) 2016   95
P. Iosifidis, M. Wheeler, *Public Spheres and Mediated Social Networks in the Western Context and Beyond,*
DOI 10.1057/978-1-137-41030-6_5

Such hybridity is reflective of the fragmentation of the media audience, the dissolution of centralised party systems, the growth of grassroots political activity, the rise of generic 24/7 news channels and citizen journalism, the global consumption of infotainment and the greater fluidity within political ideologies, presentation and marketing (Chadwick 2013:12). In this respect, the US Democratic presidential candidacies of Howard Dean in 2004 and Barack Obama in 2008 and 2012 proved to be 'game changers' in shaping the political employment of the social media. While Dean showed how the web could announce his candidacy, Obama demonstrated how to 'run an Internet campaign that uses all the relevant media, most notably television, to blend centralisation, control and hierarchy with decentralisation, devolution, and horizontality' (Chadwick 2013:209).

We begin this chapter by considering how US politicians have employed the social media to effect major changes in recent presidential campaigns.[1] We first provide a short history of the early adoption of the Internet and electronic communications that occurred in the race between Democratic President Bill Clinton and his Republican opponents. Republican President George W. Bush also used online techniques to undermine the Democratic nominee Senator John Kerry in 2004. And it was in the 2004 Democratic primaries that Howard Dean demonstrated that an online 'citizen initiative' campaign could reconfigure the relationship between the candidate and his support base. While Dean's candidacy collapsed, as he could not sustain his electoral base, Barack Obama's establishment of *mybarackobama.com* (MyBo) as a communitarian democratic social network enabled him to extend his reach to the electorate. Furthermore, Obama understood that he could construct a personal discourse with community organisers, while simultaneously establishing a more populist political image within the spectacle of the traditional media.[2]

Second, this chapter will analyse how this asymmetrical interdependence of the mass media and social media has been taken up in UK electoral politics. As British campaigns have been 'Americanised', it had been

---

[1] There are several examples of the Internet being used at the congressional and gubernatorial level—for instance, the former WWF wrestler Jesse Ventura stood as the independent candidate for governor of Minnesota, who was able to build an email network of more than 3000 supporters to facilitate voter registrations, events and rallies.

[2] This type of political candidacy has been only partially attempted in other modern democracies, and may be seen to have been truly successful only in extreme scenarios, such as the rise of the comedian Beppe Grillo as a political player in the middle of the Italian economic and political crisis concerning debt and malfeasance. See Chap. 6 for further details.

predicted that the 2010 general election would be the 'first Internet election' and that social media activism might increase exponentially. However, due to the UK party systems, different electoral rules and the political elite's reluctance to engage with community activism, the online campaign proved to be far less extensive in terms of grassroots mobilisation (Kavanagh and Cowley 2010:185). Yet Chadwick's hybrid media model shows that there was significant integration of Web 2.0 techniques within the UK parties' political marketing tools and, in particular, their attempts to shape the coverage of the campaign (Chadwick 2013; Wring and Ward 2010; Gibson et al. 2010). This was mirrored by the incorporation of social media into newsgathering routines for the sourcing of material via Twitter and by the ways that conventional media stories were complemented by online coverage (Newman 2010:3).

Finally, we will discuss how such forms of hybridity continued to characterise the political parties' deployment of social media in the 2015 UK general election campaign. In many respects, their use of social media remained limited to a party 'advocacy' model with respect to websites, online messages, the employment of YouTube for replicating electoral broadcasts and reaching out to the wider public. These techniques, however, were accompanied by a more interesting use of the social media to track the electorate's political sentiments. In particular, the Conservative Party engaged in the tactical use of Facebook by importing the Obama campaign strategist Jim Messina to 'micro-target' the attitudes of swing voters through the site. Conversely, the Labour Party attempted to win a 'ground war' battle for online community-based 'conversations' through the extensive use of Twitter. However, despite this considerable social media activity, many questions remain about the extent to which these techniques truly effected strategic political change or succeeded in closing democratic deficits.

US Presidential Elections: The Internet from the Periphery to the Centre of Campaign Operations

In the 1992 presidential campaign, the Democratic challenger Bill Clinton and President George H.W. Bush utilised email systems to disseminate speeches and position papers through a Clinton Listserv and the White House Communications Office. In the 1996 campaign, both Clinton and his Republican opponent Bob Dole would develop political websites. Moreover, Dole invited viewers of the first televised presidential debate to become involved in his campaign by issuing its website address on air. In 2000, Al Gore established an electronic 'town hall' movement and included an 'Instant MessageNet' for online chatting on his website. Alongside their websites, presidential candidates including George W. Bush and John Kerry began developing blogs through which to connect to the public.

Yet the reach of such electronic campaign operations remained limited. Instead, the principle innovation in the utilisation of electronic communication referred to the Clinton team's employment of the Excalibur database. This was an off-the-shelf electronic filing software system which was developed by a San Diego-based company, Excalibur Technology Corp. It was employed by Clinton's campaign manager James Carville to quash any bad news stories and to undermine the credibility of his opponents. For instance, Clinton's war room team successfully rebutted comments made by Vice President Dan Quayle in a 14-page booklet which was distributed to the political press.

More negative forms of political communication occurred when George W. Bush's operatives, including Karl Rove, used the Internet to direct smears against his opponents. In the 2004 presidential campaign, the Democratic nominee Senator John Kerry was confronted with a 'Kerry Gas Tax Calculator' on Bush's website, which purported to demonstrate how he would increase fuel prices. Moreover, Kerry became the recipient of further negative attack ads focusing on his Vietnam War record when the Republican National Committee placed critical banner adverts across 1000 websites (Davis et al. 2009:19).[3]

Throughout these early Internet campaigns, the social media were seen as a supplementary medium to television. Invariably, presidential candidates continued to pour their resources into traditional spot adverts and the buying up of airtime. Consequently, political consultants sought to incorporate the social media into the hierarchical professional model of campaign management. The Internet was also seen as an effective mechanism for small campaign contributions. However, this attitude changed when the little-known Governor of Vermont, Howard Dean, ran for the presidential nomination in the 2004 Democratic primaries.

---

[3] More critically, a Section 527 campaign backed by Bush supporters made a series of television attack adverts concerning Kerry's war record in Vietnam. The so-called Swift Boat Veterans for Truth used the Internet for financial contributions and to raise public suspicion about Kerry's military heroism.

Dean not only used the Internet for funding drives and campaign communications, but also to pave the way for a 'citizen-initiated' approach (Gibson 2010:7). In 2002, Dean had had marginal exposure on the national scene and was only notable for his outspoken opposition to the war in Iraq. Within the opinion polls, he appeared at a margin of error of 0 %, and was woefully short of campaign monies. Throughout 2003 and 2004, he constructed an online presence by establishing several networks of political support through the collaborative use of blogs, social networking sites and user-driven videos. Thus he hosted several blogs, including Dean Nation, Change for America, Howard Dean 2004 Call to Action Weblog and the Blog for America, to operate as 'user–controller' forums for decision-making in his campaign. These blogs were updated on a daily basis and, along with his supporters' sites such as *Meetup.com*, allowed Dean to mobilise 600,000 online activists. Consequently, he pioneered a model of grassroots campaigning comprising independent and self-organising teams of volunteers (Rice 2004; Gibson 2010). As Dean's manager, Joe Trippi contended:

> Other campaigns in the past had talked about being decentralized, moving decision making out to people in the field, but this was different. We didn't turn the campaign over to organizers in Iowa or in Michigan. We just turned the thing loose.... (Trippi 2004:94)

This had a dramatic effect, as Dean raised $27 million to become the most successful fundraiser in Democratic Party history and the front runner in the Iowa Caucus and the New Hampshire Democratic primary. Yet, while Dean could successfully announce his campaign, it eventually collapsed, as he finished behind Kerry and John Edwards in Iowa and New Hampshire. Dean's bid would fully 'crash and burn' when he committed an extraordinary media gaffe known as the 'Dean Scream' during his Iowa concession speech, in which, due to his problems with a unidirectional microphone, he appeared loud, overly emotional and unpresidential. Despite his ability to mobilise a grassroots movement, Dean's support base had proven unsustainable. However, his devolved digital campaigning had shown the way for Barack Obama, who would take significant advantage of social media while continuing to employ the political communication principles drawn from the television age (Chadwick 2013:199).

BARACK OBAMA'S 2008 PRESIDENTIAL CAMPAIGN
AND THE REALISATION OF A HYBRID MEDIA CAMPAIGN:
MESSAGE, SPECTACLE AND OUTREACH

In 2008, the Democratic Party presidential nominee Senator Barack Obama, as an articulate African-American politician, became the personification of a progressive movement (Sanders 2009:96). As the first black man to win either of the US political parties' nominations, Obama's ethnicity and cool intellect offered a sharp break from his predecessor, the gung-ho President George W. Bush. Moreover, his cosmopolitanism contrasted with the Democratic Party primary front runner Senator Hillary Clinton, and his youth compared well with the septuagenarian Republican nominee Senator John McCain.

Obama had begun the campaign as the underdog. While he was a reasonably well-known figure, who had announced himself on the national stage with his well-received speech at the 2004 Democratic National Convention, and was serving as Illinois senator, he appeared to have little chance of defeating Clinton, the former first lady and current New York senator. To offset this disadvantage, Obama built himself up as a legitimate political leader, who was accompanied by a photogenic wife and family, and who appealed to young voters (Green 2011). To develop his multicultural appeal, he provided an intriguing narrative that mixed his international status with his Americanism as the son of an African father, Barack Obama, Sr., from Kenya, and a white American mother, Stanley Ann Dunham, from Kansas.

Thus Obama presented himself as a force to purify the 'American democratic experiment' by mediating between the darkness of a sullied past and the light of a bright future. Consequently, his candidacy was perched on the 'very hinge of history' and his heroic status was mediated through the iconic 'Hope' poster designed by artist Shepard Fairey (Alexander 2010:68; Kellner 2009:725). During the primaries, Obama, with his catchphrase of 'yes we can', promised the US electorate, with a palpable yet undefined sense of 'togetherness', that he would deal with the nation's economic, political and foreign policy ills. Within the general election, this phrase was refined to become 'change we can believe in'. Obama's appeal increased during the US global financial crisis that began in September 2008, as he made measured and intelligent statements about the economy.

Obama's rhetoric focused upon a communitarian response to the fear-inducing terrors of the modern age and was framed through the utilisation of the media spectacle. His campaign managers employed a series of must-see events and urged their candidate to make well-received speeches, which were globally televised, to heighten his public worth (Kellner 2009:716). In this respect, the Obama team was aided by the Lexalytics automatic sentiment tracking system which analysed the 'emotional' content of the thousands of Twitter messages that appeared during the candidate's televised speeches. This new branch of computer science set out to 'follow what the world [was] thinking in real time' (Newman 2010:37).

To further enhance his image as a force for change, Obama presented himself as technologically literate. In this respect, he was aided by the remarkable rise of social media networks such as Facebook, Twitter and YouTube that had emerged in the intervening years from 2004 to 2008. Consequently, Obama popularised his appeal through a variety of podcasts, YouTube speeches and BlackBerry messages. He was frequently shown using SMS/texting to remain informed and to mobilise his support base. Obama's political speeches remained popular on YouTube, and the electorate responded enthusiastically to his longer speeches, which sometimes lasted well over 40 minutes (Zaleski 2008).

These Web 2.0 tools allowed Obama's team to effect online political advertisements such as the Jewish comedienne Sarah Silverman's 'The Great Schlep', imploring Jewish grandchildren to fly to Florida to force their grandparents to leave their condominiums and their prejudices behind to support Obama's candidacy. Other film and music stars including Scarlett Johansson, Kelly Hu, John Legend, Herbie Hancock, Kareem Abdul Jabbar, Adam Rodriquez, Amber Valetta and Nick Cannon produced a pro-Obama video with The Black Eyed Peas entitled *Yes We Can*, which became one of the most downloaded items on YouTube. Moreover, the campaign spread its message virally by emphasising the horizontal linkage of a range of non-traditional political actors. For instance, there was the user-generated YouTube video in which a young woman, Amber Lee Ettinger (the 'Obama Girl') sang 'I've got a crush on Obama' interspersed with images drawn from his speeches. This proved to be one of the site's most popular items, receiving five million hits (Kellner 2009:4).

In tandem, the Obama campaign targeted email messages, which appeared to be 'sent' from the candidate to members of the electorate at key periods during the election campaign (Cogburn and Espinoza-Vasquez 2011:202). A total of one billion in-house emails were sent out, alongside 8000 to 10,000 unique messages targeted to specific segments of their 13-million-member-strong email list. In this capacity, the staff created content and tested the communications by segmenting email lists. Moreover, by its conclusion, Obama's workers had garnered a further three million mobile and SMS subscribers (Chang 2009:3).

MyBo

A significant change in political campaign management occurred, as Obama realised that, while it remained necessary to ensure spectacle both within the traditional media and Web 1.0 communications, the social media could facilitate a 'shift...toward a looser "hybrid" mode of operation that incorporated the network tactics of protest movements' (Gibson 2010:5). Thus he employed the key elements of Dean's citizen-initiated campaigning to empower local activists to carry out core tasks, while introducing the appropriate mechanisms through which to command the deployment of social media resources (Milki and Rhodes 2009:9; Wolf 2004).

In 2007, the Obama campaign established the MyBo site which, after a straightforward registration process, offered users a wide degree of involvement in an online political community. It encouraged recruitment drives and enabled local associations, invariably drawn from youth groups, college students and non-traditional political actors, to organise as grassroots activists, thereby working in an inclusive and relational manner (Bang 2009:132). This incorporation of information technology was driven in part by the greater dollars that could be raised online to fund the campaign. To this end, the social media placed a focus on building a critical mass of small donors who could contribute sums of $200 or less. Subsequently, the MyBo website was transformed into a networking zone with a strong donations component. Consequently, $35 million was raised online, although this accounted for only 6 % of the total $729 million raised in campaign funds (Straw 2010:43; Green 2011).

More crucially, Obama's campaign managers David Axelrod and David Plouffe sought out one of the co-founders of Facebook, Chris Hughes, to develop MyBo's software so that it focused on real-world organising with the electorate. At the same time, Obama's background as a community organiser had given him the requisite political skills to understand how to mobilise such grassroots forms of self-organisation. He thus established a 'vast intricate machine' to coordinate campaign operations in which his managers could organise field operatives, train volunteers and monitor the success of this voluntary activism. As such, Obama's network of campaign teams placed themselves at the centre of a movement composed of activist groups and lay persons (Cogburn and Espinoza-Vasquez 2011:201). In this respect, Obama's team had learned some lessons from Dean's disintegration, and so reported contacts were spot-checked, and special online training was required for those signing up.

Across the battleground states, Obama's utilisation of social networking technologies enabled his campaign organisation to swell to 1.5 million community organisers. To aid their door-to-door canvassing, volunteers accessed constantly updated databases through field offices and via MyBo to obtain information about potential voters' political leanings (Lai Stirland 2008). Additionally, Obama activists were issued an 80-page instruction manual to illustrate the organisational focus of the campaign, and were assigned as team and data coordinators to lead cadre operations in specific states. This blend of volunteering, gumshoe canvassing and information processing became the hallmark of the Obama campaign, as it:

> [built, tweaked and tinkered] with its technology and organisational infrastructure…to successfully integrate technology with a revamped model of political organisation that stresses volunteer participation and feedback on a massive scale. (Lai Stirland 2008)

However, Obama's team realised that there needed to be some latitude in its blend of legwork and information technology. They allowed activists a greater degree of autonomy in rooting out the opinions of non-specifically targeted members of the electorate. For instance, an Orlando-based field manager, Ashley Ball, encouraged her Florida activists to utilise MyBo to construct local 'watch parties' during the 2008 Democratic National Convention, and also employed social media to effect outreach initiatives with African-American, Jewish, Latino and youth groups (Ball 2014). Ball quoted the maxim of the social media campaign as 'Obama will bring the voters to the campaign but they will stay because of the volunteers' (Ball 2014). In turn, citizen participants were invited to solve common challenges and to scrutinise Obama's response to the range of problems faced by Americans, thereby enabling them to organise 'in new political communities for the exercise of good governance' (Bang 2009:133).

Through these inclusive techniques, Obama remained in constant touch with his core support and attracted online activists who experienced him in both a public and private sense:

> Obama articulated an image of himself as an inspiring political authority who does not expect a 'blind' or rationally motivated form of obedience.... He spoke about authority as a reciprocal and communicative two-way power relationship ... in order to get people with different ... identities and projects freely to accept cooperation across all conventional boundaries. (Bang 2009:132)

In effect, through the wide number of 'social' portals, Obama defined a political image founded on reciprocity to encourage the popular scrutiny of his ideas. Therefore, the often disaffected 'mobile youth' gravitated towards him and his message of change, hope and identity (Redmond 2010:92). The social capital drawn from Obama's online supporters became a pressing concern for Clinton in the primaries. For his opponents, his social media campaign represented more than just 'Obama as a candidate', as it was transformed into a growing social movement motivated by 'Obama as a cause' (Heilemann and Halperin 2010:52). This grassroots support base enabled Obama to defeat both Clinton in the primaries and his Republican opponent McCain in the presidential election. His devolved digital campaign was thus able to connect with those Americans who had become disenfranchised by machine politics (Redmond 2010:82).

Obama would take the MyBo operations into the 2012 presidential election against Republican candidate, former Governor Mitt Romney. While he continued to use the site and expanded his use of Twitter, as an incumbent chief executive, Obama faced different challenges in defending his record. While his team once again employed grassroots activists, there was no longer the same sense of intoxication or renewal connected with his candidacy. Furthermore, Obama's campaign managers turned to a more centralised use of social media and maintained a far more systemic form of control over the messages delivered (Ball 2014). Yet, despite Romney's attempts to close the gap between the Republican and Democratic Parties' use of social media, Obama remained far ahead in his deployment of social networks, and galvanised support for his candidacy among Hispanic members of the electorate. Throughout the 2008 and 2012 campaigns, Obama's approach demonstrated how Internet campaigning matured, and that the inclusive mobilisation of activists had become a major factor in the formulation of contemporary US political communications strategies:

> All the other candidates had the same access to these tools, but the Obama campaign...leveraged the tools to support its bottoms-up grassroots campaign strategy that tapped into the hearts of the voters. What resulted was not only a victory for the Democrats and Obama, but also the legacy of what was widely regarded as one of the most effective Internet marketing plans in history—where social media and technology enabled the individual to activate and participate in a movement. (Chang 2009:2)

THE BRITISH EXPERIENCE: THE 'FIRST INTERNET CAMPAIGN'—PREDICTIONS AND PARTY PRETENSIONS

In the run-up to the UK 2010 general election, bloggers and web specialists announced the realisation of the 'first Internet campaign' (Harris 2010). British politicians looked across the Atlantic to how they could import online campaign techniques into their own electoral practices. Despite substantive differences between US presidential and UK elections due to the requirements of voting for a party majority rather than for a candidate, a compressed campaign period, and a focus on local constituency battles as well as a national campaign, it was anticipated that UK politicians would build social media relations with Facebook friends, Twitter users and networks like Mumsnet.org.

All the main parties (Conservative, Labour and Liberal Democrat) were said to have employed members of the Obama campaign to realise the digital dividend that could be achieved from such devolved forms of political communications. Moreover, the then Conservative Party blue-sky thinker Steve Hilton believed that the social media could convey a greater degree of openness and transparency to the public, thereby humanising David Cameron's political leadership (Chadwick 2013:195). The Labour Party coordinator Douglas Alexander glowingly predicted that social media would defy old media logic to make for 'a much more exciting and anarchic environment in this campaign than ever before' (Newman 2010:5).

The Conservative Party had reportedly spent a significant amount of its campaign monies on viral marketing and advertising on Facebook. At the beginning of 2010, Cameron established a website entitled MyConservatives.com (MyCon) to aid supporters in self-organising and mobilising local campaign networks. MyCon was designed to energise non-members, and party candidates were encouraged to place their profiles on the site. The Conservatives were also energetic users of Twitter and had over 30,000 followers, the most of any party. Furthermore, the party spent its time and energies on integrating bloggers such as Ian Dale and Guido Fawkes, and ConservativeHome activists including Tim Montgomerie and Jonathan Isaby, to establish clear lines of communication between online opinion leaders and party leadership (Chadwick 2013:195).

Similarly, the Labour Party promised that it would engage in a 'massive drive' for grassroots activists, would incorporate blogs such as Left Foot Forward, created by Will Straw, and would seek online funds, although this initiative was led by the unlikely figure of David Blunkett (Harris 2010; Straw 2010). Throughout previous years, the party had invested in a rudimentary social network called Membersnet, which included 35,000 members, and the software enabled activists to organise their own events and share best practices. Labour also imported software from the USA that was used to embed an online phone banking system. This enabled members to make over 60,000 calls from their work, domestic and even iPhones to floating voters in marginal constituencies, and then submit public responses into a central database. Elsewhere, the Fabian Society— the Labour Party's left-leaning intellectual forum—argued that there was much to learn from Obama's social media success in terms of campaign organisation and the democratisation of the party's structure:

> politics...should go deeper: it should change more fundamentally not just how the Party competes for election but how it is organized and how it mobilizes support...Obama showed that a successful campaign requires a mixture of a centrally managed core message alongside decentralized tools of self-organisation and a culture where it is OK to openly challenge policy and strategy. (Anstead and Straw 2009:95)

UK PARTY PHILOSOPHIES AND THE PRACTICAL EMPLOYMENT OF THE SOCIAL MEDIA IN THE 2010 GENERAL ELECTION CAMPAIGN

Despite such lofty aspirations, the most innovative use of social media during the pre-election campaign phase of the 2010 general election can be ascribed to mischief-makers such as Clifford Singer. Notably, Singer doctored spoof artwork images of Cameron to parody his empty rhetoric about austerity measures. When Cameron appeared on billboard posters claiming, 'We can't go on like this. I'll cut the deficit, not the NHS', Singer produced two mock-ups which distorted the strapline, and placed them on a website entitled mydavidcameron.com. His spoofs were speedily replicated across Twitter and Facebook, and an online generator was created so that the public could easily type in a wide range of parody slogans. While some of the 150,000 designs comprised personal insults and employed the rhetoric of class warfare, more humorous and subtle variations provided a satirical investigation into the worth of the Conservative Party's political messages.

In another case of the mismatch between the political elite and the online community, the parties' failure to effectively address their new audiences was thrown into sharp relief when then Prime Minister Gordon Brown disastrously employed the user-generated website YouTube to perpetuate his image to younger voters. His manic attempts to put a smile on his face became the subject of particular ridicule, not only from his opponents but from his allies as well. For example, the former Deputy Labour Party Leader John Prescott described Brown as having 'the worst bloody smile in the world' (Summers 2009). Consequently, in the run-up to the election, Labour spin doctors became increasingly concerned about Brown's toxicity with to the electorate.

In the wake of this avalanche of parody material and Brown's ineffective use of social media, the lessons for the mainstream parties were clear— avoid the anarchistic potential of social media, minimise citizen-initiated campaigning, use Web 2.0 for strategic advantage to market the party, facilitate intra-party communications and keep a deliberate spin control over the leaders' online and offline messages (Wring and Ward 2010:813– 814). Indeed, the most significant shift in the UK parties' online strategies related to the amount of time and resources all the parties spent on rebuilding their websites to ensure that they would appear prominently on the Google search engine (Chadwick 2013:198). As such, they bought Google AdWords keywords, which allowed web users to readily access the parties' main websites and also enabled local candidates to piggyback their sites onto the party search items. In effect, this was a form of agenda-setting, as the Conservative Party spokesman Craig Elder explained:

> The centre of the project was we took a decision...to rebuild Conservatives. com around 26 key policy areas, to make sure that everything on the site pointed via a database to reference those 26 key policy areas, to make sure

the Conservative Party first and foremost won on search, so people could search 'Conservative Education', 'Conservative Immigration' and find that...Google search, Google ads, were a massive, massive part of our strategy. (Chadwick 2013:197)

Furthermore, there were profound philosophical differences between the values that underpinned the party managers and those of campaign workers who proposed Web 2.0 solutions. These often related to questions about fundraising, and revealed the conservative logic exhibited by the political strategists in their employment of social media. For example, the Conservative Party treasurer wanted to use traditional methods to raise funds, while the party communications team pressed to experiment with online forms of financial engagement. At the same time, the Labour Party spin doctors felt that the social media were far more effective in re-energising the traditional support base than in seeking to win over any undecided voters.

Darren Lilleker and Nigel Jackson have provided a critical content analysis of the 2010 British election party websites which demonstrates that the parties were principally concerned with effecting internal forms of marketing (Lilleker and Jackson 2013:259). Hence they noted that, at the surface level, the parties had set up their homepages to act as shop fronts that could attract potential floating or uncertain voters who were surfing the Internet. In drilling down, however, they contended that the sites' interactive nodes were designed to convert existing supporters into activists by placing an emphasis on donations, endorsements and offline campaigning. They concluded that despite some evidence of a limited degree of outreach, the political mainstream preferred to keep citizen input to a minimum. Therefore, the opportunities for any truly reciprocal forms of communication were assiduously avoided:

[T]he nature of the talk that filtered through to political party websites was solidly on message and enhanced the campaign; thus, within these spaces the public voice became an extension of the party brand. Thus, we find a normalisation of political communication within party-built spaces. It is hard to argue that party online presences have any role in enhancing broader democratic engagement. (Lilleker and Jackson 2013:259)

Consequently, while the UK parties used the Internet more extensively in 2010 than before, this employment of social media was absorbed into the hierarchical model of top-down political communications. For instance, there was more sophisticated employment of databases and social software to target campaign messages to marginal constituencies. However, employment of more decentralised and personalised forms of content remained limited, as candidates used the Web 2.0 tools in an ineffective and largely superficial manner. As Rosalynd Southern and Stephen Ward noted, by:

> [s]imply making regular or even very regular updates is many ways no different from certain forms of older, Web 1.0 types of campaigning, such as sending out an email newsletter. Indeed, often a lot less effort will have gone into a Facebook wall update or a Tweet than into a campaign e-newsletter. The flow of information is still largely one-way and top-down, from the candidate to potential constituent. (Southern and Ward 2011:230)

Moreover, while the Labour, Conservative and Liberal-Democratic Parties operated an extensive 'ground war' campaign through the use of information technology, the UK general election was characterised by 'air war' techniques in the conventional media (Gaber 2011:274). Although blogs, tweets, Facebook and websites had some bearing on the campaign, they proved to be add-ons rather than key tools for the mobilisation of grassroots political support (Lilleker and Jackson 2013:245). Essentially, for many commentators, the 2010 'internet election' was the 'dog [that] failed to bite' (Gibson et al. 2010:1).

Despite these disappointments, Rachel Gibson, Andy Williamson and Stephen Ward contend that the Internet successfully channelled public interest into the general election by moving the conversation onto discussions of 'politics' with a small 'p' (Gibson et al. 2010:1–2). Furthermore, Nic Newman maintains that the social media operate most effectively through a series of small personal interactions that may add up to more than the sum of their parts. He suggests that the online community effected social discovery and added perspective to the political classes that sat alongside the more linear stream of information provided by television coverage of the campaign (Newman 2010:50). Thus, while television remained the dominant medium, most of the younger voters between the ages of 18 and 24 gained their information about the campaign from party and news websites. As such, the Web 2.0 tools of social media were perhaps most effective when they were wrapped around television news stories and employed in 'sharing thoughts and opinions' about the televised prime ministerial (PM) leadership debates (Newman 2010:3).

The Social Media and the Mass Media: News Stories, Twitter Feeds, Journalistic Blogging and the Online Coverage of the UK Prime Ministerial Election Debates

Throughout the 2010 campaign, newspaper and broadcast journalists normalised their use of the social media as source material. As Ivor Gaber commented, the parties' use of conventional news conferences and press releases declined, and reporters found that their daily email inboxes were overflowing with party communications (Gaber 2011:267). This was accompanied by the parties' extensive employment of Facebook, Twitter feeds and blogs. For instance, the Channel 4 News anchor Krishnan Guru Murthy described Twitter's real-time delivery of information as akin to a wire service. For many political journalists, Twitter acted as a newsfeed, becoming their first port of call, and they subsequently used the social network for viral marketing of their messages (Gaber 2011:268).

Web 2.0 tools were extensively employed by citizen bloggers and newspaper journalists to cover the campaign. Andrew Sparrow of *The Guardian* provided a daily blog throughout the election, monitored a range of online newsfeeds and, with the support of his colleagues, weaved many thousands of viewpoints into his correspondence. Sparrow argued that 'if journalism is the first draft of history, live blogging is the first draft of journalism. It's not perfect, but it's deeply rewarding' (Newman 2010:17). In particular, Sparrow's blog increased from 100,000 to 350,000 page views per day during the occurrence of 'Bigotgate'—the fallout from the incident in which Brown was infamously caught off-air with his radio microphone on by Sky News, condemning the 'bigotry' of the Rochdale pensioner Gillian Duffy.

As the televised PM election debates were the principal form of innovation in the 2010 election, the online community effected an alternative, real-time commentary to complement the conventional news media coverage. While it was predicted that the effect of the three PM debates would be mitigated by the detailed rules that had been negotiated by the political classes, their impact was significantly enhanced by the energetic social media conversations surrounding their broadcast. Richard Allan, Facebook's European director of policy, commented, 'You want to watch the debate on TV, because that is the right medium, but you also want to chatter about it with your friends on social media' (Newman 2010:32). Therefore, for many Web 2.0 users, social media provided 'water-cooler' moments, in which it became unthinkable not to post a link to a YouTube video.

Similarly, the Tweetminster political website reported that 36,000 people posted 184,000 tweets during the first debate at a rate of 29 tweets per second. It was further suggested that such 'Twittering' counteracted electoral passivity, leading to a greater level of efficacy and engagement within the social media classes who linked in with one another through a range of retweets and online forums. This was complemented by the use of Lexalytics analysis of the emotional content of the tweets made during the debates, demonstrating that the overall score of approval received by Cameron was balanced out by the Liberal Democratic leader Nick Clegg, while both stood well ahead of Brown.

This result was replicated in the subsequent telephone polls, and these results were duly reported in the British Broadcasting Corporation (BBC) television news bulletins and on the BBC websites. Furthermore, immediately after the debates, Independent Television's (ITV) *News at Ten* showed a selection of tweets and Facebook messages to a television audience of six million people, demonstrating how the social media coverage had become a news story in its own right and had served to set the agenda about the debates' winners and losers (Gaber 2011; Wring 2011).

Thus, in another variation of Chadwick's hybrid media model, the UK political parties, media organisations and Web 2.0 proponents, in concert, demonstrated how traditional culture norms and new political communication practices determined their importation of social media into the 2010 campaign (Chadwick 2013:196–199). The question remained, however, whether this employment of social media really afforded a greater level of participation and public efficacy, or whether it was merely another form of ephemera in an era of late modernity or post-democracy (Crouch 2004). These concerns would carry through to the political parties' use of social media in the 2015 UK general election.

The Social Media and the 2015 UK General Election: The Political Parties' Hybrid 'Old' and 'New' Media Information Campaigns

The 2015 UK general election was similarly declared to be a social media campaign. With the significant increase in Facebook and Twitter usage, it was again predicted that the parties would engage in a more 'people-led' process (Cellan-Jones 2015). Indeed, there were some notable examples of the employment of information technology. As in 2010, the leadership debates (wherein the Conservatives forced the combined set of broadcasters to operate under an arcane set of rules, which were radically reconfigured due to the rise of the UK Independence Party [UKIP] and the Scottish National Party [SNP]) were accompanied by the constant online monitoring of the leaders' political performance. Most notably, the Twittersphere was aglow with positive responses to SNP leader Nicola Sturgeon's strong showing during the two debates in which she appeared (Jones 2015).

In addition, there was the peculiar Twitter-based personality cult attempt to present the former Labour Party leader Ed Miliband as an unlikely sex symbol, through the hashtag '#Milifandom', to counterbalance his 'nerdy' image in the mainstream media. In a further attempt to improve Miliband's credibility, he was interviewed by the anti-corporate comedian Russell Brand, who had decried voting on Brand's YouTube series, *The Trews*, with its 1,000,000 subscribers. The Labour leader spoke to Brand about the inequities of global capitalism, the protection of working rights and media owners and the lasting value of voting. While Cameron castigated 'Milibrand' as a joke, the Labour strategists hoped that Brand's endorsement, with his 9.5 million Twitter followers, could provide a conduit to young, disengaged voters (Wheeler 2015:82).

However, despite the noise and hyperbole surrounding these specific examples of online party activity, Chadwick's hybridity model continued to characterise the political parties' deployment of their online and offline resources (Chadwick and Vaccari 2015:69). As Anstead commented, the notion that the 2015 election was played out on the social media to the exclusion of all other forms of mass communications was wildly inaccurate (Anstead 2015:68). Rather, old and new media fed off one another in the light party communications and the trending of political issues. In many respects, with an electoral result in which the Conservative Party successfully achieved a small overall majority, it was shown that within a social media election, the traditional rules of communication applied:

> The Conservative campaign, straight from the tried and trusted Lynton Crosby textbook, combined relentless attack on Labour's weak points with strong core vote messages...the basic underlying focus on economic competence and fear of Labour, propped up by the SNP, was consistent, comprehensible and apparently resonant. Across the country the political tectonic plates may have shifted, but this was political communication as usual. (Scammell 2015:39)

Therefore, the vast majority of the mainstream party's use of the social media was limited to a traditional 'advocacy' model. Instead of following

Obama's interactive approach, the UK political parties ran tightly controlled campaigns in which they deployed social media to remain on message. The party leaders remained gaffe-free, so they could not be mocked online. Instead, they maintained a relentlessly top-down utilisation of social media when it came to propagating their message.

In varying hues, the parties used tried and tested methods of positive and negative positional videos, a number of which went viral. The Green Party election broadcast (PEB) 'Change the Tune' (which had actors portraying Cameron, Miliband, Clegg and UKIP's Nigel Farage as members of an extremely unattractive and venal boy band) and several Labour Party electoral broadcasts garnered significant second audience numbers on YouTube. Such a second life for conventional PEBs was also apparent for the Conservatives' 'It's working—don't let them wreck it' video, which achieved online traction, as did the filmmaker Paul Greengrass' biopic of Miliband (Lilleker 2015:70).

Inevitably, despite such deployment of the social media, the parties continued to view their online political communications as 'add-ons' to their traditional media air war campaigns. In March 2015, YouGov founder Stephan Shakespeare declared that the UK parties' online strategies were effectively using 'social media to deliver leaflets' (Bold 2015). However, this 'monological' approach was hardly surprising, as the advertising agency Saatchi & Saatchi had declared that the influence of social media had been wildly overrated (Charles 2015:67).

A feeling emerged that online political party discourse was merely preaching to the converted, perpetuating an 'echo-chamber' effect and serving only to reinforce existing bias and preconceptions (Sunstein 2007). On one hand, this meant dismissing the influence of social media on the political attitudes of the much-sought-after 'floating voters' within the key marginal seats:

> The attention given to social media usage [was] massively disproportionate when compared to...the ground war...where...personal connections and conversations have much more impact than those carried out electronically. Activists talking to voters influence elections in a way that, at present, social media simply does not. (Clapperton 2015)

Yet, on the other hand, the social media sites' ability to track the political sentiments of the electorate proved to be where the parties' online resources would be most potent in shaping voters' opinions. Both the Conservative and Labour parties employed an arsenal of digital tools to interact with voters throughout the election campaign. However, with regard to the various emphases that the mainstream British parties placed on micro-targeting and community organising through social media, their contrasting digital campaigns would have a significant effect on the electoral outcome.

SENTIMENT ANALYSIS: MICRO-TARGETING VERSUS COMMUNITY ORGANISING—THE COMPETING CONSERVATIVE AND LABOUR PARTIES' SOCIAL MEDIA TACTICS

The Conservative Party imported advanced data science techniques which had been used by Obama's campaign teams. These technologies enabled party managers to understand how their policy announcements were received and, more crucially, to micro-target a very small numbers of voters. Therefore, under the leadership of Jim Messina, the data strategists mined the information gleaned from social media sites of 'likes' and 'preferences' to ensure that the party was talking to the 'right people' on a continuous basis. To effect this strategy, the Conservatives focused on Facebook as their social medium of choice.

The Tories spent ten times as much as their Labour opponents to place adverts and to buy data from the platform, enabling them to identify Facebook users' political preferences, activities, geolocation and demographic characteristics. The Conservatives' digital director Craig Elder explained that, while Facebook had been an interesting way to reach young voters in 2010, by 2015 it was recognised as a 'massive driver of activity' through which over half the electorate could be contacted (*Channel 4 News* 2015). Importantly, the Facebook 'behemoth' had moved beyond a concentration of young users in urban centres and into a far wider generational array of subscribers throughout the nation.

This was a top-down strategy which involved data mining by Messina of the key concerns of a small number of undecided voters and thereby responding with targeted advertising aimed at these groups (Margetts and Hale 2015). During the campaign, the target audience of Facebook subscribers was refined to 100,000 people in the most decisive constituencies. In the final days of the campaign, this figure was reduced to just a few hundred key voters, who were repeatedly contacted via websites, phones and doorsteps. In addition, the Conservatives transformed their 2010 website, which had been an unfocused source of information, into a tool that could drill down to individual constituencies. As such, their persuasion of a mere 900 swing voters to support them in the seven marginal seats helped them achieve a majority (*Channel 4 News* 2015).

This approach proved vital in an election whose outcome was determined by only a few thousand votes. Through its information communication strategies, the party utilised political branding techniques to reach out to 'regular people' to 'get [the] right messages to the right people at the right time' (*Channel 4 News* 2015). As the Conservative peer and pollster Lord Andrew Cooper declared on his Twitter account, 'Big data, micro-targeting and social media campaigns just thrashed "5 million conversations" and "community organizing"' (Margetts and Hale 2015).

The Labour Party employed in-house package tools such as Contact Creator to maintain records on voters and off-the-peg software, including NationBuilder, to organise and mobilise volunteers to canvass the electorate (Bland 2015). As the party pursued such online 'ground war' techniques, it complemented this activism using Twitter. The strategists believed that the continuous supply of tweets, combined with its army of street canvassers and community organisers, would work to advance its vote in the marginal constituencies.

At the start of 2015, Miliband had asked Labour activists to engage in millions of on- and offline conversations to judge public sentiment, and according to the Oxford Internet Institute, during the month leading up to the general election, Labour candidates sent more than 120,000 tweets, while the Conservatives produced only 80,000 (Margetts and Hale 2015). At a surface level, through retweeted memes such as #VoteCameronOut or #Milibrand (in response to Brand's interview of Miliband), it appeared that Labour was far more successful than its opponents in generating bottom-up activity in its deployment of the microblogging site. However, unlike the Tories in their use of micro-targeting, the Labour Party had no idea how these tweets were being taken up and by whom. Therefore, Twitter proved to be a digital tool with limited effect when it came to tracking public sentiment. As the journalist Suzanne Moore commented:

> One of the biggest shocks of this election is the realisation that you can't get a socialist paradise on... Earth by tweeting....Who knew? Actually, as people who do this kind of thing all follow each other, it seems that many of them still don't realise. In the echo chambers some of us inhabit online,

everyone not only votes Labour but crows about it in 140 characters....
Declaring one's allegiances is fine if you understand who you are declaring
them to. No one really does. Hope soon changed on election night into
disbelieving, angry tweets....All of this happened in self-selecting universes.
(Moore 2015)

CONCLUSION

This chapter has provided a review of how the political elites within the
USA and UK have incorporated the Internet and, particularly, the Web 2.0
tools of social media into their campaigns over the last 20 years. Initially,
US presidential candidates treated such communications media with cir-
cumspection, as they remained unconvinced that a greater outreach to the
electorate was possible. However, as the Internet rapidly expanded, the
new communications formats offered politicians greater opportunity to
reconfigure their campaign strategies. The most significant breakthrough
occurred with the rise of the 'citizen-initiated' campaigns associated with
Democratic presidential candidates Howard Dean and Barack Obama in
2004 and 2008, respectively.

Dean and Obama demonstrated how a little-known governor and a
barely recognised junior senator, respectively, could announce their arrival
on the national scene, and also laid out the principles of online fundraising. Although the Dean campaign collapsed in 2004, Obama was to
realise the full worth of these campaign strategies in 2008. He employed
a hybrid media approach using more traditional forms of image management along with a communitarian-inspired approach to social media to
effect a political movement. Through his intricate machine of a network
of volunteers, he won key states in the Democratic primaries from the
front runner Senator Hillary Clinton and, in the general election, against
his Republican opponent Senator John McCain. Although Obama's use
of social media was less pronounced in his re-election victory in 2012, he
remained manifestly ahead of Governor Mitt Romney, and through Web
2.0 techniques was able to garner strong Hispanic support.

In the run-up to the 2010 UK general election, there was some initial
evidence of a limited citizen-initiated approach to the mainstream parties'
online campaigns. However, as the parties preferred to maintain centralised
control over the content and organisation of their campaigns due to a combination of ideological predisposition, structure and values, the online campaigning was confined to marketing and attempts to set the political agenda
(Dale 2010). In 2010, social media were principally employed in journal-

istic practices in terms of blogging and using real-time communications as effective newsfeeds, and in this capacity, they were most profitably employed when wrapped around a conventional news story, such as the coverage of the three televised PM debates. In this manner, Twitter proved to be important in providing online commentary on the media-generated events within the campaign.

In the 2015 UK general election, the social media were predicted to prove even more instrumental in shaping the nature of the parties' political communications. However, the mainstream parties continued to use online platforms to advocate their party positions and to undermine the political opposition. They remained fixed in developing a hybrid model between the old and new media, in which the latter was seen very much as an add-on to the conventional 'air war' played out by the leaders on television. Conversely, the most interesting deployment of social media was demonstrated in the comparative techniques used by the Conservative and Labour parties in mobilising the vote in the targeted marginal constituencies.

Thus it was within the 'ground war' of the campaign that the Tories' use of Facebook in micro-targeting swing voters and Labour's more activist-based approach proved decisive. Here, Messina's data mining, in which he drilled down into the concerns that defined voting intentions, allowed the Conservatives to gain a unique understanding of their constituents' interests. In contrast, the Labour Party's employment of Twitter was less effective in tracking public sentiment. However, in both cases, such deployment of social media for targeting marginal seats may be seen to have exacerbated the inequities of an unrepresentative system wherein a few thousand votes can determine electoral success or failure.

Therefore, a mixed picture has emerged with regard to the use of online techniques in representative democracies, and there are many lingering questions as to whether they actually promote greater public efficacy. For the social media to effect meaningful change, and to overcome the perception of a gaping democratic deficit, their normative function should be to enhance civic virtues. Consequently, in the next chapter, we will need to address how new or alternative social movements have emerged through real-time communications to take on autocratic state structures and effect new forms of accountability in matters of state security.

Bibliography

Alexander J.C. 2010. *The Performance of Politics: Obama's Victory and the Democratic Study for Power.* Oxford: Oxford University Press.

Anstead N., and W. Straw. 2009. *The Change We Need: What Britain Can Learn from Obama's Victory*. London: Fabian Society.

Anstead, N. 2015. "Was This a Social Media Election? We Do Not Know Yet". In *UK Elections Analysis 2015: Media, Voters and the Campaign: Early Reflections from Leading UK Academics*, ed. D. Jackson and E. Thorsen. Bournemouth: Centre for the Study of Journalism, Culture and Community, Bournemouth University and Political Studies Association (PSA) Media and Politics Group.

Bai M. 2010. "Internet Populism Buffets Politics". In *New York Times* articles selected by *The Observer*, November 7. 1–4.

Bang H.P. 2005. "Among Everyday Makers and Expert Citizens". In *Remaking Governance: Peoples, Politics and the Public Sphere*, ed. J. Newman, 159–179. Bristol: The Policy Press.

Bland, A. 2015. Online and On the Streets: Labour Tests Modern Methods in Southampton Marginal. *The Guardian*. May 2. http://www.theguardian.com/politics/2015/may/02/online-labour-modern-methods-southampton-marginal (accessed June 5, 2015).

Bold, B. 2015. 2015 General Election Won't be a 'social election', says YouGov founder. *Marketing Magazine*. March 24. http://www.marketingmagazine.co.uk/article/1339881/2015-general-election-wont-social-election-says-yougov-founder (accessed June 5, 2015).

Cellan-Jones, R. 2015. Election 2015: It Wasn't Social Media 'wot won it.' *BBC News: Technology*. May 11. http://www.bbc.co.uk/news/technology-32689145 (accessed Jube 6, 2015).

Chadwick A. 2006. *Internet Politics: States, Citizens and New Communications Technologies*. Oxford: Oxford University Press.

Chadwick, A., and C. Vaccari. 2015. "Citizen Engagement in the Dual Screened Election Campaign". In *UK Elections Analysis 2015: Media, Voters and the Campaign: Early Reflections from Leading UK Academics*, ed. D. Jackson and E. Thorsen. Bournemouth: Centre for the Study of Journalism, Culture and Community, Bournemouth University and Political Studies Association (PSA) Media and Politics Group.

Chandrasekhar R. 2012. "Don't Kill Freedom of Speech", *Times of India*, November 30. http://rajeev.in/News/Dont_Kill_Freedom/Times_of_India.html (accessed November 20, 2014).

Channel Four News. 2015. The ruthless reality of the Election 2015 digital campaign. *Channel Four News*. May 23. http://www.channel4.com/news/conservative-snp-election-victory-social-media-behind-scenes (accessed June 6, 2015).

Charles, A. 2015. "The Politics of the Social Media". In *UK Elections Analysis 2015: Media, Voters and the Campaign: Early Reflections from Leading UK Academics*, ed. D. Jackson and E. Thorsen. Bournemouth: Centre for the Study of Journalism, Culture and Community, Bournemouth University and Political Studies Association (PSA) Media and Politics Group.

Clapperton, S. 2015. Comment: This Isn't a Social Media Election and the Next One Won't Be Either. *Politics.co.uk*. April 7. http://www.politics.co.uk/comment-analysis/2015/04/07/comment-this-isn-t-a-social-media-election-and-the-next-one (accessed June 6, 2015).

CNNIC (China Internet Network Information Centre). 2014. *Statistical Report on Internet Development in China*. January. http://www1.cnnic.cn/IDR/ReportDownloads/201404/U020140417607531610855.pdf (accessed December 29, 2014).

Crouch C. 2004. *Post-Democracy*. Cambridge: Polity.

Dahlgren P. 2009. *Media and Political Engagement: Citizens, Communication and Democracy*. Cambridge: Cambridge University Press.

Dale I. 2010. "This was meant to be the Internet Election—So What Happened?" *The Daily Telegraph*. April 27. http://www.telegraph.co.UK/news/election-2010/7640143/General-Election-2010-This-was-meant-to-be-the-internet-election.-So-what-happened.html (accessed February 26, 2014).

Gaber I. 2011. "The Transformation of Political Campaign Reporting: The 2010 UK Election, Revolution or Evolution". In *Political Communication in Britain: The Leaders' Debates, the Campaign and the Media in 2010 General Election*, eds. D. Wring, R. Mortimore, and S. Atkinson. Basingstoke: Palgrave MacMillan.

Gibson R.K. 2010. "Parties, Social Media and the Rise of 'Citizen-Initiated' Campaigning". Paper presented at the American Political Studies Association.

Gibson R.K., A. Williamson, and S. Ward. 2010. *The Internet and the 2010 Election: Putting the Small p Back into Politics*. London: Hansard Society.

Green P.M. 2011. *Interview with Mark Wheeler*. Chicago, IL: Roosevelt University. August 1.

Harris, J. 2010. "Welcome to the First e-election". *The Guardian*. http://www.theguardian.com/politics/2010/mar/17/labour-conservatives-general-election-online (accessed February 26, 2014).

Heilemann J., and M. Halperin. 2010. *Race of a Lifetime: How Obama Won the White House*. New York: Viking Penguin.

Jones, G. 2015. How Social Media Reacted to the Leaders' Debate. *New Statesman – Election site*. April 14. http://www.may2015.com/featured/election-2015-back-to-a-tie-as-possible-rogue-poll-puts-tories-ahead-by-6-points/ (accessed June 6, 2015).

Kavanagh D., and P. Cowley. 2010. *The British General Election of 2010*. Basingstoke: Palgrave Macmillan.

Keane J. 2009. *The Life and Death of Democracy*. New York: Simon and Schuster.

Kellner D. 2009. "Barack Obama and celebrity spectacle". *International Journal of Communication* 3(1): 715–741.

Lai Stirland S. 2008. Obama's Secret Weapons: Internet, Databases and Psychology. *Wired Magazine*, October 29. http://www.wired.com/threatlevel/2008/10/obamas-secret-w/ (accessed November 20, 2013).

Lilleker D.G., and N. Jackson. 2013. "Reaching Inward Not Outward: Marketing via the Internet at the UK 2010 General Election". *Journal of Political Marketing* 12(2–3): 244–261.

Lilleker, D.G. 2015. "The Battle for the Online Audience: 2015 as a Social Media Election?". In *UK Elections Analysis 2015: Media, Voters and the Campaign: Early Reflections from Leading UK Academics*, ed. D. Jackson and E. Thorsen. Bournemouth: Centre for the Study of Journalism, Culture and Community, Bournemouth University and Political Studies Association (PSA) Media and Politics Group.

Margetts, H., and S. Hale. 2015. Digital Disconnect: Parties, Pollsters and Political Analysis in #GE2015. *Elections and the Internet: Research from the Oxford Internet Institute.* May 12. http://elections.oii.ox.ac.uk/digital-disconnect-parties-pollsters-and-political-analysis-in-ge2015/ (accessed June 6, 2015).

Milki, S.M., and J.H. Rhodes. 2009. Barack Obama, the Democratic Party, and the Future of the "New American Party System". *The Forum* 7(1). www.bepres.com/forum/vol7/iss1/art7 (accessed February 26, 2014).

Moore, S. 2015. We Thought We Could Tweet Our Way to a Socialist Paradise. The Election Changed That. *The Guardian.* May 11. http://www.theguardian.com/commentisfree/2015/may/11/tweet-socialist-paradise-election-changed-that (accessed June 6, 2015).

Newman N. 2010. #UKelection2010, Mainstream Media and the Role of the Internet: How Social and Digital Media Affected the Business of Politics and Journalism. Reuters Institute for the Study of Journalism Working Paper. Oxford: University of Oxford.

Redmond S. 2010. "Avatar Obama in the Age of Liquid Celebrity". *Celebrity Studies* 1(1): 81–95.

Rice, A. 2004. *Campaigns Online: The Profound Impact of the Internet, Blogs and E-Technologies in the Presidential Politics Campaigning.* Baltimore: Johns Hopkins University.

Sanders, K. 2009. *Communicating Politics in the Twenty-First Century.* Basingstoke: Palgrave MacMillan.

Scammell, M. 2015. Extraordinary Election, Political Communication as Usual. In *UK Elections Analysis 2015: Media, Voters and the Campaign: Early reflections from leading UK academics*, ed. D. Jackson and E. Thorsen. Bournemouth: Centre for the Study of Journalism, Culture and Community, Bournemouth University and Political Studies Association (PSA) Media and Politics Group.

Southern R., and S. Ward. 2011. "Below the Radar? Online Campaigning at the Local Level in the 2010 Election". In *Political Communication in Britain: The Leaders' Debates, the Campaign and the Media in 2010 General Election*, eds. D. Wring, R. Mortimore, and S. Atkinson. Basingstoke: Palgrave MacMillan.

Straw W. 2010. "Yes We Did? What Labour learned from Obama". In *The Internet and the 2010 Election: Putting the Small p Back into Politics*, eds. R.K. Gibson, A. Williamson, and S. Ward. London: Hansard Society.

Summers D. 2009. Politics Blog: Gordon Brown has the Worst Smile in the World. *The Guardian.* May 5. http://www.guardian.co.uk/politics/blog/2009/may/05/brown-smile-prescott (accessed November 20, 2013).

Sunstein C. 2007. *Republic.com 2.0.* Princeton, NJ: Princeton University Press.

Tripp, J. 2004. *The Revolution Will Not Be Televised: Democracy, the Internet and the Overthrow of Everything.* New York: Harper Collins.

Wheeler, M. 2015. "Celebrity Endorsement and Activities in the 2015 UK General Election Campaign". In *UK Elections Analysis 2015: Media, Voters and the Campaign: Early Reflections from Leading UK Academics,* ed. D. Jackson and E. Thorsen. Bournemouth: Centre for the Study of Journalism, Culture and Community, Bournemouth University and Political Studies Association (PSA) Media and Politics Group.Wolf G. 2004. How the Internet Invented Howard Dean. *Wired Magazine.* January 1. http://www.wired.com/wired/archive/12.01/dean.html (accessed February 26, 2014).

Wring D., and S. Ward. 2010. "The Media and the 2010 Campaign: The Television Election?". *Parliamentary Affairs* 63(4): 802–817.

Wring D. 2011. "Introduction". In *Political Communication in Britain: The Leaders' Debates, the Campaign and the Media in 2010 General Election,* eds. D. Wring, R. Mortimore, and S. Atkinson. Basingstoke: Palgrave MacMillan.

Zaleski K. 2008. Participant. *Youthquake: Elections, Media and Voters.* November 12. New York: Paley Center.

CHAPTER 6

The Public Sphere and Network Democracy: The Arab Spring, WikiLeaks and the Edward Snowden Revelations

Introduction

For many Internet advocates, the social media provide an electronic agora to allow a variety of issues to be raised, framed and effectively debated. As the Internet provides an instant global communication resource, citizens can enjoy real-time interactive access with one another to exchange ideas, bypass authority, challenge autocracies and effect greater means of expression against state power. Thus, the social media allow for 'many-to-many' or 'point-to point' forms of communication. In particular, the unprecedented expansion of online social networks such as Facebook, LinkedIn and Twitter has created major opportunities for grassroots communication, deliberation and discussion.

These new forms of the public sphere have been associated with the rise of network democracy. This concept suggests a dispersal of concentrated communications power and a horizontal network of links that allows for the viral spread of information, thereby effecting greater levels of public engagement, participation and ideological representation. Manuel Castells, in *Communications Power* (2009), argues that the information networks give rise to new forms of meaning by encouraging causal linkage between members' private expression and public discourse. This enables an ever-expanding set of digital citizens to engage in processes

© The Editor(s) (if applicable) and The Author(s) 2016

P. Iosifidis, M. Wheeler, *Public Spheres and Mediated Social Networks in the Western Context and Beyond,*
DOI 10.1057/978-1-137-41030-6_6

of 'communicative abundance' to resist dominant forces within society (Keane 2013:1; Fenton 2012:163):

> In our society, which I have conceptualised as a network society, power is multi-dimensional and is organized around networks programmed in each domain of human activity of empowered actors. Networks of power exercise their power by influencing the human mind predominantly (but not solely) through the multimedia networks of mass communication. Thus, communications networks are decisive sources of power-making. (Castells 2012:7)

In this chapter we will analyse the democratic possibilities of technological innovations associated with Web 2.0 tools, first by addressing the first and second 'waves' of academic debate concerning social media and the public sphere, the networked individual and society. The initial optimism associated with a virtual public sphere was quickly replaced by doubts about whether this model was appropriate for the development of democratic values. Consequently, Castells' contention that the information communications networks have enabled a more personalised form of politics has proven vital to the discussion of citizen efficacy and participation. He suggests that grassroots networks have the capacity to build social movements characterised by new types of solidarity, political resistance and the circumvention of national borders by facilitating 'wider spaces' of power in the global society (Couldry 2012:115).

Second, these concerns have led to considerable attention focused on the application of networked power relations during the 'Arab Spring' movement that occurred in 2011. For instance, Philip Seib has argued that the new communications environment was instrumental in forging the conditions for the revolutions in Tunisia and Egypt, along with the mobilisation of other forms of opposition in Libya and Syria (Seib 2012). Moreover, the revolutionary fervour was found to be contagious, and to have spread across previously rigid national boundaries. In turn, the social media may be seen as a forum in which the controls over international information are being contested. Since the Al-Qaeda terrorist attacks of 9/11, Western security institutions have become increasingly concerned about the dangers of cyberterrorism and asymmetric warfare. These organisations have sought to simultaneously increase their control over the surveillance of data, while contending that the individual right to free information should be checked for the 'common good' of state security. Along these lines, this analysis will also consider the implications of the actions of Julian Assange's WikiLeaks network of citizen journalists, along with whistle-blowers such as the former US Private Bradley (now Chelsea) Manning and Central Intelligence Agency (CIA) agent Edward Snowden, in the dissemination of classified US defence and national surveillance materials, in relation to the democratic value of the social media.

Third, a debate has arisen as to whether the social media are truly a force capable of reconfiguring power relations in terms of economic, political and social organisation (Couldry 2012:116). For instance, the fallout within the states involved in the Arab Spring has given rise to difficult questions—not least of which is whether information communications technologies (ICTs) have been more effective in mobilising voices for protest than in creating sustainable democratic institutions for nation-building. The illiberal actions of the Turkish government in banning YouTube between 2007 and 2010 and its ban of Twitter and YouTube sites in March 2014 demonstrates that autocratic executives have remained vigilant in protecting their interests. Thus the key question remains as to whether the social media are forces of democracy, revolution and expansion of the public sphere, or whether they are instruments of power and control.

This has led several writers, including Richard Barbrook and Andy Cameron (1996), to question whether the neo-liberal ideologies that have combined to facilitate the growth of the Internet and the contemporary social media have produced a combination of individualist ignorance and utopianism. These arguments have been taken up by John Keane (2013) who contends that elite power has been enhanced by data collection, censorship, spin and new mechanisms of surveillance. In addition, concerns have been raised about the trivialisation and unreliability of ICTs, and whether such dislocation will lead to a highly individualistic and polarised set of political outcomes. Nick Couldry (2012:118) in turn, has asked whether the social institutions of the Internet have preserved the existing order rather than promoting change. Similarly, Natalie Fenton (2012) remains sceptical about the networked forms of communications, questioning whether they can challenge the concentration of monopolistic ownership and neo-liberal values of social media. Therefore, in this chapter, we will examine whether the democratic forms of participation organised by 'e-activists' have been effective, or rather have been subject to an uneven redistribution of power.

THE DEMOCRATIC VALUES OF THE INTERNET: FROM THE DUTIFUL CITIZEN TO THE NETWORKED INDIVIDUAL

In the first wave of enthusiasm for the political implications of the Internet, some predicted that a digital democracy would emerge along the lines of an electronic agora or public sphere. This model followed Jurgen Habermas' critique of the rise of an organic public sphere accompanying the democratic dissemination of information in the press that had emerged in the eighteenth century. He argued that the public sphere (the space between the state and the public in which mass communications operated) had demonstrated how private expression could be transformed into public opinion. Through a range of 'rational' discourses within the public arena, the media expedited a process wherein private citizens debated ideas such that collective decision-making could occur and tyrannical political power might be challenged. Consequently, the hierarchical relations between political elites and the masses were broken down:

> The economic independence provided by private property, the critical reflection fostered by letters and novels, the flowering of discussion in coffee houses and salons and, above all, the emergence of an independent, market-based press, created a new public engaged in critical political discussion. From this was forged by a reason based consensus which shaped the direction of the state. (Curran and Gurevitch 1992:83)

With regard to Habermas' deliberative arguments, it was predicted that the growth of Internet interactivity and decentralisation of power relations would allow for rational and informed debate. For instance, *Wired* magazine's media correspondent Jon Katz compared the burgeoning 'Net' to the eighteenth-century pamphleteers of the American Revolution (Katz 1995). It was argued that, because the Internet was a global medium, not only would digital citizens be able to express their individual ideas, but they would create a diverse and cohesive virtual community to facilitate agency and reform (Wheeler 1997:224).

However, this wave of optimism was quickly replaced by more critical accounts suggesting that the Internet was conditioned by prevailing economic, social and political interests (Street 1996). Furthermore, questions arose about the value of the virtual democracy, as post-modernist perspectives about the 'simulacrum' or the implosion between subjective and objective meaning meant that the social media came to be seen as a means of narcissistic self-interest rather than collective activity. Other cultural critiques emerged regarding the value of the public sphere model as a means to engage the wider political community. It was contended that gender and race issues had not been addressed, as the 'rational' communications within the multimedia realm favoured wealthy white men to the exclusion of others (Loader and Mercea 2011:758).

Despite these difficulties, a new wave of social and political theories emerged in the wake of the development of Web 2.0 platforms. This second generation of writings about Internet democracy has been distinguished by the displacement of the public sphere model with a networked citizen perspective. Instead of Habermasian concomitants from dutiful citizens, the drivers of democratic innovation have been the networks of everyday citizens who are engaged in lifestyle politics (Bennett 2003; Dahlgren 2009; Papacharassi 2009). At the same time, it has been argued, alternative forms of cognitive behaviour are occurring as new generations engage with the software technologies of the social media. For instance, Margaret Wertheim has argued that cyberspace may lead us to construct an image of an expansive sense of 'self', becoming 'almost like a fluid, leaking out around us all the time and joining each of us into a vast ocean or web of relationships with other leaky selves' (Wertheim 1999).

Therefore, the private identities of autonomous citizens may be used to advance a multitude of publicly realised political ideas and values (Loader and Mercea 2011:759). In his empirical study of Catalan Internet users, Manuel Castells maintained that personal autonomy is enhanced by the use of social media in relation to societal rules and institutional power (Castells 2007). He argued that these actors will engage in collective activity within the networked society to facilitate a reconfiguration of political solidarity through the dissemination of knowledge, the representation of alternative forms of social capital and the construction of grassroots engagement:

> Enthusiastic networked individuals ... are transformed into a conscious, collective actor. Thus social change results from communicative action that involves connection between networks ... from a communication environment through communication networks. The technology and morphology of these communication networks shapes the process of mobilization, and thus social change, both as a process and an outcome. (Castells: 2012:219–220)

THE NETWORKED SOCIETY AND SOCIAL REVOLUTION

From this perspective, the networked society comprises autonomous individuals who connect with one another in an ever-widening space within politics. Consequently, non-traditional political actors have effected new forms of consciousness through blogs, tweets, Facebook activities and online petitions. Thus virtual technology can facilitate a more 'virtuous' citizenship, to reconnect the public with the democratic process, allowing a 'civic commons' to emerge (Putnam 2000; Chadwick 2006:25). In some respects, this transformation reflects the pluralism in governmental decision-making that Robert Dahl identified when he predicted a diffusion of centralised power relations (Dahl 1961). For Castells, however, power:

> is no longer concentrated in institutions (the state), organizations (capitalist firms), or symbolic controllers (corporate media, churches). It is diffused in global networks of wealth, power, information and images, which circulate and transmute in a system of variable geometry and dematerialised geography. (Castells 2007:359)

These concerns about the location of power have led to questions about how such forms of representation have segued into the contested principles of late modernity or post-democratic behaviour (Crouch 2004). These ideas are comparable to, but contest the notion of, post-modernism in that they suggest a self-referring modernism and fragmentation in which 'social practices are constantly examined and reformed in the light of incoming information about those very practices, thus constitutively altering their character' (Giddens 1991:38). In terms of post-democratic activity, late modernists contend that such changes reflect a replacement of hierarchies with networks: the rise of discursive network governance, the expansion of the social media and a constantly reformed version of contemporary democracy (Marsh et al. 2010:326).

Clay Shirky has argued that within the networked society it becomes 'ridiculously easy' to break down the barriers that have previously closed off collective action (Shirky 2009). Instead, the social media encourage the formation of self-directed open-source or hacking groups to engage in their own activities and to collaborate. Therefore, the old hierarchies of repression, corporate interest and hermetically sealed ideologies are removed to allow for an alternative expression of grassroots political behaviour. Such a dispersal of power allows cyberspace to create a public space, which ultimately becomes a political space, enabling 'sovereign assemblies to meet and...recover their rights of representation, which have

been captured in political institutions predominantly tailored for the convenience of the dominant interests' (Castells 2012:11).

Accordingly, ICT networks will facilitate a networked public to construct
their values, meaning and identity, giving rise to new forms of solidarity. The
Internet makes it easier to organise and agitate, as people can participate in
reality TV votes, support a petition with the click of a mouse, or even force
out undemocratic governments. This has led to the formation of networked
social movements which have largely ignored the political elite, distrusted
the established media and rejected any leadership, hierarchy or formal organisation, using open forums for collective debate and social dialogue. This is
reflected in a 'division of labour' within activism that has been defined by
the available social media platforms to build political consciousness:

> If you look at the full suite of information tools that were employed to
> spread the revolutions of 2009–2011, it goes like this: Facebook is used
> to form groups, covert and overt—in order to establish those strong and
> flexible connections. Twitter is used for real-time organization and news
> dissemination, bypassing the cumbersome 'newsgathering' operations of the
> mainstream media. YouTube and the Twitter-linked photographic sites—
> Yfrog, Flickr and Twitpic—are used to provide instant evidence of the claims
> being made. Link-shorteners like bit.ly are used to disseminate key articles
> via Twitter. (Mason 2012:75)

In turn, in a variation of the Canadian philosopher Marshall McLuhan's
adage that the 'medium is the message', Castells theorises that the social
media's power lies in the images of representation that are produced by
people's consciousness (Castells 2012). This understanding of the cognitive
power of the social media accords with Lee Salter's (2003) arguments that
the Internet is a novel technological asset for democratic communications
'because of its decentred, textual communications system, with content most
often provided by users' (Fenton 2011:40). Informal new social movements
(NSMs) have emerged from the dealignment of partisan allegiances and networks of action. These NSMs may contradict the previous dominant logic, to
effect a new social structure (a networked society), a new economy (a global
informational economy) and a new culture (a culture of 'real virtuality'):

> The technological and inter-personal revolutions of the early twenty-first
> century [mean]...it [is] now possible to conceive of living this 'emanci-
> pated' life as a fully connected 'species-being' on the terrain of capitalism
> itself—indeed on the terrain of a highly marketized form of capitalism.
> (Mason 2012:143)

The political power of social media is striking. On 17 January 2001, during the impeachment trial of Philippine President Joseph Estrada, loyalists in the Philippine Congress voted to set aside key evidence against him. Less than 2 hours after the decision was announced, thousands of people, angry that their corrupt president might not be charged, organised a protest chiefly by forwarding text messages that read 'Go 2 EDSA. Wear blk'. Over one million people arrived on Epifanio de los Santos Avenue over the next few days, demonstrating the public's ability to coordinate such a massive and rapid response (close to seven million text messages were sent that week). Alarmed by this massive protest, the country's legislators reversed course and allowed the evidence to be presented, eventually sealing Estrada's fate, who fled the country on 20 January 2001 (Shirky 2011). The event marked the first time that social media was a catalyst in deposing a national leader:

> Suddenly dictatorships could be overthrown with bare hands of the people, even if their hands had been bloodied by the sacrifice of the fallen. Financial magicians went from being the objects of public envy to the targets of universal contempt. Politicians became exposed as corrupt and as liars. Governments were denounced. Media were suspended. Trust vanished. (Castells 2012:1)

The Philippine strategy has since been adopted several times, as networked social movements erupted against the mismanagement of the economic crisis by US and European governments. Spain's spontaneous grassroots protest movement, called Los Indignados—'the indignant ones'—began with thousands of mainly Spanish youth camping out in Madrid's central square, Puerta del Sol, Tunisia, in May 2011, and then spread across the country. With similar symbolism, Greece's 'outraged' (aganaktismenoi) occupied Syntagma, the central square of Athens opposite the Greek Parliament, the area around the White Tower in Thessaloniki and public spaces in other major cities in June 2011, in protest of the strict fiscal measures imposed by the International Monetary Fund (IMF), European Union (EU) and European Central Bank.

In 2005, the Italian comedian Beppe Grillo set up a blog site, 'www.beppegrillo.it', which rapidly gained a greater following than other Italian political party websites, with a larger audience than the ailing newspapers. In response to a combination of the collapse of the Italian political economy, the corrupt behaviour and sexual peccadillos of Silvio Berlusconi and the EU's anti-democratic imposition of the technocratic leader Mario Monti, Grillo used his site to construct online petitions and to mobilise his followers to take to the streets on V (an Italian expletive) Day (Turner 2013:180–181).

On the basis of this success, in 2009, Grillo established his anti-technocratic and anti-EU Five Star Movement through Twitter, Facebook and an online television channel. From 2012 to 2013, the popularity of the comedian-blogger's movement rose from polling at 5 % of the population to 25 % of the votes in the 2013 Italian general election. Grillo provided an effective mix of social media, anti-establishment rhetoric and old-fashioned rallies to disseminate his criticism of an anti-democratic Italian political establishment. While he had over one million Facebook and Twitter followers, he encouraged his supporters to meet and discuss his blogs in real-world 'meet-up' groups:

> Grillo's message has resonated in a country where faith in government, parliament and the media is low and falling....Social media politics as pioneered by Grillo—citizen-led, brazen, open, democratic—is what happens when politicians appear too distant, too elite, too different from the people they represent. (Bartlett 2013)

Across the Atlantic, Occupy Wall Street, the name given to a protest movement that began in September 2011 in New York's Wall Street financial district, was another example of a cyberspace-driven movement, calling for social and economic equality and for curbing of the perceived corporate influence on government—particularly from the financial services sector. Elsewhere, the Communist Party lost power in Moldova in April 2009 following public protests coordinated by text messages, Facebook, Twitter and LiveJournal after the announcement of preliminary election results that showed it was winning approximately 50 % of the votes in an obviously fraudulent election (Splichal 2009:392).

Web 2.0 has thus been *the* mechanism informing new types of political resistance, and has been the means through which revolts have occurred in Western democracies and illiberal societies and against autocratic regimes. These changes have resulted from the deployment of digital communications within the workplace and their growth throughout the public's social lives. Due to the unprecedented exponential take-up of these social media tools by online participants, these trends have enhanced individual and collective behaviour, confirming the revolutionary potential of the new technologies, and thereby expanding political consciousness and amplifying 'the crucial driver of all revolutions—the perceived difference between what could be and what is' (Mason 2012:85).

The Arab Spring: The Tunisian and Egyptian Social Media Revolutions

As digital networks have reduced costs in terms of both finances and resources, they have allowed individuals and groups to effect a wider range of public expression with greater ease. Shirky has described how social media have enabled insurgents to adopt new strategies which have been crucial for change and reform (Shirky 2011). Importantly, the social media networks have challenged the repressive capacity of the state to control mass communication. As Philip Seib commented:

> Governments around the world were caught unaware because they did not understand how media were changing national and global political dynamics by empowering citizens to the point at which they could do something about the circumstances that were making their lives miserable. (Seib 2012:31)

Using Web 2.0 tools, Middle Eastern activists realised that they could establish a significant presence. It was in Tunisia that the first social media-driven protests of the Arab uprisings were witnessed. The catalyst for the Tunisian protests proved to be the self-immolation of a street vendor, Mohamed Bouazizi, who was selling fruit at a roadside stand in the city of Sidi Bouzid on 17 December 2010. After a confrontation with a corrupt city inspector who had confiscated his weighing scales, Bouazizi protested to the city governor but was turned away. He returned to the governor's office with his cart, demanding to know how he could be expected to make a living. Once he had confiscated his wares, he covered himself in paint stripper and set himself on fire. This was followed by a protest from Bouazizi's family, which was uploaded on YouTube and became a national sensation.

When Bouazizi died on 4 January 2011, it was the 'last straw' for many Tunisians, and the coverage of his death was amplified by social media. This led to various dissatisfied groups, comprising the unemployed, political and human rights activists, labour and trade unionists, students, professors and lawyers, coming together and combining forces, ushering in the Tunisian revolution. The so-called Jasmine Revolution led to the first ousting of a Middle Eastern dictator, President Zine El Abidine Ben Ali, who despite his attempt to censor Facebook in 2008, discovered that the tides of change were being driven via many proxy sites.

The revolutionary fervour was contagious. It sparked the Arab Spring, which used the viral power of social media to bring down Hosni Mubarak's long-standing dictatorship in Egypt, reverberating through Libya, Syria, Yemen and Bahrain. The protests in Cairo's symbolic Tahrir (Liberation) Square were organised by activists who used social media as their principle means of communication. These collective techniques emerged from the long-standing use of blogs and user-generated videos (vlogs) placed on YouTube and Facebook, which helped to generate online dissent. Again, the protest would be sparked by a specific incident—the self-immolation of six protesters against a rise in food prices. This was conveyed through a Facebook 'vlog' by a female student, Asmaa Mahfouz, who declared:

> People have some shame! I, a girl, posted that I will go down to Tahrir Square to stand alone and I'll hold the banner....I am making this video to give you a simple message: we are going to Tahrir on January 25th....If you stay at home, you deserve all that's being done to you, and you will be guilty before your nation and your people. Go down to the street, send SMSs, post it on the Net, make people aware. (Mahfouz quoted from Castells 2012:54–55)

This was uploaded to YouTube and virally propagated to many thousands, and would come to be known as the 'Vlog that Helped Spark the Revolution (Wall and El Zahed 2011). As the call to action spread across local networks of friends, families and associations, it was picked up by other networks, not the least of which were the Al-Ahly SC and Zamalek Egyptian football clubs fan networks, which had a long history of fighting against the police. On 25 January 2011, over 100,000 demonstrators descended upon and occupied Tahrir Square. They resisted the police attacks and transformed the square into a highly visible space through which to advertise the aims of the revolution. According to Castells, Tahrir Square became the physical manifestation of the protest 'space' that had been initially occupied by the virtual demonstrators drawn from social media sites. As such, it illustrated how 'hybridity' could exist between the online and offline domains:

> Indeed, activists created a 'media camp' in Tahrir, to gather videos and pictures produced by the protesters. In one instance, they collected 75 gigabytes of images from people in the streets. The centrality of this hybrid

> public space was not limited to…Tahrir Square. It was replicated in all major
> urban centres in which hundreds of thousands of demonstrators mobilised
> at different points in time during the year. (Castells 2012:60)

Moreover, when the street protests began in earnest, the Facebook sites were already operational, calling upon protesters to display only Egyptian flags, to bring plenty of water, to put vinegar and onions under their face scarves to offset the effects of tear gas and to desist from disrupting traffic (Seib 2012:51). In the midst of the demonstrations, Twitter, which was made available on the demonstrators' mobile phones, proved to be the ideal tool for providing continuous updates about the nature of the protest, boosting morale and counteracting the negative stories drawn from the state-run news channels.

In a desperate attempt to stem the protests, Mubarak's regime tried to force Vodafone, Egypt's major mobile phone supplier, to intimidate its customers by distributing government-written messages. These demanded not only that the protesters desist, but that 'Egypt's honest and loyal men confront the traitors and criminals' (Seib 2012:52). Furthermore, Mubarak made the unpopular decision to sever the country from the global Internet. This blanket ban lasted only 5 days, as the blackout had detrimental implications for the international businesses based in Egypt. Moreover, the momentum for change had swung in favour of the protesters. In some respects, the social media had served their purpose, as the protesters took to the conventional media channels. For instance, during a radio phone-in programme, a caller denouncing Mubarak exclaimed, 'Listen to that. The revolution is already here' (Seib 2012:52). Shortly afterwards, Mubarak's 28-year reign was over.

The collapse of the Ben Ali and Mubarak regimes in 2011 amid the protests propagated through the social media raised further hope that democracy would spread throughout the Middle East. In 2013, young left-wing Turkish demonstrators were mobilised via Web 2.0 tools to occupy Istanbul's Taksim Square to protest the creeping Islamic influence being advanced by the increasingly autocratic Prime Minister Recep Tayyip Erdogan (Mason 2012) (see Chap. 11). However, while deep-seated grievances came to the fore, in the illiberal democracy of Turkey and within other dictatorships, such activities were met either with the banning of the social networks YouTube and Twitter or with extremely violent forms of repression (Letsch and Rushe 2014).

Undoubtedly, the Web 2.0 tools proved to be instrumental in the popular uprisings in Libya and Syria. Yet, while Libyan dictator Colonel Muammar Gaddafi's regime was toppled, its removal was precipitated by a bloody civil war in which the Western powers had armed insurgents, and not by the actions of a popular grassroots movement. Similarly, the Syrian uprising transmogrified into an ongoing vicious civil war which has seen the rise of the Islamic State of Iraq and the Levant (ISIS), both within Syria and in adjacent territories in northern Iraq. ISIS has also proven to be adept in its simultaneously brutal and sophisticated use of social media to engender fear in its opponents, strengthen its international quest for a worldwide caliphate and recruit Western-based Muslims to its regressive form of Islam (see Chap. 11). Furthermore, the fallout from ostensible processes of 'democratisation' within Egypt has been problematic, and demonstrates the strengths and weaknesses of utilising ICTs for political change. Despite their positive attributes in formulating a public resistance to repression, these social movements have also demonstrated that such an outpouring of resolve requires a hierarchical organisation for attainable outcomes (Gladwell 2010). Such concerns would also become apparent as the controversial social network of activists, WikiLeaks, and the whistle-blowers Bradley Manning and Edward Snowden challenged the USA in matters of international security and accountability.

WikiLeaks, Afghanistan and Iraq War Logs, Cablegate and Edward Snowden's National Security Agency Revelations

The development of Web 2.0 tools has enabled advocates of open government to challenge closed information systems and to become effective agenda-setters. In 2006, Australian 'hacktivist' Julian Assange, who had been connected with a range of 'cyberpunk' movements, set up a global infrastructure of online activists called WikiLeaks. This represented an underground movement or form of 'networked journalism', which shared the characteristics of a networked society—the diffusion of centralised power structures and the facilitation of new types of newsgathering and propagation of ideas.

Assange built the WikiLeaks model on the changes that had occurred within legacy media organisations. Newspapers and television news channels had commonly assimilated new forms of citizen participation within their dissemination of communication. Previously, such public involvement would have been considered reprehensible and potentially libellous in the formation of objective analysis. Yet, throughout the 2000s, these newsgathering and dissemination techniques had become ubiquitous, and even considered democratically desirable:

> Instead of lofty columnists handing down opinions, there is a lively and often rude exchange of views through online comment and forums. This reaches its formal apogee in the "live blog" where a journalist or news team covers a single event or issue with a continuous, multi-dimensional online web-page story. As it updates its links and recycles other sources— video clips, Tweets, agency information, official statements, reader emails and anything else that can add detail, context or drama to the narrative. It is the journalist as a facilitator of an information flow rather than the main witness or author of the final version of reality. (Beckett and Ball 2012:37–38)

Therefore, it was the intention of Assange and his collaborators (including Daniel Domscheit-Berg) to create a digital 'fifth estate' which would enable a worldwide network of activists to capture and disseminate vast amounts of data. However, under the terms of network journalism, it was also WikiLeaks' intention to challenge the conventional wisdom and hierarchies of power. By maintaining the anonymity of its contributors through encryption mechanisms, WikiLeaks would not only be a muckraking vehicle to hold the powerful to account, but would construct an online form of political agency to allow for new expressions of political consciousness. It was both a grassroots movement and an online publisher that would disrupt the state's hegemonic control over surveillance mechanisms (Beckett and Ball 2012:13).

WikiLeaks successfully intervened in cases related to corporate malfeasance (Barclays Bank tax avoidance schemes, Bilderberg Group meetings and the Bank Julius Baer fraud) and state crimes (Somali assassinations, killings by the Kenyan police and toxic dumping in Africa). However, Assange (to the personal and legal enmity of Domscheit-Berg) became obsessed with using WikiLeaks to prosecute the US government in the court of public opinion. He believed that the US defence and security agencies had used the 'War on Terror' to withhold damaging information behind an array of classified information constraints. Moreover, WikiLeaks had been frustrated by President Barack Obama's proclamations to effect governmental transparency in his 2008 election campaign, only to discover when he came to power that Obama chose not to close Guantanamo Bay, escalated the war in Afghanistan and broke many of his promises by advocating 'smart power'':

> WikiLeaks was guided by the theory of hypocrisy and democracy. Its attempt to construct an 'intelligence agency of people' supposed that individual employees within any organization are motivated to act as whistleblowers not just because their identities are protected by encryption, but especially because their organization suffers intolerable gaps between its publicly professed aims and its private *modus operandi*. (Keane 2013:54)

These whistle-blowing activities were most spectacularly realised in 2010 when WikiLeaks released hundreds of thousands of logs, cables and online videos about US defence and military capacities. To maximise the impact of such network journalism, Assange and Berg collaborated with several major newspapers—*The Guardian*, *The New York Times*, *Le Monde*, *El País* and *Der Spiegel*. This vast amount of data was released in several tranches: the Afghanistan and Iraq War logs and the US diplomatic cables. On 18 February 2010, WikiLeaks published a cable leaked from the US Embassy in Reykjavik related to the 'Icesave' scandal concerning the bankruptcy of the Icelandic Landsbanki which had failed to pay out its customers and its creditors. This cable, known as 'Reykjavik 13', would thus launch an avalanche of classified documents.

In April 2010, WikiLeaks released the infamous video of the 12 July 2007 Baghdad airstrike which graphically showed US pilots mistakenly killing two Reuters employees whom they believed were carrying weapons. In reality, the men were holding their cameras. Furthermore, the video demonstrated the helicopter pilots' callous attitudes towards their targets as they continued to slaughter Iraqi civilians. This was met with an intense political vilification of what became known as the *Collateral Murder* video, illustrating WikiLeaks' spectacular impact upon the public consciousness.

In July 2010, WikiLeaks released 92,000 documents related to the war in Afghanistan from 2004 to the end of 2009. These documents detailed civilian casualties and incidents of so-called friendly fire, in which allied forces were shot down by their own side. Shortly afterwards, in October 2010, there was further leaking of approximately 400,000 documents relating to the Iraq War, many of which involved the Bush administration's tolerance of the Iraqi authorities' use of torture. The US Department of

Defense claimed that these logs represented 'the largest leak of classified documents in its history'.

However, significantly more was yet to come. On 28 November 2010, WikiLeaks and its newspaper partners jointly published the first 220 of 251,287 leaked American confidential diplomatic cables. This massive amount of data, which would be leaked in its entirety over several months, dwarfed everything in its wake. The contents of these diplomatic cables included numerous unguarded comments and critiques about the host countries of various US embassies, resolutions towards ending the ongoing tension in the Middle East, efforts and resistance regarding nuclear disarmament, actions in the War on Terror, assessments of threats around the world and US intelligence and counter-intelligence efforts.

'Cablegate' proved to be highly embarrassing for the State Department, the Department of Defense and the Pentagon. The fallout for WikiLeaks and the collapse of relations between Assange and Berg would also prove to be a defining event, as there had been a failure to redact significant portions of the online documentation. This occurred despite Assange's assurance to Berg and his agreements with his newspaper partners to do so. In this context, the American government argued that WikiLeaks had placed the lives of many of its intelligence operatives and cooperative agents in mortal danger. More vitriol came from American politicians, including the 2008 Republican Vice Presidential candidate Sarah Palin, who argued that Assange was a cyberterrorist who should either be assassinated or tried for treason and executed (Chadwick 2013:92).

These calls led to a spiralling of events in which Assange effectively became a 'stateless' person, technically 'on the run', although very much residing in West London. In 2011, Assange was accused of several rape charges by the authorities in Sweden. He claimed that these were trumped-up charges to undermine his credibility, and that if he went to Sweden he would be extradited to the USA to face more dangerous charges. Assange thus fought the Swedish extradition in the British courts on the basis that these were false accusations and that it would place him in significant jeopardy. On failing to win the case, Assange fled to the Ecuadorian embassy, which has no bilateral extradition orders with Sweden. At the time of this writing, he remains 'exiled' and is confined to living in the embassy offices in Knightsbridge, London.

The WikiLeaks disclosures also led to calls by the US military and defence authorities to investigate how such a breach of classified information could occur on such an unprecedented scale. In this respect, the US Army already had their (wo)man, Bradley (now Chelsea) Manning, in custody. Manning was a private soldier who had been arrested in June 2010 when authorities received chat logs from a former hacker, Adrian Lamo, in which Manning had confided that (s)he had leaked the *Collateral Murder* video, in addition to a video of the Granai airstrike and about 260,000 diplomatic cables, to WikiLeaks. That such a lowly private could have accessed the entire US defence network and had downloaded top-secret data onto one CD, which (s)he had passed off as a collection of Britney Spears songs, demonstrated to a shocked America that its security apparatus was severely compromised. In 1971, Daniel Ellsberg had taken many weeks to photocopy the Pentagon Papers about the Vietnam War, and could make the information available only through *The New York Times*. In contrast, in 2010, Manning could download and distribute this information at the click of a mouse, and the US government was powerless to stop the flow of data across the global Internet. However, despite these differences in speed, scale and effect, the army still convicted Manning as a traitor, and (s)he is now serving a 35-year sentence in prison.

Yet the WikiLeaks revelations would be overshadowed by a former CIA operative, Edward Snowden, who leaked intelligence information concerning the US National Security Agency (NSA) surveillance of international Internet and mobile phone traffic. The scale of these state intrusions were again met with incredulity, and the USA was forced to apologise to foreign leaders, including German Prime Minister Angela Merkel, who had been victims of these intrusions. Snowden, who remains on the run, has argued that his revelations forced the US government's hand in passing the USA Freedom Act of 2014, thereby reforming its surveillance operations with regard to transparency and accountability. In turn, Obama confirmed that the Snowden revelations had caused trust in the USA to plunge around the world. He added that the mass surveillance programmes, which had remained secret from the public and were defended out of reflex rather than reason, should be ended:

> We have got to win back the trust not just of governments, but, more importantly, of ordinary citizens. And that's not going to happen overnight, because there's a tendency to be sceptical of government and to be sceptical of the US intelligence services. (Ackerman 2014)

A CRITIQUE OF THE SOCIAL MEDIA: INDIVIDUALISM,
UNRELIABILITY, POLARISATION AND THE
RECONFIGURATION OF POLITICAL POWER?

Online social networking sites have often been perceived as revolutionary new media tools, because they allow greater citizen participation in
the dissemination of information and creation of content. The networked
population is gaining greater access to information, enhanced opportunities to engage in public speech and an ability to undertake collective
action. However, as Zygmunt Bauman has argued, such forms of 'liquid
modernism', in which individual practices of social behaviour create new
opportunities for the self-realisation of participation, may also exacerbate
uncertainties in the human condition. Most notably, the new patterns of
social activity have paradoxically facilitated increasing fluidity in people's
behaviour, while producing existential fears of being imprisoned by such
freedoms (Bauman 2000:8).

Principally, the Marxist hypermedia scholars Richard Barbrook and
Andy Cameron have argued that the 'Californian Ideology', which
emerged from the technophiles in Silicon Valley, encompassed a range of
neo-liberal economic principles forged by individualistic and deregulated
forms of free market enterprise (Barbrook and Cameron 1996). In effect,
such techno-populist libertarianism created a labour aristocracy or 'virtual class' who benefitted from an inequitable distribution of resources, as
there was a commodification of individual thought through a supply-side
market transaction between entertainment providers and users (Wheeler
1998:228–229). According to Barbrook and Cameron, this meant that:

> [d]espite its radical rhetoric, the Californian Ideology is ultimately pessi-
> mistic about fundamental social change....The social liberalism of New Left
> and the economic liberalism of New Right have converged into an ambig-
> uous dream of a hi-tech...version of the plantation economy of the Old
> [American] South. Reflecting its deep ambiguity, the Californian Ideology's
> technological determinism is not simply optimistic and emancipatory. It
> is simultaneously a deeply pessimistic and repressive vision of the future.
> (Barbrook and Cameron 1996:14)

These concerns underpin John Keane's analysis of what he describes as
the 'decadent media'. Public expression has been restricted to individual discourse, and the concentration of power within the new media has

undermined the substance of democratic behaviour. Keane thus identifies the disparities which exist between the normative expectations associated with 'media abundance', such as openness, plurality, inclusion and equality, with a more tarnished reality in which the social media promote the intolerance of opinions, restrict the scrutiny of power and promote an acceptance of the way things are heading. In this respect, Keane contends that elite business and state power has been enhanced by data collection, censorship, spin and new mechanisms of surveillance (Keane 2013):

> Message-saturated societies can and do have effects that are harmful for democracy. Some of them are easily spotted. In some quarters, most obviously, media saturation triggers citizens' inattention to events. While they are expected as good citizens to keep their eyes on public affairs, to take an interest in the world beyond their immediate household and neighbourhood, more than a few find it ever harder to pay attention to the media's vast outpourings. Profusion breeds confusion. (Keane 2009)

In trying to comprehend the sheer mass of information, users are further confronted with the fact that much of the Internet's content is unreliable. As a widespread information source, the Internet should provide reliable, authentic and up-to-date information, but user-generated content—and blogs in particular—are often deemed unreliable sources, containing personal and one-sided opinions. While it is fair to say that common sense (house rules) and common decency should be the rule or acceptable practice when posting material on the Internet, because this is largely a self-regulated area, reaction comes only when someone complains. There is clearly a need for a better balance in enforcing appropriate online behaviour, assigning liability and protecting freedom of speech. Frankly, providing an informed (and safe) online experience is important for both consumers and businesses.

Dahlberg (2007) found online debate to be polarising, with a general lack of listening between people. He noted that the Internet and social media fail to adequately consider the asymmetries of power through which deliberation and consensus are achieved, the intersubjective basis of meaning, a centrality of respect for difference in democracy, and the democratic role of 'like-minded' deliberative groups. What is often absent in online deliberations is a consensus-based, justifiable and rational decision, let alone the inclusion of everyone affected by that decision. With the 'echo-chamber' (Sunstein 2007) effects of the social media, agreement becomes impossible, issues become 'inflamed' and decision-making is subjected to a greater polarisation of opinion:

> A political process in which like-minded people talk primarily to one another poses a great danger for the future of a democracy. This kind of process can lead to unwarranted extremism. When various groups move in opposite directions to extreme positions, confusion, confrontation, accusation, and sometimes even violence may be the ultimate result. (Sunstein 2001:7)

Therefore, some have questioned whether, rather than promoting change, the Internet has reinforced the social institutions of economic, political and social power. Couldry has argued that instead of a networked society creating opportunities for change and reform, the existing power relations have remained firmly in place. First, he questions whether the power within the network can transform or effect other forms of power that exist outside the network. Second, he asks whether network analysis fails to address matters of context and resources necessary for the development of any sustainable political agency. Third, and most fundamentally, he proposes that economic, military and legal authority cannot be reduced to network operations, and rather, that state and corporate interests retain their central place in society and combine to undermine individual autonomy and agency (Couldry 2012:116–118).

In this context, Fenton contends that networked forms of communication cannot really challenge the multimedia concentrations of capital which define the political economy of the Internet (Fenton 2012). She argues that political solidarity is shaped by the material experience of labour relations, struggles and conflicts rooted in the exploitation of labour in the pursuit of capital. Thus, solidarity is a modernist concept based on the principles of a political economic order, and workers continue to be exploited by the hegemonic forces of capital. Therefore, for grassroots solidarity to be effective, it is necessary to reorganise global capitalist relations such that they are not monolithic forces of impenetrable domination (Fenton 2011:53). The commercial power of the Internet must thus be understood as a significant barrier to the proletariat's political expression, and for collective identities to emerge, we must realise that:

> [w]hile it is true that social media provide a pleasurable means of self-expression and social connection, enable people to answer back to the citadels of media power and in certain situations…may support the creation of

radical counter-public...[s]ocial media are more often about individual than collective emancipation, about presenting self (frequently in consumerist... terms) rather than changing society, about entertainment and leisure rather than political communication...and about social agendas shaped by elites and corporate power rather than a radical alternative. (Curran, Freedman and Fenton 2012:180)

CONCLUSION

In this chapter, we have considered the implications and democratic potential of the social media in forming new types of power relations, determining alternative social movements and effecting changes in political consciousness. We have shown how Web 2.0 tools have advanced a greater plurality of expression and enabled the construction of horizontal networks of communication. According to Castells, these information networks represent the diffusion of centralised power and the democratisation of political expression (Castells 2012). In this respect, the process is as important as the outcome, as the social media allow for the aggregation of a multi-dimensional range of opinions and values in shaping political behaviour and outcomes.

Within this context, the social media can be instrumental in realising the potential power of revolutionary groups and forces. In Western societies and the states of the Global South, there have been numerous examples, from the ousting of the corrupt Philippine President Joseph Estrada, to the electoral success of the Italian comedian Beppe Grillo, to the American Occupy movement in which populist uprisings have been inspired and alternative voices have been raised. Web 2.0 tools have allowed social movements to respond to public grievances and to mobilise oppositional forces. This was in evidence during the Arab Spring, as an array of previously repressed groups combined forces through the new communications mechanisms to effect massive protests and to topple the autocratic regimes of Ben Ali in Tunisia and Mubarak in Egypt.

Here we have seen the rise of political consciousness, informed by a growing number of hacktivists and whistle-blowers, including Bradley (Chelsea) Manning and Edward Snowden, who challenged state power in the 2000s. The use of the online publisher WikiLeaks by Julian Assange and Daniel Berg was shown to be particularly instrumental in promoting activism across cyberspace. Its creation of a user-generated fifth estate consisting of encrypted leaked information from anonymous parties demonstrated that the diffusion of political power was now truly possible. The revelations of 'Cablegate' and the dissemination of the shocking *Collateral Murder* video were examples of how an underground group of activists might challenge the legitimacy and constitutionality of the actions of the US defence and security agencies. Moreover, WikiLeaks' collaboration with legacy media partners demonstrated another variation of the associative power of networks:

> But overall, WikiLeaks and its professionals innovated together, effectively blending pre-existing technologies, genres, norms, behaviours and organizational forms to create new hybrid approaches to news making. They have shared these resources among themselves and, in some case, networked publics. (Chadwick 2013:112)

Yet these changes have been controversial. The motivations of figures such as Assange have been called into question, and ambiguity has muddied the waters. While Assange has been venerated by the public for his exposure of state and corporate malfeasance, he has been criticised for his cavalier dissemination of non-redacted information, with serious implications for the lives of many US operatives. Thus, the questions of power and responsibility that have permeated the traditional media remain pertinent for the social media and the democratic potential, or lack thereof, within this context. Questions abound concerning individualistic forms of participation: the trivialisation of information, the inability to distinguish between 'real' and 'virtual' communication and the saturation of information that is endemic in an overabundant social media world.

Effectively, can people make sense of the wide range of information they receive? Furthermore, have the echo-chamber effects of a pluralistic yet highly individualistic discourse led to a stratified and polarised rather than collective form of political activity? More instrumentalist critiques have also questioned the economic, political and social constraints that still abound within cyberspace, and suggest that communications networks reinforce rather than challenge the institutions of capitalism. In particular, Fenton argues, technological utopianism masks the fact that 'the Internet does not transcend global capitalism but is deeply involved with it by virtue of the...discourses of capitalism...that people who use it are drenched in' (Fenton 2012:124). Therefore, the democratic potential of the social media has yet to be established, and it remains the purpose of this review to consider how these developments are being realised within the arena of diplomatic politics and the international community.

BIBLIOGRAPHY

Ackerman, S. 2014. "Snowden welcomes Obama's plans for NSA reform as 'turning point'". *The Guardian*, http://www.theguardian.com/world/2014/mar/25/edward-snowden-welcomes-obama-nsa-reforms (accessed April 7, 2014).

Barbrook R., and A. Cameron. 1996. "The Californian Ideology". *Science as Culture* 6(1): 44–72.

Bartlett J. 2013. "How Beppe Grillo's Social Media Politics Took Italy by Storm Grillo's Five Star Movement Won 25% of the Votes in Italy's Election Through Mixing New Technology with Old-Style Activism", *The Guardian*, February 26. http://www.theguardian.com/commentisfree/2013/feb/26/beppe-grillo-politics-social-media-italy (accessed April 7, 2014).

Bauman Z. 2000. *Liquid Modernity*. Cambridge: Polity.

Beckett C., and J. Ball. 2012. *WikiLeaks: News in the Networked Era*. Cambridge: Polity Press.

Bennett W.L. 2003. "Lifestyle Politics and Citizen-Consumers: Identity, Communication and Political Action". In *Media and the Re-Styling of Politics: Consumerism, Celebrity and Cynicism*, eds. J. Corner, andD. Pels. London: Sage.

Castells M. 2007. "Communication, Power and Counter-power in the Network Society". *International Journal of Communication* 8: 238–266.

Castells M. 2009. *Communications Power*. Oxford: Oxford University Press.

Castells M. 2012. *Networks of Outrage and Hope: Social Movements in the Internet Age*. Cambridge: Polity.

Chadwick A. 2006. *Internet Politics: States, Citizens and New Communications Technologies*. Oxford: Oxford University Press.

Chadwick A. 2013. *The Hybrid Media System: Power and Politics*. Oxford: Oxford University Press.

Couldry N. 2012. *Media, Society, World: Social Theory and Digital Media Practice*. Cambridge: Polity Press.

Crouch C. 2004. *Post-Democracy*. Cambridge: Polity.

Curran J., and M. Gurevitch. 1992. *Mass Media and Society*. London: Edward Arnold.

Dahl R. 1961. *Who Governs? Democracy and Power in an American City*. New Haven: Yale University Press.

Dahlberg L. 2007. "Rethinking the Fragmentation of the Cyberpublic: From Consensus to Contestation". *New Media and Society* 9(5): 827–847.

Dahlgren P. 2009. *Media and Political Engagement: Citizens, Communication and Democracy*. Cambridge: Cambridge University Press.

Fenton N. 2011. "Mediating Solidarity". *Global Media and Communication* 4: 37–57.

Fenton N. 2012. "Internet and Radical Politics". In *Misunderstanding the Internet*, eds. J. Curran, N. Fenton, and D. Freedman. London: Routledge.

Giddens A. 1991. *The Consequence of Modernity*. Stanford, CA: Stanford University Press.

Gladwell, M. 2010. "Small Change", *New Yorker*, October 4. http://www.newyorker.com/reporting/2010/10/04/101004fa_fact_gladwell (accessed March 22, 2014).

Katz, J. 1995. "The Age of Paine", *Wired*, May. 154–214.

Keane J. 2009. Monitory Democracy and media-saturated societies. *Griffith Review, Edition 24: Participation Society*. <http://www.griffithreview.com/edition-24-participation-society/222-essay/657.html> (accessed November 20, 2014).

Keane J. 2013. *Democracy and Media Decadence*. Cambridge: Cambridge University Press.

Letsch, C., and D. Rushe. 2014. Turkey Blocks YouTube Amid 'national security' Concerns, *The Guardian*. http://www.theguardian.com/world/2014/mar/27/google-youtube-ban-turkey-erdogan (accessed April 7, 2014).

Loader B., and D. Mercea. 2011. "NETWORKING DEMOCRACY? Social Media Innovations and Participatory Politics". *Information Communication and Society* 14(6): 757–769.

Marsh D., P. 't Hart, and K. Tindall. 2010. "Celebrity Politics: The Politics of the Late Modernity?". *Political Studies Review* 8(3): 322–340.

Mason P. 2012. *Why It's Kicking Off Everywhere: The New Global Revolutions*. London: Verso Press.

Papacharassi Z. 2009. *A Private Sphere: Democracy in a Digital Age*. Cambridge: Polity Press.

Putnam R.D. 2000. *Bowling Alone*. New York: Simon and Schuster.

Salter L. 2003. "Democracy, New Social Movements and the Internet: A Habermasian Analysis". In *Cyberactivism: Online Activism in Theory and Practice*, eds. M. McCaughey, andM.D. Ayers. London: Routledge.

Seib P. 2012. *Real-Time Diplomacy: Politics and Power in the Social Media*. Basingstoke: Palgrave MacMillan.

Shirky C. 2009. *Here Comes Everybody: The Power of Organising without Organisations*. London: Penguin.

Shirky, C. 2011. The Political Power of Social Media: Technology, the Public Sphere, and Political Change, *Foreign Affairs*, January/February issue. http://www.foreignaffairs.com/articles/67038/clay-shirky/the-political-power-of-social-media (accessed March 21, 2014).

Splichal S. 2009. "'New' Media, 'Old' Theories: Does the (National) Public Melt into the Air of Global Governance?". *European Journal of Communication*. 24(4): 391–405.

Street, J. 1996. "Remote Control: Politics, Technology and Culture". In *Contemporary Politics Studies 1996* (Volume 1), ed. I. Hampsher-Monk and J. Stanyer: Political Studies Association.

Sunstein C. 2001. *Republic.com*. Princeton, NJ: Princeton University Press.

Sunstein C. 2007. *Republic.com 2.0*. Princeton, NJ: Princeton University Press.

Turner E. 2013. "The 5 Star Movement and its Discontents: A Tale of Blogging, Comedy, Electoral Success and Tensions". *Interface: A Journal for and about Social Movements* 5(2): 178–212.

Wall M., and S. El Zahed. 2011. "'I'll Be Waiting for You Guys': A YouTube Call to Action in Egyptian Revolution". *International Journal of Communication* 5: 1333–1343.

Wertheim M. 1999. *The Pearly Gates of Cyberspace: A History of Space from Dante to the Internet*. New York: W.W. Norton.

Wheeler M. 1997. *Politics and the Mass Media*. Oxford: Blackwell Publishers.

Wheeler M. 1998. Democracy and the Information Superhighway, *Democratization and the Media: Special Edition*. ed. V. Randall. Frank Cass Journal, 5(2). Summer: 217–239.

CHAPTER 7

Public Diplomacy 2.0 and the Social Media

INTRODUCTION

This chapter addresses how the social media have become a more profound force in shaping international values throughout the wider diplomatic community. It examines the changing nature of public and cultural diplomacy (PCD) within the context of evolving global communications. In light of these changes, many countries, including the USA and the UK, have come to realise that they must employ Web 2.0 tools to curry favourable opinion among the international public:

> Technological developments in the field of digital communication have revolutionized the practice of public diplomacy. A considerable number of countries have recognized the many opportunities offered by these new technologies and have embraced them. Each year, both the number of states with such programmes and the amount of resources dedicated to these activities grow. Countries that fail to understand the importance of digital public diplomacy are greatly disadvantaged, and this is widely recognized. (Mytko 2012)

In turn, modern forms of 'new public diplomacy' have reflected the interaction of political leaders, journalists and the wider public in determining cultural relations and exchanges, international forms of broadcasting and nation branding. Brian Hocking suggests that PCD embraces

© The Editor(s) (if applicable) and The Author(s) 2016
P. Iosifidis, M. Wheeler, *Public Spheres and Mediated
Social Networks in the Western Context and Beyond*,
DOI 10.1057/978-1-137-41030-6_7

the theories of strategic political communications, which indicates 'a high level of awareness of ... human behaviour determined by culture and patterns of media utilisation as well as a deep knowledge of over-seas news organizations and political systems' (Hocking 2005:36). Therefore, the impact of social media on international public discourse has affected global forms of 'social capital' and knowledge such that:

> [t]he diplomatic pouch became largely obsolete as foreign ministries turned first to open sources such as the BBC, CNN and, more recently, Twitter and its siblings to find out what was going on in distant parts of the world. (Seib 2012:2)

In this chapter, we explore the nature of such international forms of political communication, first by discussing the social media techniques through which states and non-state actors (NSAs) have promoted cultural interchange as a means to mobilise public opinion to advance their cause. These developments are compared and contrasted with the traditions of diplomacy and previous forms of PCD, which may be characterised as state-centric and invariably propagandist. According to Nicholas J. Cull, the establishment of diplomatic relations via online social networks has created a range of user-generated content and interactivity between states, NSAs and the public, and has facilitated a more democratic information infrastructure (Cull 2012:2). Consequently, it has been argued, governments will improve their use of the web, engage in new forms of statecraft and relinquish their control over PCD strategies to facilitate people-to-people communication (Hayden 2012:3).

Second, we analyse the ways in which states have developed 'public diplomacy 2.0' techniques, with specific reference to the USA and UK.[1] Although PCD was part of the superpower struggle in evidence during the Cold War, Al Qaeda's 9/11 terrorist attacks signalled to US leaders that they were engaged in a new battle for 'hearts and minds'. As such, PCD has been part of the 'soft power' (Nye 2004) processes in operation under the presidencies of both George W. Bush and Barack Obama. While Bush used cross-cultural forms of diplomacy to deflect the negative US image, until the arrival of James K. Glassman as Under Secretary of State

---

[1] It should also be noted that other nation-states such as Sweden and Switzerland have developed sophisticated public diplomacy 2.0 policies.

for Public Diplomacy and Public Affairs (2008–2009), the Bush administration's employment of PCD was overly reliant on public relations techniques. Conversely, Obama's employment of PCD has ostensibly demonstrated a more inclusive use of social media. This response was designed to facilitate new forms of statecraft based on dialogue and outreach. Similarly, the UK's Foreign and Commonwealth Office (FCO) has engaged in digital forms of diplomacy in terms of nation branding and online networking.

Third, such use of social media has accorded with the transformational changes from state-centric to more cosmopolitan forms of PCD. NGOs have utilised online media to advance public interest and engagement in their direct action campaigns. NGOs have been disadvantaged in mainstream media coverage, as states have claimed credibility, legitimacy and public attention as sources of information. Therefore, these organisations have taken advantage of the diffusion of horizontal communications to act as online agenda-setters (Thrall et al. 2014:10). These grassroots forms of PCD have included charity initiatives to mobilise public response to natural disasters, including the 2010 Haiti earthquake, and campaigns against human rights abuse by groups such as the Lord's Resistance Army (LRA) under the brutal warlord Joseph Kony.

The chapter thus considers the extent to which the social media may facilitate the use of new 'currencies' of dialogue, outreach and propagation of opinions as key bargaining tools within PCD initiatives. We conclude by considering whether such employment of soft power truly equates with a democratisation of foreign policies, or rather, reflects a reconfiguration of elite interests within the international order. Moreover, we examine whether the social media have, in fact, effected substantive public interest in international issues.

PCD: Propaganda and Public Relations

The traditions of diplomacy have been seen as the coordination of state interests with the broader concepts of collective security and economic power. The mechanisms of bargaining, interest and cooperation have been utilised as diplomatic 'currency' by British Foreign Office mandarins, ambassadors and US State Department officials. This has been presented as part of a realist discourse on international issues in which the matters of ethics must be balanced against the complexities of the global state system. Within this Westphalian tradition, secret and sensitive information was carefully husbanded by diplomats who maintained insider power:

> In the days of the old diplomacy it would have been regarded as an act of unthinkable vulgarity to appeal to the common people upon any issue of international policy. (Nicolson 1939)

At the same time, there has been a long-standing practice of importing technology within the evolution of diplomacy. The innovations of the telegraph, telephone, automobile and airplane, for example, eliminated the many weeks that had been required to exchange over-seas diplomatic cables. Moreover, with the growth of radio, film and television there arose accompanying state-centric forms of PCD in which governments propagated their national ideologies and values to influence the foreign public. With the arrival of mass media, PCD was often conflated with the more pernicious effects of the propaganda perpetuated by fascist or totalitarian states (Pigman 2010:122–123). For instance, during World War II, Hitler's Nazi Germany employed the American-born William Joyce, known colloquially as 'Lord Haw-Haw', as a radio broadcaster of propaganda designed to demoralise and sap the will of the British public (Seib 2012:113).

Elsewhere, the well-known Hollywood trade organisation, the Motion Picture Association of America (MPAA), was referred to as the 'little State Department', as its methods were so in line with the US government's propagandist aims in the early days of the Cold War (1945–1990) (Segrave 1997:144). President Harry Truman (1945–1952) viewed films as crucial ideological weapons for the re-education of the peoples of Germany, Italy and France against the evils of Communism, to the virtues of free enterprise and democracy, and to American democracy in particular (Puttnam 1997:213). This offensive in creating 'a world-wide Marshall plan in the field of ideas' (Puttnam 1997:213) was reflected in the MPAA's choice of representatives such as Frank McCarthy, who represented the organisation in Paris, and who had been General George Marshall's aide and a former assistant to the secretary of state (Puttnam 1997:203).

Throughout the Cold War, PCD played a major role in defining the bipolar forms of propaganda employed by the USA and the Soviet Union (USSR). Governmental ministers, embassy diplomats and consular officials thus used public relations strategies to set agendas within the international media. Furthermore, during this period, cultural, arts and exchange-based diplomatic initiatives were purposively developed by state-sponsored institutions such as the US Information Agency (USIA), the British Council, the Voice of America and the BBC World Service.

Eric M. Fattor has written that the battle for ideological supremacy was fought out in the world's fairs of the 1950s and 1960s and, most strikingly, during the 1959 'Kitchen Debate' series between then Vice President Richard M. Nixon and Soviet Premier Nikita Khrushchev (Fattor 2014:118). In particular, the technology of that ubiquitous consumer durable—the television set—was celebrated by Nixon:

> Subsequent to this conversation, Nixon was severely criticized...for trying to equate the banal technology...with the strategically more relevant technology of ballistic rockets. However, this criticism was misinformed. Whether he knew it or not, Nixon was celebrating the primary mechanism through which the American Empire expanded throughout the later twentieth century. (Fattor 2014:118)

The technological imperative of the cathode-ray tube outlived bipolarity and, with the inclusion of digital technologies, witnessed the exponential expansion of media coverage. Most notably, in terms of international affairs, we have seen the emergence of the so-called CNN effect, in which public opinion has been mobilised through the rise of 24/7 global news programming. As far back as 1968, Leonard Marks (then head of the USIA) predicted that a 'golden age of world peace' could be afforded by a global communications process resulting from the networking of computers (Cull 2012). Moreover, as Richard Barbrook demonstrated, the coordination of US military and industrial forces in constructing an embryonic vision of the Internet in the 1960s effected a utopian vision of a computerised future in which global emancipation founded upon the American version of free market modernity would predominate (Barbrook 2007:182–183). However, it was not until the 2000s that the diplomatic classes came to realise the potential for social media as such a liberating force.

PUBLIC DIPLOMACY 2.0: THE FACILITATION OF A 'CONVERSATION'—CULTURAL, DEMOCRATIC AND SOFT POWER

The social media, by circumventing national boundaries and the 'gatekeeping' controls of the past, has been the perfect medium through which to realise new public diplomacy initiatives. Web 2.0 networks enable the views of the public to be transmitted back to state players or

NSAs through the blogosphere, tweets and postings. Such interactivity has encouraged a greater dialogue among a wider range of actors to effect listening, citizen advocacy and cultural practices. Moreover, social media provide a continuous real-time newsfeed via Twitter, while establishing alternative platforms for the distribution of international broadcasts. As Philip Seib noted, the leisurely processes of diplomacy have been replaced by instant demands in which the social media's coverage of events has determined 'the new pace and reach of information flow' (Seib 2012:3).

In addition, as Web 2.0 social networks distribute information in a viral manner, they allow for new forms of exchange diplomacy to emerge. In this respect, people-to-people forms of communication have enabled 'memes'—units of ideas, styles or cultural practices that are designed to permeate the public's international consciousness—to operate through hyperlinks, websites or re-tweeted messages, complete with their own hashtags. Therefore, states and other international actors have developed new forms of outreach to influence the foreign public.

Through such a fragmented and decentralised range of information sources, alternative voices have emerged from transnational civil society constituencies to effect a 'polylateral' or non-hierarchical form of PCD (Wiseman 2010). Public diplomacy 2.0 thus refers to the construction of horizontal webs to engage the public, NSAs and civil society organisations (CSO) that are relevant to foreign policy objectives. As such, grassroots Web 2.0 communication techniques may facilitate digital and citizen-led types of diplomacy. As Cull commented:

> [t]he task of public diplomacy...evolve[d] from one of speaking to one of partnering around issues with those who share the same objectives and empowering those who will be credible with their target audience. (Cull 2011:7)

According to Jan Melissen, states can no longer use public information channels as a one-way mechanism through which to talk to the public (Melissen 2011:1). Consequently, while noting that governments have increased their use of e-bulletins, tweets and foreign ministerial blogs, advocates of new public diplomacy contend that states must relinquish their control over PCD strategies. Indeed, some commentators argue that any attempt to maintain centralised power will prove to be counterproductive, as the social media do not accord with the controls of the past (Zaharna and Rugh 2012:2). As Joseph S. Nye Jr. contends:

> [t]he Internet creates a system in which power over information is much more widely distributed...What this means is that foreign policy will not be the sole province of governments. Both individuals and private organizations, here and abroad, will be empowered to play direct roles in world politics. The spread of information will mean that power will be more widely distributed and informal networks will undercut the monopoly of traditional bureaucracy. (Nye 2002:61–62)

However, despite these claims for greater openness, concerns remain as to whether governments are prepared to cede their control over PCD initiatives. State-centric forms of public diplomacy 2.0 in which governments engage in public relations or 'spin' techniques have continued to exist. For instance, in 2006, the Israeli state constructed a series of official blogs dedicated to 'lifestyle' products designed to influence international opinion. These blogs were accompanied by the creation of IsraelPolitik.org and by 'citizen press conferences' on Twitter. Foreign Affairs Advisor David Saranga argued that such Web 2.0 communications enabled Israel to advance its position, shape the political agenda and engage with interested parties. In this context, 'engagement' was a 'mushy' term and should be questioned in terms of its validity in opinion formation (Seib 2012:120) (*see* Chap. 11).

These concerns segue into a broader critique of the power relations which exist between online disseminators (leaders) and the receivers (followers) of information through social networks. Web 2.0 tools have reinforced state power over political communications by effecting 'primary' and 'secondary' forms of definition (Hall et al. 1978). In this respect, 'virtual' agenda-setters have constructed ideologically loaded but apparently consensual positions to propagate the interests of the elite. In turn, the 'followers' mistakenly believe they can express their opinions autonomously when they are subject to the hegemonic values of state or corporate power:

> What would make the Propaganda Model more 'marginal in its applicability' is not the rise of blogging, podcasting and other potential media vehicles, but rather the diminution of class and hierarchically organized social orders, and the spread and deepening of egalitarianism. As long as highly unequal and unfair economic and social orders persist, their dominant elites will have to justify themselves and they will continue to need supportive propaganda. (Herman and Chomsky 2009:20)

Thus, while states have embraced new forms of technological delivery, it remains necessary to question the deeper motivations which have defined their use of PCD practices. Such a concern underpins any investigation of the US State Department's PCD strategies which have emerged in the wake of social media.

PUBLIC DIPLOMACY AND THE USA: THE BUSH DOCTRINE, THE 'SHARED VALUES INITIATIVE' AND THE WAR ON TERROR

The American government rediscovered PCD after the 9/11 Al-Qaeda attacks on the World Trade Center in New York City and the Pentagon in Washington D.C. Shortly after the terrorist atrocities, President George W. Bush's administration hired advertising guru Charlotte Beers to effect new PCD strategies. Bush's Secretary of State Colin Powell charged Beers with developing the 'Shared Values Initiative' to win over Middle Eastern audiences to the cause of US democracy:

> I wanted one of the world's greatest advertising experts, because what are we doing? We're selling. We're selling a product. That product we are selling is democracy. It is the free enterprise system, the American value system. It is a product very much in demand. It's a product that is very much needed. (Powell 2001)

Beers thus took a 'public relations' (Bernays 1928) approach to PCD and she introduced her fellow Madison Avenue branding expert Steve Hayden to inform State Department officials on how they could counter the negative US international image (Pigman 2010:128). Her programme resulted in five television mini-documentaries focusing on 'real' American Muslims ('Baker', 'Doctor', 'School Teacher', 'Journalist' and 'Firefighter'), who were shown to be fully participating in US life. In each film, these interviewees provided voiceovers to invoke a sense of US community and credibility. The shorts were shown in several Islamic Middle East and Asian states, and with State Department approval, airtime during Ramadan was bought at a cost of $5 million. In conjunction with these films, the US government sponsored speaking tours across Kuwait, Lebanon, Jordan and Indonesia. Finally, the campaign established a promotional website www.opendialogue.com, which encouraged naturalised Muslim Americans to 'share' their thoughts, comments and experiences. Over 1000 stories were posted during the event.

However, in part because of Beers' hierarchical approach to PCD, and more importantly, due to the Bush administration's overarching military adventurism:

> [w]hen [these] platforms of information were used, they more often than not supplemented the deployment of violence and brute force by conveying the images of strength and power associated with the American military apparatus....With such a backdrop, it is easy to see why the efforts of...Beers failed since media campaigns designed to arouse sentimentality...about common values cannot hope to compete with the sights of falling bombs, rolling tanks and the bloody carnage of civilian casualties. (Fattor 2014:163)

With the failure of the Shared Values Initiative with sceptical Middle East audiences, the State Department's PCD strategies effectively collapsed. These problems were exacerbated by the huge military expenditure, which dwarfed all other Bush administration programmes, including the $10 billion spent on PCD. Furthermore, the administration's sporadic leadership concerning PCD led to a series of half-thought-through ideas which failed to win international favour. The poor international US reputation was only made worse by the revelations of torture, rendition and injustice meted out to Arab nationals in the asymmetric 'War on Terror'.

The result was that subsequent under secretaries of state for public diplomacy, including Karen Hughes (2005–2007), another political communications expert, were hampered by the negative international perceptions of the Bush presidency. Hughes' attempts to saturate Middle Eastern audiences with 'positive messages' about the USA proved to be highly counterproductive. Conversely, her decision to set up the Digital Outreach Team (DOT) in 2006 demonstrated the growing realisation within the diplomatic classes that an intelligent deployment of social media would be crucial in any further PCD efforts.

JAMES K. GLASSMAN AND PUBLIC DIPLOMACY 2.0

In 2008, former journalist and political commentator James K. Glassman replaced Hughes to lead the US PCD strategies to win the 'war for hearts and minds'. Although Glassman would be in office only a short time, he oversaw profound change in the cultural values associated with the deployment of public diplomacy 2.0. Consequently, Glassman supported a number of existing programmes, but more importantly, effected a greater realisation among State Department officials that they could no longer use persuasive techniques to manipulate the reception and outcome of their messages. His philosophy was to 'bring people in contact with America... not to tell them what to think' (Newsweek 2009).

Through the social media, he argued, the US government would use Web 2.0 communications to facilitate a 'holistic' approach to PCD based upon creating a dialogue with interested parties through listening, understanding and engagement. Glassman contended that US public diplomacy should act as a reciprocal 'platform for cooperation, mediation and reception—a mode of being informed as well as informing' (Glassman 2008). As such, he advanced smaller digital forms of 'engagement' in which PCD officers contributed to online forums concerning US foreign policy. Moreover, the State Department cooperated with NBCUniversal, the Directors Guild of America (DGA) and the Tisch School of the Arts at New York University to launch the 'Democracy Video Challenge' for international participants. In this competition, entrants were invited to produce three-minute videos that would be posted on YouTube, in which they were to complete the phrase, 'Democracy is...' The winning entries were determined by an Internet vote.

These initiatives were complemented by another Glassman-led project regarding shared 'social media best practices' with those NGOs that had contributed to US public diplomacy under the banner of the Alliance of Youth Movements. Participants within the alliance included Web 2.0 activists like Oscar Morales, who founded the Facebook group 'One Million Voices against the FARC', which coordinated protests against terrorism in Colombia. Rather than force the hand of Colombian liberals, Glassman had allowed Morales to create a grassroots movement which articulated an ideological position that accorded to US values and needs.

Moreover, Glassman utilised a mixture of Middle Eastern journalists, faith groups, local students and social networks, including Twitter and Second Life, to reach out to Arab audiences. He deployed State Department officials to act as surrogates within blogs, chat rooms and message boards, where, speaking in Urdu, Farsi, Arabic and Russian, they identified themselves as US representatives who were prepared to explore a range of ideas. In this transparent and congenial manner these online operatives dropped 'memes' into cyberspace to counteract any distortions concerning US positions. For instance, one Glassman proxy became involved in a lengthy debate with the media adviser to the former

Iranian Prime Minister Mahmoud Ahmadinejad, on the adviser's website. This online conversation was subsequently reprinted in Iran's national newspapers.

Through this deployment of social media communications, Glassman encouraged the State Department to win a series of small victories rather than attempt to impose its views wholescale on a sceptical Middle Eastern audience. As these 'winning discourses' accumulated, they developed their own momentum, thereby garnering more favourable reception by online constituencies in the Middle East:

> Glassman, as they say in Washington, gets it. The Under Secretary of State for Public Diplomacy has been on the job for only six months, but he has already scored small successes in the US effort to win over 'hearts and minds' in the Muslim world, a hard sell if ever there was one. (Newsweek 2009)

Yet, while Glassman had reconfigured the modes of US foreign policy communications, it remained unclear whether he had truly transformed American political motives. More optimistic public diplomacy commentators predicted that Glassman had laid the foundation for a new approach to PCD that would be fully realised with the inauguration of incoming President Barack Obama.

BARACK OBAMA'S DIGITAL DIPLOMACY: TWENTY-FIRST CENTURY STATECRAFT—DIALOGUE AND OUTREACH

Obama's 2008 electoral victory appeared to signal a significant change in the direction of US foreign policy. In the election campaign, he had promised to end the war in Iraq, withdraw troops from Afghanistan, stop the use of torture to gain intelligence and close down the illegal extradition process of rendition. Obama argued that the USA needed to improve its international standing by becoming a 'world policeman' practising 'smart' power (Nye 2004). Moreover, Obama's reputation as a 'social media president', who had incorporated many Web 2.0 techniques in his election campaign (*see* Chap. 5), meant that he was favourably inclined towards public diplomacy 2.0 (Harris 2013).

In this respect, his Secretaries of State Hillary Clinton (2009–2013) and John Kerry (2013–) were keen to play up the online development of PCD. Indeed, Clinton was called the 'godmother of digital diplomacy', as she advocated Internet freedom and new types of diplomatic statecraft. She argued that, because the 'geometry of global power' was more diffuse, 'building coalitions for common action [was] becoming both more complicated and more crucial' (Sandre 2013). This led to her appointment of a close ally, Judith McHale, former President and Chief Executive Officer (CEO) of Discovery Communications (the parent company of the Discovery cable channel), as Under Secretary of Public Diplomacy and Public Affairs (2009–2011). McHale's media background as CEO of a company with over 1.4 billion subscribers across 170 countries was both an advantage in terms of 'selling US messages' and a drawback due to her limited background in public service. Moreover, her close affiliation with Clinton as a campaign funder was heavily criticised, with accusations of cronyism and the apparent public relations direction of US PCD. Nevertheless, McHale demonstrated a conversance with the transformation in global power relations ushered in by the rise of social media:

> In a world where power and influence truly belongs to the many, we must engage with more people in more places. That is the essential truth of public diplomacy in the Internet age....The pyramid of power flipped because people all around the world are clamouring to be heard, and demanding to shape their own futures. They are having important conversations right now—in chatrooms and classrooms and boardrooms—and they aren't waiting for us. (McHale 2011)

Additionally, Clinton's appointment of a 'network diplomacy' advocate, Princeton professor Anne-Marie Slaughter, as Director of Policy Planning (2009–2011) reflected the administration's belief that digital diplomacy was the way forward. Slaughter had written extensively on the 'collaborative' power of networks to effect a creditable and accountable set of diplomatic outcomes. Clinton also retained the services of Condoleezza Rice's new technology adviser, Jared Cohen, while acquiring advisers who had made their reputations in the 2008 presidential campaign, including Alec Ross and Katie Jacobs Stanton. On Clinton's watch, roughly 150 full-time domestic staff and 900 international diplomats used Twitter, Facebook, YouTube and blogs to conduct forms of public diplomacy (Mytko 2012). This resulted in several programmes targeting online audiences to engage in dialogue in their native language and in US embassies developing social media services and ultimately gaining over 300,000 Facebook followers (Seib 2012:121).

In tandem, the State Department created a number of partnerships with industrial and academic players, along with NGOs, to harness the connective power of the social media technologies. This effort included the deployment of mobile phone applications and Web 2.0 technologies to foster relations with civil society organisations and government officials and people-to-people contact. It was complemented by high-profile programmes such as the 'Virtual Student Foreign Service', composed of university students; the Tech@State conferences, which drew together technology developers and NSAs; and the 'Apps4Africa' competition, designed to promote the development of mobile technological solutions for regional issues (Hayden 2012:9).

Furthermore, during the president's second term, the former US ambassador to Russia, Michael McFaul (2012–2014), demonstrated the effectiveness of Twitter, using it to comment about official US stances, political issues and cultural concerns, and to reply to questions from the public. His openness appeared in stark contrast to Russian leader Vladimir Putin's decidedly propagandist use of social media. Craig Hayden describes the combined effect of these developments as 'twenty-first century statecraft', whose agenda:

> complements traditional foreign policy tools with newly innovated and adapted instruments that fully leverage the networks, technologies, and demographics of our networked world. (Hayden 2012:11)

Hayden argues that changes in the orientation of PCD enabled new actors to be fully integrated into the communications process as 'stakeholders' and 'opinion leaders'. These views were augmented by Ross' belief that State Department officials should match the new technologies to the appropriate NGOs to resolve international problems through online dialogue. Thus, through public diplomacy 2.0 strategies, the US government would be able to reach out to a wider international audience to facilitate international political consensus (Harris 2013:22).

Within this context, the State Department extended the activities of the DOT to engage with Middle Eastern online users. The DOT comprised ten civil servants who, as native Arabic, Persian and Urdu speakers, posted comments on popular regional websites. Rather than hide behind false identities, the members of the DOT identified themselves as State Department representatives who would respond to other users in an individual capacity. The DOT was responsible for the online dissemination of Obama's 'Cairo speech' in June 2009, in which the president set out his Middle Eastern policy objectives to demonstrate more equitable relations with Arab states and to reconfigure America's relationship with Israel. One hundred eighty-one posts were disseminated across 30 discussion threads to explain how the new turns in US foreign policy would advance regional international relations. As a result of these online initiatives, the DOT garnered begrudging respect from foreign audiences, as it provided a 'space' wherein Middle Eastern audiences could articulate their disagreements with US foreign policy:

> The efforts of the DOT to join the conversation seem to stir counter-messages, but they also enable those reading these sites, including the undecided among the lurkers, to hear alternative perspectives. It is important that diplomats around the world recognize the potential of joining two-way conversations about controversial issues in the age of networks, but also systematically explore strategies for grappling with often hostile and emotional arguments where there is a lack of trust among the adversaries. And regardless of how much the US invests in developing public diplomacy methods, the best way to change attitudes and gain trust in the Middle East is through foreign policies that link words and deeds that evoke broad public support. These are some of the major strategic challenges facing public diplomacy 2.0. (Khatib et al. 2012:471–472)

The extent to which these social media connections resulted in any real change in Arab attitudes remained unclear (Khatib et al. 2012:453–472), and the issues of 'equitability' and 'trust' in online PCD discourse between the USA, activists and the foreign public remained problematic. Despite the ostensible pursuit of dialogue and outreach with international audiences, McHale still hoped to use more covert forms of 'persuasion' to influence public opinion. Furthermore, the Twitter accounts of senior social media policy advisors including Ross, Cohen and Stanton focused on insights drawn from fellow US-centric 'tech circles'. Consequently, in developing 'insider networks', they showed little or no interest in feeding back global opinion to the American diplomatic community. This parochial inability to facilitate proper dialogue with non-American actors exemplified the 'echo-chamber' effect that Cass Sunstein had identified as detrimental to online democratic practices (Sunstein 2007) (*see* Chap. 6). In addition, Ross' preference for the term 'twenty-first century statecraft' lacked the relational values implicit in Glassman's phrase 'public diplomacy 2.0':

> The default setting of US public diplomacy has always been advocacy. Congress, the White House and arguably the American people have all

looked to public diplomacy to 'push' messages out to the world rather than to provide feedback on the state of international opinion, which might shape policies in the first place. It is hardly surprising that official diplomatic Twitter accounts have been used to push out messages rather than to create or enhance a community around an issue of interest to the United States. (Cull 2013:136)

Consequently, in the Obama era, those tasked with effecting US social media strategies have struggled to strike an appropriate balance between maintaining the national interest and the demand for greater reciprocity. This has been driven in part by the dilemma that exists for a government that has wanted to open up track 3 (person-to-person) types of diplomacy, but has also faced the myriad problems of having its state secrets disseminated across cyberspace (*see* Chap. 5). However, it also shows that the Obama administration, despite its rhetorical pledges, has remained reluctant to fully engage in an online dialogue with the international community. This reflects the mixed outcomes of the 'Obama Doctrine', in which there have been as many continuities as changes in US foreign policy directions inherited from the Bush era. Therefore, a more balanced approach to PCD and to Web 2.0 technologies is needed to demonstrate the full effect of networked communications.

UK PUBLIC DIPLOMACY 2.0: NATION BRANDING AND GLOBAL OUTREACH

The UK was the other early adopter of digital public diplomacy strategies. The British FCO recognised the advantages provided by social media in reaching out to a wider foreign audience, the targeting of politicians and the expedient management of declining resources. Britain has 'punched above its weight' by taking a more pragmatic approach to public diplomacy 2.0 than that of the USA. For instance, Tom Fletcher, the UK ambassador to Lebanon, contends that social media enabled Britain to carry out its core diplomatic goals, including information harvesting, analysis, the promotion of English as the language to unlock cyberspace, crisis management and the extension of commercial interests (Fletcher 2012). The social media have been a valuable channel through which to advertise UK products, to achieve inward and outward investment and to mediate trade relations. This attitude has been dictated by the UK's reduced post-colonial role in the international order. In this capacity, Britain was able to build upon its membership in the EU and its relations with the Commonwealth of Australasian, African and Asian states formerly occupied by the British Empire.

The FCO has access to over 120 Twitter channels and 120 Facebook pages, enabling UK diplomats to augment their communications infrastructure with the inclusion of tens of thousands of Facebook friends and more than 220,000 Twitter followers (Mytko 2012; Quinn 2014). For instance, UK officials in the Netherlands tweeted about a London-based conference on Somalia, which was picked up by *The Guardian* and subsequently re-tweeted to 26,000 people. In turn, the original tweet was propagated across the social media to be read by Dutch residents, UK citizens and interested parties working on Somalian issues (Mytko 2012).

The UK government has thus developed a well-structured, flexible and efficient approach to social media. For British diplomats, the most effective online PCD programmes have been those established on the basis of trust and cooperation, such that all participants consider themselves equal partners:

> Digital media has become an essential part of our work and allowed us to not only explain what we think but also to engage more widely. One of the most positive things about social media is the ability to interact with people, to hear their views and positions and to respond on their needs and requests....Our blogs, Twitter, and Facebook profiles are a direct window to explain the work we do. And at the same they are a platform for people to make themselves heard by Ministers and senior public servants. (Quinn 2014)

Moreover, while the FCO has established broad guidelines and training and evaluation programmes for diplomats in their use of Web 2.0 technologies, UK ambassadors have enjoyed significant leeway concerning the information they could send out. Therefore, British diplomats have been at the forefront in setting up blogs and creating Twitter handles to target foreign audience segments. Importantly, they have established Web 2.0 links with youth groups and ethnic diasporas to advertise the 'attractiveness' of the UK in terms of nation branding (e.g., online communications regarding the 2012 London Olympics) and to facilitate greater openness in people-to-people relations.

For instance, the ambassador to Thailand, Mark Kent (2012–), has been one of the UK's leading 'Twiplomats', with his online commentary promoting the attractiveness of UK brands to Thai audiences. Kent has blogged, tweeted and posted YouTube videos about his support of the Arsenal Football Club (Arsenal FC) to engage with those segments of the Thai population who follow the club, in order to raise the international profile of the FA Premier League. He has also provided posts about the increased popularity of Thai food and of Thailand as a holiday destination for the British public, and thus has cultivated a reciprocal relationship with Thai businesses (Kent 2013).

In a more controversial capacity, Kent used his Twitter feed to denounce the 2014 military coup in Thailand and its effect on the democratic functioning of the nation's political institutions. Similarly, when Kent was the ambassador to Vietnam, he supported the introduction of a free and democratic Internet within the country. These examples show that diplomatic social media channels of communication may act as a conduit through which the foreign public can participate with UK diplomats to engage in critical forums concerning their governments. These more vital forms of engagement have invariably occurred as public diplomacy 2.0 initiatives have increasingly operated within the purview of independent NGO.

THE SOCIAL MEDIA AND NGOS: MOBILIZATION, AGENDA-SETTING AND ONLINE CAMPAIGNING

The growing influence of NGOs represents another dimension of the diplomatic power associated with the rise of social media. NGOs have become vehicles for a multitude of causes, including economic justice, fair trade, climate change and the promotion of human rights. The International Red Cross and Red Crescent Movement, the International Rescue Committee and the World Wildlife Fund have extended their global reach through the Internet. This was apparent when the Red Cross received $8 million in US donations via text messaging in the wake of the catastrophic Haiti earthquake in 2010, a response that was influenced by the voluminous texts and photos appearing on social media sites and videos posted on YouTube. It also demonstrated how NGOs have used 'crowdsourcing' techniques to coordinate disaster relief programmes:

> Crowd-sourcing allows capable crowds to participate in...a form of collective wisdom and information sharing that strongly leverages participatory social media services and tools....[T]he Haiti crisis map had more than

2500 incident reports, with more reports being added every day. The large amount of nearly real-time reports allows relief organizations to identify and respond to urgent cases in time. (Gao et al. 2011:10–11)

Traditionally, NGOs have been reliant on the mainstream news media to draw attention to their causes and to mobilise public support for campaigns exposing human rights violations. However, they have enjoyed only limited news coverage due to their restricted role in foreign policy processes. For instance, reports show that between 2010 and 2012, of the 257 NGOs surveyed, 40 % had not appeared in a news story during a given year, and 25 % were not covered at all during the period (Thrall et al. 2014:10–11). Because they lack funding, credibility and close relationships with the political establishment, NGOs have struggled to make themselves heard within the conventional media. And when they have received media coverage, the focus has been skewed towards those organisations with access to a greater amount of resources, such as Amnesty International, Human Rights Watch and Oxfam. These groups accounted for 50 % of all NGO news appearances between 2010 and 2012 (Thrall et al. 2014:10–11).

Therefore, for many NGOS, the use of Web 2.0 technologies to communicate directly with the public has been appealing. Their public diplomacy 2.0 strategies have included online petitions, hosting of campaign websites, charitable engagements and partnerships with interested parties to effect international protests. Amnesty International has increased its presence on Twitter by linking up with university student unions and 'eminent person diplomats' such as those within the Elders programme (including the late South African President Nelson Mandela and former US President Jimmy Carter). By establishing a strong online presence, it has directed public attention to its activities to engender diplomatic action regarding human rights abuse.

THE KONY 2012 CAMPAIGN

The wider use of social media for the mobilisation of public interest was evident in the KONY 2012 campaign. *KONY 2012* was a 30-minute film that was posted on popular video-sharing sites, including YouTube and Vimeo, by Invisible Children, a San Diego-based non-profit organisation. It detailed the atrocities in northern Uganda committed by the

LRA, led by the warlord Joseph Kony. The film showed how Kony's rebel militia had forced child soldiers to take up arms, and it outlined Invisible Children's mission to have the brutal insurgent imprisoned as a war criminal. Towards the end of the film, President Obama was shown authorising the deployment of 100 US Special Forces advisors to assist the Central African countries' efforts to remove Kony. The film concluded by asking its viewers to publicise its online campaign to fight the LRA's human rights abusers. Throughout the film, the makers reminded viewers of the global power of the World Wide Web to press for change in governments' foreign policies.

By 1 March 2014, *KONY 2012* had received over 120 million views, with 1.3 million 'likes' on YouTube and over 21.9 thousand 'likes' on Vimeo. Indeed, the intense global interest engendered by the video led to the Invisible Children website crashing shortly after the film had been placed on the site. In the immediate aftermath of the release of *KONY 2012*, polls indicated that more than half of America's young adult population had accessed the programme, and *Time* declared it the most 'viral video in history'. In turn, *KONY 2012* was picked up by the conventional news media, which had previously ignored the topic. In March 2012, the Kony story appeared 28 times in *The New York Times* and on 603 occasions in the major world publications (Thrall et al. 2014:15).

However, in the fallout, *KONY 2012* received significant criticism from other NGOs and regional specialists. It was accused of providing an oversimplified account of the region rather than addressing the complex power relations that exist within Central Africa. Alex De Waal contended that the video was 'naïve' in its 'peddling [of] dangerous and patronizing falsehoods', turning 'Kony [in]to a global celebrity, the embodiment of evil', instead of 'reducing him to [the status of] a common criminal and a failed provincial politician' (De Waal 2012). It was further argued that the film's 'consumerist' approach provided a 'feel-good' response to conflict resolution, to assuage the guilt of Western audiences. At the time of this writing, Kony has yet to be caught. The Invisible Children programme has collapsed in the shadow of one viral moment, conventional media coverage has returned to pre-*KONY 2012* levels of neglect and public interest has moved on to the next item of 'disposable' foreign affairs.

Therefore, despite NGOs' greater access to the means of communication, the social media appear to provide a more challenging environment for those groups seeking global attention. Within a quantitative survey of social media coverage of 257 human rights organisations, A. Trevor Thrall, Diana Sweet and Dominik Stecula (Thrall et al. 2014) discovered that:

- Rather than solving the problem of coverage, the Internet has further polarised the attention of the global public. For example, the top 10 % of the NGOs sampled accounted for 90 % of YouTube views, 81 % of Facebook likes and 92 % of Twitter followers.
- There was a direct relationship between the size of an NGO's budget and its ability to generate attention within traditional news outlets and social media, with results indicating a threshold of around $10 million annually before an NGO started to receive attention.
- Most NGOs lacked the organisational resources to effectively compete for public attention, and the Internet was unlikely to resolve the problem of global communication.
- The continuing fragmentation of the mass audience was leading to a shorter public attention span, providing greater problems for all NGOs (Thrall et al. 2014:14–15).

Thrall et al. explained these results in terms of the 'zero-sum nature of public attention'. They argued that the Internet had effectively traded one attention-seeking medium (e.g., television) for another. To capture the fleeting attention of the public, NGOs must have the resources to create content that is compelling for the media and the public, thus favouring larger over smaller organisations (Thrall et al. 2014:17):

> We conclude that most NGOs lack the organizational resources to compete effectively for either traditional news coverage or for public attention and that the Internet is unlikely to resolve the problem of global communication. (Thrall et al. 2014:1)

CONCLUSION

In this chapter we have considered the implications of social media for states, NSAs and NGOs in forming new types of diplomatic relations. We have seen how Web 2.0 tools have advanced a transformation in foreign policy practices, from that of a closed community of state diplomats to one that is more open and transparent. PCD strategies are being reconceived as governments realise that they should engage in conversations with a variety of NSAs and grassroots actors to be more favourably received by the international public. These forms of public diplomacy 2.0 reflect the changing geometric flow of communication, as vertical hierarchies of expression are being replaced by an equitable web of horizontal links. Therefore, states have realised that their leaders, ambassadors, diplomats and officials should be fully conversant within the blogosphere, Facebook, Flickr and Twitter.

Consequently, the USA and UK have effected new forms of diplomatic statecraft to enhance alternative types of information management, consular communication and response, and assurance of Internet freedom. In turn, governments must understand that they are no longer perceived as the most powerful and credible sources of public information. Rather, they must empower other players in their target network to engage within the electronic public sphere. As such, an online agora may facilitate a range of ideological and political agendas which will contribute to the formation of a global diplomatic consensus. Ultimately, governments must act in a reciprocal manner within online communities comprising NSAs, NGOs, corporate players and public representatives:

> Most urge the would-be digital diplomat to go to the sites where one's desired audience is located and to engage them in their own language with due attention to the dominant practices of that site. Many also acknowledge that in a networked world one must create information not as an impressive show for a one-time end user...but on the assumption that it will live or die as a 'meme': be passed along a peer-to-peer network; variously 'liked', shared and 're-tweeted'. While one can never call up a 'viral' message to order one can at least create messages in a succinct form that is easy to pass on to others. (Cull 2011:26)

This expansion of Internet-based social networks has placed greater emphasis on person-to-person communications, from which a 'new public diplomacy' has emerged. These principles of public diplomacy 2.0 have been defined by Clay Shirky's proposition that the social media may provide 'access to a conversation...[rather]...than access to information' (Shirky 2011).

However, as information bestows knowledge rights, there is the danger that an ill-informed conversation, prejudiced by prevailing hegemonic relations, will undermine diplomatic affairs. For instance, many of the new forms of communication require short messages, which are much easier to 'spin' and misrepresent. Furthermore, it remains unclear whether powerful states such as the USA are prepared to cede control of their PCD messages. Instead, they have sought the covert use of social media, under the cloak of openness and transparency, to propagate their own interests:

> Yet there is an unresolved tension in the way US public diplomacy policy-makers have articulated the relationship of technology to public diplomacy. While Glassman and McHale explained the demands of the contemporary media ecology—that to be credible and influential is to be *present* in social media spaces and time frames associated with those platforms—these arguments nevertheless imply that such technologies *are the more efficient means of dissemination available to states.* (Hayden 2012:7–8)

This has led to a greater emphasis on the use of public diplomacy 2.0 techniques as practiced by NGOs. It has been suggested that social media will enable these organisations to become truly autonomous in their ability to mobilise public opinion and direct attention to a multitude of causes. At one level, Web 2.0 technologies have facilitated opportunities for NGOs to coordinate disaster relief programmes such as the 2010 Haiti earthquake response. At another, NGOs have been liberated from media filters, using social media to target specific segments of the public. For example, NGOs have propagated information across cyberspace about matters of climate change, environmentalism and human rights. Notably, the KONY 2012 campaign used the video-sharing sites YouTube and Vimeo to post its content, achieving immediate global coverage and widespread public attention.

However, the KONY 2012 initiative was as widely criticised as it was praised. The campaign ultimately proved to be ephemeral, as public interest quickly dissipated, moving on to the next international scandal. The problems associated with competing media and related claims on public attention have become manifest as the demand for instant gratification has intensified. As Thrall et al. concluded in their survey of social media coverage of NGOs, online campaigns have enjoyed only fleeting success (Thrall et al. 2014:20). While the social media have the potential to bring about a greater degree of public consciousness, it remains unclear whether lesser-known NGOs have adequate social capital to lay claim to long-term public commitment.

Therefore, in this this chapter we have shown that the use of Web 2.0 technologies in state, NSA and NGO forms of public diplomacy has yielded mixed results. While the principles of public diplomacy 2.0 have become normative aims for most modern governments, the full implication of these changes in diplomatic communications is only beginning to be realised. Moreover, public attention has already reached a saturation point, and it is difficult to evaluate whether more complicated international concerns can be distilled into a series of 'likes', 'number of views' and 're-tweets' as a measure of success. Finally, the international focus predominantly on the Global North must be reconsidered, and it is the purpose of this analysis to uncover the extent to which the social media have created new public spheres within the Global South.

BIBLIOGRAPHY

Barbrook R. 2007. *Imaginary Futures: From Thinking Machines to the Global Village*. London: Pluto Press.

Bernays E. 1928. *Propaganda*. New York: Horace Liveright.

Cull N.J. 2011. "WikiLeaks, Public Diplomacy 2.0 and the State of Digital Public Diplomacy". *Place Branding and Public Diplomacy* 7(1): 1–8.

Cull N.J. 2012. "The Long Road to Public Diplomacy 2.0: The Internet in U.S. Public Diplomacy", Paper Presented to the workshop on 'International Relationships in the Information Age,' International Studies Association, Harvard University. http://www.ash.harvard.edu/extension/ash/docs/cull.pdf (accessed June 18, 2014).

Cull N.J. 2013. "The Long Road to Public Diplomacy 2.0: The Internet in U.S. Public Diplomacy". *International Studies Review* 15(1): 123–139.

De Waal, A. 2012. Don't Elevate Kony, *World Peace Foundation*, March 10. http://sites.tufts.edu/reinventingpeace/2012/03/10/dont-elevate-kony/ (accessed June 18, 2014).

Fattor E.M. 2014. *American Empire and the Arsenal of Entertainment: Soft Power and Culture Weaponization*. Basingstoke: Palgrave MacMillan.

Fletcher T. 2012. "The Naked Diplomat", *Foreign and Commonwealth Office Global Conversation Blog*, October 2. http://blogs.fco.gov.uk/tomfletcher/2012/10/02/the-naked-diplomat (accessed June 18, 2014).

Gao H., G. Barbier, and R. Goolsby. 2011. "Harnessing the Crowdsourcing Power of Social Media for Disaster Relief". *Cyber-Physical-Social Systems* 26: 10–14. Arizona: IEEE Computer Systems.

Glassman J.K. 2008. "Public Diplomacy 2.0: A New Approach to Global Engagement", *United States State Department Archive*, December 1. http://20012009.state.gov/r/us/2008/112605.htm (accessed June 18, 2014).

Hall S., C. Critcher, T. Jefferson, J. Clarke, and B. Roberts. 1978. *Policing the Crisis: Mugging, the State and Law and Order*. London: MacMillan.

Hayden C. 2012. "Social Media at State: Power, Practice, and Conceptual Limits for US Public Diplomacy". *Global Media Journal* 11(12): 1–21.

Harris B. 2013. "Diplomacy 2.0: The Future of Social Media in Nation Branding". *Exchange: The Journal of Public Diplomacy* 4(1): 17–32.

Herman, E., and N. Chomsky. 2009. "The Propaganda Model after 20 Years: Interview with Edward S. Herman and Noam Chomsky" by Andrew Mullen, *Westminster Papers in Communication and Culture*, November. http://www.chomsky.info/interviews/200911--.htm (accessed June 18, 2014).

Hocking B. 2005. "Rethinking the 'New' Public Diplomacy". In *The New Public Diplomacy: Soft Power in International Relations*, ed. J. Melissen. Basingstoke: Palgrave MacMillan.

Kent, M. 2013. Invited Talk to London Metropolitan University Diplomacy Students. February 28. http://www.londonmet.ac.uk/news/news-stories/university-news-2013/university-news-february/lmnews-ambassador-visit-sums-up-diplomacy-course (accessed June 18, 2014).

Khatib L., W. Dutton, and M. Thelwall. 2012. "Public Diplomacy 2.0: A Case Study of the US Digital Outreach Team". *The Middle East Journal* 66(3): 453–472.

McHale J.A. 2011. *Opening Remarks at the Council on Foreign Relations: A Review of U.S. Public Diplomacy*. New York. June 21.

Melissen J. 2011. Beyond the New Public Diplomacy. Clingendael Paper No. 3. October 2011. Amsterdam: Netherlands Institute of International Relations.

Mytko G. 2012. The United Kingdom and the Rise of Digital Public Diplomacy, *Exchange: The Journal of Public Diplomacy*, September 28. http://www.exchangediplomacy.com/the-united-kingdom-and-the-rise-of-digital-publicdiplomacy (accessed June 18, 2014).

Newsweek Staff. 2009. The Man Who Sells America Abroad, *Newsweek*, February 2. http://www.newsweek.com/man-who-sells-america-abroad-77853 (accessed June 18, 2014).

Nicolson H. 1939. *Diplomacy: a Basic Guide to the Conduct of Contemporary Foreign Affairs*. London: Harcourt Brace & Co.

Nye J.S. 2002. "The Information Revolution and American Soft Power". *Asia-Pacific Review* 9(1): 60–76.

Nye J.S. 2004. *Soft Power: The Means to Success in World Politics*. New York: Public Affairs.

Pigman G.A. 2010. *Contemporary Diplomacy: Representation and Communication in the Global World*. Cambridge: Polity Publishers.

Powell C. 2001. quoted from Selling a Nation, *Marketing Week*, November 8.

Puttnam D. 1997. *The Undeclared War: The Struggle for Control of the World's Film Industry*. London: HarperCollins.

Quinn G. 2014. Speech Almaty Kazakhstan: British Diplomacy in the Information Age, *Gov.UK*, April 3. https://www.gov.uk/government/speeches/british-diplomacy-in-the-information-age (accessed June 18, 2014).

Sandre A. 2013. Global Interconnectivity, Social Diplomacy and Non-state Actors, *Huffington Post*. April 12. http://www.huffingtonpost.com/andreas-sandre/global-interconnectivity-_b_3071557.html (accessed June 18, 2014).

Segrave K. 1997. *American Film Abroad: Hollywood Domination of the World's Movie Screens*. Jefferson, NC: McFarland & Co.

Seib P. 2012. *Real-Time Diplomacy: Politics and Power in the Social Media*. Basingstoke: Palgrave MacMillan.

Shirky C. 2011. The Political Power of Social Media: Technology, the Public Sphere, and Political Change, *Foreign Affairs*, January/February issue. http://www.foreignaffairs.com/articles/67038/clay-shirky/the-political-power-of-social-media (accessed March 21, 2014).

Sunstein C. 2007. *Republic.com 2.0*. Princeton, NJ: Princeton University Press.

Thrall A.T., D. Stecula, and D. Sweet. 2014. "May We Have Your Attention Please? Human-Rights NGOs and the Problem of Global Communication". *International Journal of Press/Politics* 19(1): 1–22.

Wiseman, G. 2010. 'Polylateralism': Diplomacy's Third Dimension. *Public Diplomacy Magazine* 1: 24–39.

Zaharna R.S., and W.A. Rugh. 2012. "Issue Theme: The Use of Social Media in U.S. Public Diplomacy—Guest Editors Note". *Global Media Journal* 11(12): 1–8.

PART III

The Rise of the BRICS and On-line Interest

CHAPTER 8

Russia and China: Autocratic and On-line

INTRODUCTION

Here we introduce the reader to the third and final section of the book, which shifts the focus from mature, liberal democracies, to non-Western, developing countries as well as authoritarian regimes, and explore the relationship between online mobilisation and policy change in these parts of the world. The proliferation of new technologies and new forms of network action are challenging traditional notions of civil society, and civic action is becoming increasingly adaptable in Brazil, Russia, India, China and South Africa (BRICS) and other southern states. While the vastly increased access to information and the ability to communicate easily and rapidly can empower citizens and contribute to democracy in the non-Western world, some voices have argued that these expectations have failed to materialise, illuminating the limitations of social media activism, as authoritarian rule has survived the arrival of the Internet and has bent the technology to its own purposes. In this chapter we consider the role of social networking tools in the creation of an online public sphere and as a means of initiating mass protests and uprisings in the authoritarian regimes of China and Russia, while the chapters that follow will focus on the postcolonial powers of India and South Africa, the post-industrialised societies of Brazil, Japan and South Korea, and the Arab Spring countries.

The Internet had been expected to help democratise countries like China and Russia. Just as earlier communications technologies may have

© The Editor(s) (if applicable) and The Author(s) 2016
P. Iosifidis, M. Wheeler, *Public Spheres and Mediated Social Networks in the Western Context and Beyond*,
DOI 10.1057/978-1-137-41030-6_8

helped topple past dictatorships (e.g., the telegraph in Russia's Bolshevik revolutions in 1917 and short-wave radio in the dissolution of the Soviet Union in 1991), the Internet would enable people to mobilise in contemporary Russia and erode China's authoritarian state. In reality, however, it often enabled the authoritarian state to get a firmer grip. Within the county's borders, the Communist Party of China (CPC) has systematically put in place projects such as the 'Great Firewall', which keeps out 'undesirable' foreign websites like Facebook, Twitter and YouTube, and the 'Golden Shield Project', which monitors activities within the vast country. Sina Weibo is now the predominant microblogging service (similar to Twitter in the West), but in contrast to Twitter's open philosophy, the Chinese version is a system of arbitrary censorship. Meanwhile, the effect of social media on democratisation in Russia is questionable, as social platforms are vulnerable to government pressure. In 2014, postmodern tsar Vladimir Putin, a former KGB operative who has since been elected twice each as Prime Minister and President, signed into law a bill that boosts government control over the Internet, despite a campaign warning that it would lead to widespread censorship. The new regulations, which went into effect in August 2014, are aimed at silencing opposition websites, while also providing the Russian government with a wealth of user data.[1]

In this chapter we discuss whether the expectations of a free Internet have been confounded in these two autocratic countries. First, we offer statistical data demonstrating social media take-up and discuss how the local citizens in these countries have embraced them, exploring the technological, economic and political factors that have shaped the Internet and social media within Russia and China. We then consider the various forms of Internet censorship practiced by the two governments and the level of online freedom of expression. Here we argue that not only have the repressive regimes survived the advancement of the Internet and social media, but both states have shown skill in bending the technology to their own interests.

INTERNET AND SOCIAL MEDIA TAKE-UP IN RUSSIA AND CHINA

Internet and Social Media Take-up in Russia

Both Russia and China have witnessed explosive growth in the number of Internet and social media users and in the number of social media chan-

---

[1] See http://asozd2.duma.gov.ru/main.nsf/(SpravkaNew)?OpenAgent&RN=428884-6&02 (accessed 8 December 2014)

nels. In 2011, Russia became the largest online market in Europe, with about 51 million Internet users, overtaking former leaders Germany (50 million Internet users), France (43 million) and the UK (37 million).[2] In 2014, the number of Internet users in Russia reached an astonishing 90 million, who spent more than 40 % of their time online on social networking sites. Interestingly, however, Facebook is much less popular in Russia than in other European countries, with only 23.2 million unique users who spend an average of 1 hour per visit. Founded in 2006, Vkontakte (now called 'VK', which literally translates to 'in contact') is the most popular Russian social networking site, with an average of 50.2 million unique visitors. VK closely resembles Facebook and offers many similar social media functions, but users can also use it to stream all types of entertainment media. While VK is more widely used by the younger 11–25 age demographic, the second most popular site, Odnoklassniki, with 45 million unique users, is preferred by adults. Also founded in 2006, the Odnoklassniki network is similar to classmates.com, and allows users to get in touch with long-lost childhood friends and family members.

Mail.ru, or MoiMir, which is focused mainly on email communication, online gaming and music sharing, holds third place among the social networking sites with just under 40 million unique monthly visitors, followed by Facebook and the frequently visited LiveJournal, which offers an online blogging service, with user interactions that include friend pages and online communities. Launched in 1999, LiveJournal. ru is the most popular blog in Russia, and it is looking increasingly like a national mass media portal. It holds a position of authority, and as a trusted source, it has become a reputable alternative platform for political discussion about prime civic events. Twitter and Instagram are also popular and growing rapidly in the Russian social media market (see Table 8.1). Other popular sites include the Russian LinkedIn equivalent, Moikrug.ru, which was founded in 2005 by graduates of Moscow State University.

Therefore, it is clear that the Russian social networks have seen strong, rapid expansion, but does this enhanced online communication offer a 'magic bullet' that can empower citizens and change regimes? In her book *Revolution Stalled. The Political Limits of the Internet in the Post-Soviet Sphere*, Oates (2013) recognises both the potential for and barriers to the Internet's ability to deliver democratisation. Her main point is that the

---

[2] See http://www.russiansearchtips.com/2012/01/russia-becomes-the-biggest-online-market-in-europe (accessed 29 December 2014)

Table 8.1 Top ten social networks among Internet users in Russia (March 2014)

Social network sites	Unique visitors (millions)	% of Internet users
VK	50.2	73.9
Odnoklassniki	45	57.9
Mail.ru	40.0	40.3
Facebook	23.2	34.1
LiveJournal	14.1	20.8
Twitter	11.8	17.4
Instagram	8.3	12.2
Google+	8.1	12.0
Fotostrana	6.8	10.0
Sprashivai.ru	6.4	9.4

democratising potential of the Internet should be assessed within the constraints of national political systems. In her view:

> ... the Russian case proves that much of the democratizing potential of the Internet may have been limited by the government's almost complete control of the national information sphere, an ingrained sense of self-censorship on the part of Russian 'netizens', as well as a general lack of interest in the internet as an authoritative voice for citizens. (Oates 2013:26)

Internet and Social Media Take-up in China

Like Russia, China has also experienced impressive growth in Internet users and (local) social networking sites over the past few years. While Russia is now the largest online market in Europe, China is the single largest market of Internet users and social media consumers in the world. In January 2014, the China Internet Network Information Centre (CNNIC 2014) reported that the number of Internet users in China had reached 618 million at the end of 2013, an increase of about 54 million over 2012. China's Ministry of Industry and Information Technology (MIIT) expects the number to grow to a new high of 800 million users by 2015 (see Yu Hong 2011). There are two drivers behind this uplift. First, Internet infrastructure has developed at a remarkable speed, whereas the country's wider 3G coverage and the growth of local smartphone manufacturers have made the Internet more accessible and affordable. Second, the blocking of social media platforms from the West, such as Facebook, Twitter and YouTube, has led to the development of home-grown social media websites including Weixin (WeChat) and Sina Weibo, with 600 million and 280 million active users, respectively, as of April 2014 (Cicero Group 2014; Social Media Fast Facts: China 2014). According to Cicero Group analysis, the social media market is vibrant and competitive, with recent developments pointing to three overarching trends:

- The user base is still growing, albeit at a slower pace. At the end of 2013, Internet penetration was highest in China's largest and most developed cities, and most subsequent growth would be in less developed regions and rural areas. In any case, there is still huge potential for growth, as Internet penetration in 2013 stood at 45.8 % of the population.
- Social media platforms are increasingly going mobile. In 2013 there were 500 million mobile Internet users, with 60 million new mobile Internet users between 2012 and 2013 alone.
- Advertising, especially on social media platforms, is quickly gaining momentum. The number of businesses advertising via social media is growing, as most platforms have an integrated advertising and marketing content management system, allowing businesses to easily promote their products (Cicero Group 2014).

Social media platforms in China are highly diverse (e.g., there are nine major operators of instant messaging tools, four microblogging platforms and four social network services), but they are more domestic than global. In terms of microblogging platforms, the service dominating the market is the Twitter-like Weibo (meaning microblog), which allows users to post short messages. The top four Weibo services in China are Sina Weibo, Tencent Weibo, NetEase Weibo and Sohu Weibo. In April 2014, these sites collectively reached 97 % penetration of the social media market, with the dominant network Sina Weibo (founded in 2009) claiming 280 million active users and 500 million registered users. However, most of these services have recently suffered a loss of active users, as netizens are moving to mobile, and the number of instant messaging platforms is growing. In fact, the Chinese instant messaging market is vibrant and even more diverse than that of its Western peers, and although most of the instant messaging tools have been available less than 3 years, the number of users is considerable, and growing rapidly. As a comparison, for example, one of the most popular instant messaging tools in the West, WhatsApp, announced in 2014 that it had exceeded 500 million active users 5 years after its launch, whereas WeChat, a major instant messaging service in China, achieved this figure within a mere 2 years. Meanwhile, social network services in the country launched before the emergence of Weibo and instant messaging platforms provide an online communication route for netizens to post, share and exchange information in the same way as Facebook and LinkedIn outside China. RenRen, introduced in 2005, is the most popular social network site, with a registered active user base of 194 million, followed by KaiXin001, Douban and Qzone (see Table 8.2).

Despite the diversity of the Chinese social media landscape, censorship is prevalent, and a sophisticated firewall has been developed to filter undesirable output. The Internet is closely monitored by the State Council Information Office and MIIT of the People's Republic of China, supervised by the CPC's Central Propaganda Department (CPD). Both are tasked with ensuring that Internet content complies with party policy. For example, the Great Firewall of China prevents Chinese users from accessing sensitive information on foreign homepages, and services like

Table 8.2 Social media landscape in China (end of 2013)

Microblogging platforms	Active users (millions)
Sina Weibo	280.0
Tencent Weibo	230.0
NetEase Weibo	120.0
Sohu Weibo	N/A
Instant messaging	Active users (millions)
WeChat	600.0
Mobile QQ	426.0
Momo	100.0
Mi Talk	40.0
YiXin	39.0
iAround	32.0
WangXin	15.0
LaiWang	10.0
WeMeet	N/A
Social network services	Active users (millions)
RenRen	194.0
KaiXin001	130.0
Douban	75.0
Qzone	63.0

Source: Cicero Group 2014; Social Media Fast Facts: China 2014

Facebook, Twitter and YouTube are not accessible within the country. The heavy censorship of the Chinese Internet also extends to Weibo, where it is enacted by host company Sina (Canaves 2011, cited in Rauchfleisch and Schafer 2015:142). Sina censors content in two ways: first, some content is automatically blocked based on a blacklist containing links and keywords, or is delayed until it has been approved by Sina; second, Sina employs a large number of human censors, who constantly scan Weibo posts for seemingly problematic content (Hui and Rajagopalan 2013, cited in Rauchfleisch and Schafer 2015:142). Some have also expressed scepticism about Weibo's potential to create an online public sphere and initiate open debate, for it is an apolitical space, where popular users and topics are centred around entertainment (Sullivan 2013). Others, though, are more optimistic, emphasising that the Chinese government allows for some degree of public discussion online. The study by Rauchfleisch and Schafer (2015) takes a middle ground, arguing that while censorship is an effective tool, and limits the potential of Weibo and other social media in China, it would be wrong to dismiss their potential altogether, as Weibo's content is not entirely apolitical, and it is not fully government-controlled or censored in all instances.

RUSSIA AND CHINA: THE HISTORICAL AND POLITICAL CONTEXT

From the Soviet Union to Putin's Russia

Russia can be considered an oligarchic regime with a free market economy, which has been performing relatively well in peaceful times because of the rapidly growing world market appetite for natural resources. After World War I, the Marxist–Leninist one-party state emerged as an ideological challenge to liberal democracy. In the 1920s and 1930s, this Marxist–Leninist model—where a power elite dictates both economics and politics—seemed to provide a feasible alternative to the laissez-faire mechanisms of free market economics and limited government prevalent in most of the Western world. With the victory of the Soviet Union and the USA in World War II, the two leading examples of these contrasting models competed for dominance, until the ideological collapse of Communism and the consequent fracturing of the Soviet Union in the early 1990s into its constituent republics. Since then, liberal democracy has been widely perceived as the 'best' system for economic and political modernisation, as evidenced by the spread of liberal capitalist democracies around the world. Seeing the 'writing on the Berlin wall', the political elites, even those in non-free states, realised that they needed to maintain the appearance of 'liberalism' to hold onto power (Partlett 2012).

But elites in certain non-free regimes were reluctant to implement liberal, pluralistic politics, and as a result they developed intricate systems of 'faking' liberal democratic politics in order to legitimise their rule with the appearance of liberal democracy while maintaining their monopoly of power. Partlett (2012) describes how Russia followed this path, first with President Yeltsin's administration and later with Vladimir Putin's rule of political governance, both characterised by electoral fraud and media manipulation. The media in Russia have historically supported government actions and never really acted as a 'fourth estate' in criticising the political elite and giving voice to the citizens, even throughout the glasnost era of 1985–1991. Russian politicians, the public and journalists alike seem to perceive the media as a political tool rather than as a watchdog keeping political power in check on behalf of the citizens (Voltmer 2000). Levitsky and Way (2002) in describing this system of combining democratic rule with authoritarian governance in Russia (but also in other post-communist Eurasia such as Serbia and Ukraine), use the terms 'diminished forms of democracy' or 'competitive authoritarianism', given the prevalence of fraud, civil liberties violations and abuse of state and media resources. They go so far as to say that 'it may be time to stop thinking of these cases in terms of transition to democracy and to begin thinking about the specific types of regimes they actually are' (Levitsky and Way 2002:51). The absence of democratic institutions and the tradition of oligarchic rule enable the Kremlin elite to manipulate the media, elections, parliament and the regions for its own interests.

Indeed, propaganda was seen as a key resource by the Bolsheviks in delivering their social revolution. Once the civil war had begun in 1918, the Bolsheviks banned the other political parties and arrested their leaders, while closing down newspapers that opposed them. Under Lenin's leadership, the Bolsheviks were ruthless (e.g., through the creation of the secret police, 'Cheka') in ensuring that they did not face rebellion. At the same time, they organised a highly effective propaganda campaign. Through speeches, newspapers and leaflets, the people were continually told that *they* were now in charge of Russia, that life would be better than it was under the old system and that the wealth would be distributed more fairly. This type of state intervention and the adoption of a highly centralised governance control model were a profound influence in shaping the cultural industries (film, the arts and the media). For instance, Eisenstein's montage theory in cinema (he is considered the father of montage) was not just about technique, but served a dialectical revolutionary purpose. He used intellectual montage in his feature films, such as *Battleship* and *October*, to portray the political situation surrounding the Bolshevik uprisings. Eisenstein believed that the montage sequence could be used to mould the thought processes in the mind of the viewer, thus representing a powerful tool for propaganda. The film *October*, for example, contains a sequence in which the concept of 'God' is connected to class structure, and several images containing overtones of political authority and divinity are edited together in descending order of impressiveness, such that the idea of God eventually becomes associated with a block of wood. Eisenstein believed that this sequence caused the viewer to subconsciously automatically reject all political class structures (Goodwin 1993).

In terms of state media, the political newspaper *Pravda* and the telegraph agency TASS were centrally controlled and allowed for no dissident expression. This is evidenced by the handling of the accident in the nuclear power complex in Chernobyl, Ukraine, on 26 April 1986, in which massive radioactive contamination spread across much of Ukraine and Belorussia. The Soviet leadership's handling of the accident was the first serious test of Gorbachev's glasnost in the mass media. The Soviet authorities met on 28 April, 2 days after the disaster, to discuss how much information to release, and decided that only a handful of highly placed and centralised sources (*Pravda*, TASS, *Izvestiya* and central television) would issue reports in a gradual manner in order to avoid greater harm and the spread of panic. 'TASS's first, brief dispatch issued some 65 hours after the accident said only that an accident had occurred at the reactor. It was followed within 45 minutes by a TASS release about nuclear accidents in the United States. Pravda's terse initial coverage ran on the lower right corner of page two of its May Day edition, headlined simply "from the USSR Council of Ministers". Gorbachev, who only recently had elaborated upon the merits of glasnost, stayed largely silent on the matter for more than two weeks' (Gibbs 1999:41–42). The Chernobyl disaster shows domestic news handling of the event that was carefully controlled and managed by the authorities and the media through the consistent omission or distortion of several points, highlighting the limitations of the policies of glasnost (openness) and perestroika (restructuring).

The Traditional Media and the Role of the ICT
in Social Movements

One might expect that the democratising power of the ICTs, the Internet and the social media, combined with the Russian government's policy of expanding online access, would enhance political and media openness. After all, the Soviet policy of glasnost in the 1980s offered Soviet leaders a way to encourage lively debate, and wound up with central media outlets that were critical of the serving elite (Michiewicz 1988, 1997). Yet the Russian administration seem to remember the central role played by the media in the collapse of the Soviet Union in 1991, and are reluctant to repeat the same mistake. In effect, the Russian state not only seeks to control the Internet, but is actively using it to expand its communicative power (Diebert et al. 2010). To be sure, the Internet has certain features that define its role as communication provider, social networking vehicle and a virtual sphere for democratic debate. But these functions manifest themselves in different ways in different societies (see Hallin and Mancini 2004), and one thus needs to determine the specific media and political ecology within which the Internet operates.

Online research vehicles should be located within specific national political institutions and communications structures. Commentators including Fossato et al. (2008), Lonkila (2008) and Oates (2013) have stated that, to assess whether the post-Soviet Internet has enhanced civic life within the country, it must be placed in its political context. For example, the work by Fossato et al. focused on three specific social movements (a nationalist and liberal movement and a citizen group campaigning for fair treatment of motorists), all inspired by blogs, and each aiming to criticise the Russian government on particular matters. Their study, which used web content analysis and interviews with bloggers, found that the blogosphere played a modest role in initiating public discussion in the online and offline worlds, largely because of the vulnerability of Russian bloggers to the pressure of the elites. The project by Oates (2013) considered the intersection between political interest and online activity, and in this context examined how political parties (United Russia, the Communist Party of the Russian Federation, the Liberal-Democratic Party of Russia, and A Just Russia) used the online sphere to garner support. One of the main findings was that, two decades after the end of Soviet rule, political parties in Russia appeared to have done little to foster democracy. On the contrary, successive Russian presidential administrations have used the media to create and manipulate political images. Specifically with regard to the Internet, the study concluded that the medium tended to 'reflect' rather than 'challenge' offline political power and political communication.

Oates' study (2013) also looked at the state of freedom of speech and information distribution in Russia as defined by its Soviet past in comparison to both Western models and to the former Soviet sphere. A number of democratic institutional failures were found, including ineffective political parties, a weak legislature, the lack of an independent judiciary and media that do not function as a fourth estate. Oates saw the young Russian non-free state as providing a 'communications paradox in that there is so much information and so little democracy. The country has a wealth of media outlets and a range of opinions that are expressed in broadcast, print and Internet outlets [but the] contemporary Russian media has more to do with the Soviet media than any Western model....[C]entral television stations in Russia retain a particular political influence [while] self-censorship is endemic in the journalism industry' (12–13).

In the run-up to the Sochi Winter Olympics in February 2014, state-owned Channel One rebranded itself as 'First Olympic' and banned the reporting of any criticism of the Olympics, Putin's greatest legacy. Meanwhile, RIA Novosti, the state news agency, which was traditionally loyal to the Kremlin but in a subtly intelligent way, changed ownership, and with a new television presenter, Dmitry Kiselev, began to transmit openly anti-American propaganda and homophobic rants that one would expect to experience during the Soviet times. Various private broadcasters, directly or indirectly, came to be under the control of the media empire owned by Yury Kovalchuk, a friend of Putin's who holds a large stake in Gazprom Media (Russia's largest media group, controlling five TV channels, seven radio stations and a publishing company). Obviously, state-run or private media with close ties to the Russian political elite cannot provide a space for critical political discussion, but instead serve as a means of reinforcing the status quo. 'Non-free Russian media can create and hunt enemies both in the country and abroad, blaming Russia's troubles on traitors and ill-wishers' (*The Economist* 15 February 2014:27–28).

Given the failings of traditional media, Oates (2013) asks whether the Internet can provide a vehicle for effective political action. As shown above, Russia has grown from relatively low Internet usage in the former Soviet region, to the largest European online presence, suggesting that the growth of online communication can be a positive force for political awareness and freedom. In fact, in 2011, Moscow witnessed the largest pro-democracy protests since the dissident movements of the 1960s and 1970s[3] and the collapse of the Soviet Union in 1991, with tens of thousands of people gathering in main squares to oppose the 2011 Russian legislative election process, which many people considered to be corrupt. New information and communication technologies such as social media played a crucial role in the organisation, mobilisation and representation of these protests. 'One key way to spur protest was the collection of video evidence of voter irregularity and fraud to post online, making it difficult for the officials to refute or manipulate the information' (Oates 2013:18). Furthermore, social networking sites such as VK and blogging sites such as LiveJournal encouraged debate and aggregation of interests. The mainstream media in the Western world regarded such collective action as a new link in the chain of global political movements that had begun in North Africa and the Middle East, and dubbed it a 'social media revolution'. But was the winter 2011 unrest the first manifestation of a rising political consciousness on the part of the Russian citizens, or was it instead a series of isolated events, specifically motivated by compelling evidence of electoral fraud?

The massive December 2011 protests in Moscow were aimed at electoral fraud, the most important aspect of Russian fake democracy, with many of the protestors expressing their dissatisfaction with distortions, cronyism and corruption, and urging Putin to take steps towards 'real' democracy, or risk undermining the regime (Partlett 2012). However, in the aftermath of the events, it became clear that the Russian authoritarian leadership had managed to overcome the protest movement by containing and controlling online dissent. Russian authorities used their leverage over domestic networks to contain online opposition to the regime. In cases where non-democratic governments have control over the content and structure of social networks, users lose the ability to access independent points of view and learn about government malfeasance. 'Not only is information sharing monitored and potentially blocked, but democracy activists avoid networks connected with government authorities for fear of reprisals'. This is illustrated by the story of Russia's most popular social networking platform, VK, which in March 2013 reportedly collaborated with Kremlin officials to gather intelligence on opposition groups that used the site. It was no coincidence that

---

[3] In the late 1960s and early 1970s, the Soviet government was subject to criticism from opposition activists who were kept as political prisoners in camps in the Perm region.

a few months before the start of the Sochi Olympics, VK had been taken over by a Kremlin-friendly oligarch, Alisher Usmanov. What this discussion suggests is that, while the Internet and social media were able to spur protest in several ways during the 'winter of discontent', their effect on democratisation is limited when domestic social platforms are vulnerable to government pressure and control of activity in the online sphere. The state is strengthening its grip on the Internet, as evidenced by the passage of new online laws (see below). The picture that emerges, according to Oates (2013:22) is at first confusing—in that Russia has invested heavily in increasing online connectivity, while simultaneously limiting free speech online—but becomes clear when it is approached from the broader perspective of the Russian state and citizen information control.

Internet Regulation and Online Censorship

The first .ru domain in the Russian Federation went online in 1994, at a time when Internet in the country was in its very early stages of life. Russian authorities largely overlooked the country's Internet sector as having any significance in economic or social terms. However, as the number of adult Internet users grew from just nine million, or 8 % of the adult population, in 2001, to 65 million, or 55 % of the adult population, at the end of 2013, the leadership thought it necessary to regulate the medium, initially by setting up clear goals and methods of use, with enhanced transparency. It later became obvious, however, that the Kremlin sought to control the content of the Internet. The battle for control started with the passage of a law in November 2012 that allowed the government to block, without a court order, websites deemed to promote suicide, illegal drugs or child pornography (other criteria initially proposed as grounds for a ban included 'propaganda of extremism' and of homosexuality, but these were dropped after public outcry). In effect, about 150 websites were on the blacklist as of July 2013, but according to independent watchdog Rublacklist.net, another 6800 unrelated sites fell victim to the ban because the government was using a flawed blocking mechanism, targeting IP addresses instead of URLs. Opposition leaders railed against the law as a 'crack' in the doorway to broader Internet censorship. The major concern was that social networks, which had been used to arrange protests against Putin, would be stifled. The heightened Internet regulation coincided with a much broader Kremlin crackdown on political activism, as Putin returned for a third presidential term in spring 2012. In fact, since the middle of 2013, authorities have filed cases against political opposition leaders and rank-and-file activists, and have tightened legislation on public rallies, media and NGOs.

Even so, in Russia there is lack of direct censorship in the manner found in China, which simultaneously censors web content and uses the Internet as a further means of identifying and punishing dissidents, thereby turning the Internet into more a tool for repression than a beacon of democracy. But the lack of direct censorship in Russia does not indicate a dearth of control, for Russia's online media management is achieved through norms of self-censorship and a fear of severe consequences for challenging elites on key issues such as the 2013 war in Chechnya (Oates 2013:23) or the 2014 military intervention in Ukraine and internationally condemned annexation of the Crimean Peninsula. Diebert et al. (2010) defined such methods as 'third-generation Internet control', wherein the use of the Internet is encouraged as a way to spread government propaganda and misinformation. Indeed, recent laws and policies have been initiated that undermine the value of the Internet as a democratising vehicle. In July 2014, Russia's State Duma (lower house of parliament) and Federation Council (upper house of parliament) adopted amendments to Russia's personal data protection act which require personal data of all Russians to be stored on Russian-based servers. This 'data localisation' requirement will have a major impact on global social networking companies such as Facebook, Twitter and Google that transmit electronic communications over the Internet. Essentially, any foreign company using the personal data of Russian nationals outside the country must locate its servers in Russian Federation territory; otherwise, access to this type of information resource will be blocked. This move is seen to bode poorly for Internet freedom in Russia.

The law was understood to come into effect in 2016, but the Kremlin decided to accelerate its implementation in order to ban most foreign web services and retain influence in light of the conflict at the time between the West and Russia over the Crimean annexation. It follows the general trend towards strict state regulation of the Internet in Russia. For example, in September 2014, the Security Council, with Putin in attendance, was debating implementing a special order of Internet governance, presuming the possibility of disconnecting Russia from the global network. If this goes ahead, it will allow the Kremlin to switch off Russia's Internet in the case of an emergency situation, such as during a war or large-scale protests (Koshkin 2014). It appears that while the authorities under Vladimir Putin largely ignored the Internet through the 2000s, allowing the spawning of a vibrant and fast-growing industry, the government has gone on a regulatory tear since late 2011, when Moscow was hit by large anti-Putin protests that were largely coordinated online. Several extrajudicial Internet blacklists have been introduced, giving rise to concerns of heightened political censorship (Eremenko 2014). According to the Kazan-based human rights watchdog Agora, 103 criminal cases were filed in 2013 against bloggers and Internet commentators based on their posts in 2012, an almost threefold year-on-year increase. Popular 'political' bloggers are now required to register with the government, evidence that the Kremlin seeks to monitor all private communications of its citizens around the clock. Nevertheless, while this move could enable the political elite to maintain their power monopoly at least in the short run, it can be viewed as an abuse of state power and a violation of civil liberties.

The Gated China

Whereas Russia can be perceived as an oligarchic regime with a free market economy, the People's Republic of China (China) is an autocratic one-party state offering an alternative model to that of democracy, at least as the notion is regarded in the West (free elections, freedom of speech and freedom to organise). The country has been reborn through a transition from the dark early decades of China to a place at the pinnacle of the modern world. Under one-party rule, China today is not only the manifestation of an economic miracle; it is also witnessing the renaissance of its ancient culture and learning, including the visible revival of Confucianism (a philosophical system developed from the teachings of the Chinese philosopher Confucius). China has survived political maelstroms and economic disasters at home, and ideological isolation and fallout internationally. From the disastrous Cultural Revolution under Mao Zedong[4] to the Tiananmen democracy crackdown[5] and the fall of the Berlin Wall in 1989, China has fought it out internally, closed ranks and moved forward

---

[4] In 1966 Mao launched the 'Cultural Revolution', aiming to purge the country of 'impure' elements and revive the revolutionary spirit. However, 1.5 million people died, and much of the country's cultural heritage was destroyed.

[5] The Tiananmen Square protests of spring 1989 were student-led demonstrations in Beijing, and received broad support from city residents but were forcibly suppressed by Chinese leaders, who ordered the military to enforce martial law in the country's capital, resulting in many casualties among unarmed civilians.

under Deng Xiao Ping's pragmatic leadership from 1978 to 1992. China left the Mao saga behind and embarked on a monumental task of building socialism with 'Chinese characteristics'. Vowing to succeed in this task, Deng introduced reforms that shifted the country from a planned to a market economy and opened China to the world after three decades of isolation. In essence, China is a politically authoritarian and powerful state that is running a liberalised market economy. Centralised political power is evidenced by the fact that the current President, Xi Jinping, is China's paramount leader, since he also holds the positions of general secretary of the Communist Party of China and chairman of the Central Military Commission. At the same time, China is now more open to the world (e.g., in 2001 China entered the World Trade Organisation and in 2008 it staged the Olympic Games in Beijing).

The powerful Chinese communist state can be said to offer a credible alternative to capitalism, given that values such as openness, social equality and participation have not always been ideally realised in Western capitalist political systems, characterised by deep social division, economic crises (especially in the Eurozone area) and concentration of economic power in the hands of just a few conglomerates. A notable setback to democracy has been the Iraq War. When Saddam Hussein's fabled weapons of mass destruction failed to materialise after the American-led invasion of 2003, then President George W. Bush shifted the rhetoric instead to justifying the war as a fight for freedom and democracy. This did the democratic cause great harm. The left wing regarded it as proof that democracy was merely a justification for American imperialism, and foreign policy realists took Iraq's growing chaos as proof that 'American-led promotion of democratisation was a recipe for instability' (*The Economist* 2014:49). Given these shortcomings, some observers (Ramo 2004) proposed China's economic development model (often called the 'Beijing model' or 'Beijing Consensus') of the pragmatic use of innovation and experimentation in the service of 'equitable, peaceful high-quality growth' and 'defence of national borders and interests' as superior and a feasible alternative—especially for developing countries—to the 'Washington Consensus' of market-friendly policies promoted by the International Monetary Fund (IMF) and World Bank. The past decade or so has witnessed stable and strong growth of the Chinese economy, with average annual economic growth of 10.7 % between 2003 and 2011, rendering China the second largest economy in the world, with its share of the global economy rising from 4.4 % in 2002 to 10 % in 2011.

Yet China's stunning advances conceal deeper problems. The elite are becoming a self-perpetuating and self-serving clique. According to *The Economist* (1 March 2014:51):

[t]he 50 richest members of the China's National People's Congress are collectively worth $94.7 billion—60 times as much as the 50 richest members of America's Congress. China's growth rate has slowed from 10 % to below 8 % and is expected to fall further—an enormous challenge for a regime whose legitimacy depends on its ability to deliver consistent growth.

The Chinese Communist Party has always sanctioned a 'patriotic' rather than 'democratic' media, and the state-run media has sanctioned and controlled the free flow of information. Propaganda is used by leadership to sway domestic public and international opinion in favour of its policies (Shambaugh 2007). Aspects of propaganda (which domestically include censorship) can be traced back to the earlier periods of Chinese history (e.g., Mao Zedong consistently adopted mass campaigns to legitimise the state and leadership policies), but today it is mainly depicted through cultivation of the economy and the cultural industries. According to Ho and Fung (2015) cultural industries (including visual arts, crafts, performing arts, heritage, film and video, television and radio, online games and new media, music, publishing, fashion, design, architecture and advertising) have made a significant contribution to economic development in modern China. As an extension of the power of 'culture', cultural industries are also regarded as a domain closely related to social cohesion and stability.

In China, state authorities still exercise strict control over the cultural industries, from publishing to music and movie businesses. However, under the backdrop of globalisation, market forces have also been able to intervene in the development of these cultural industries. The interplay between political and market forces has thus profoundly influenced the content and products of these cultural industries, which in turn play a crucial role in shaping the national identity. Internally, the Chinese government aims to develop the domestic cultural market and cultural industries. In the report delivered at the 17th National Congress of the CPC (Xinhua News Agency 2007, cited in Ho and Fung 2015) and the 'Report of the Work of the Government' in 2009 (Xinhua News Agency 2009, cited in Ho and Fung 2015), the government focuses on 'adapting the cultural and creative industries to the specificities of the domestic market and to the specific "local culture"'. Externally, the Chinese government sets its eyes on global markets, to become a leading centre regionally and world-wide. 'Go global' was discussed in the relevant documents as a strategy for China's cultural industries: China should focus on the international scene and enhance its cultural impact internationally through the creation of cooperative platforms, and should export more cultural products 'created in China' than 'made in China' (Keane 2006). In short, China's external cultural policy agenda is to expand the cultural influence of the country and thus increase its 'soft power' (Ho and Fung 2015).

With the belief in the importance of state intervention, the Chinese government has adopted a highly centralised governance model, and controls cultural industries through different administrative bodies such as the Ministry of Culture (MOC), which mainly oversees general cultural activities. Connecting its cultural policy to the ultimate goal of building a harmonious society, the government has set its cultural policy agenda both internally and externally (Ho and Fung 2015). Nevertheless, a country where freedom of expression is suppressed and human rights are not always respected,[6] where the press is censored and where there is no strong opposition party, is a country where the presence of culture and democracy are at least questionable. In terms of the Internet and social media platforms, China is the most relevant and interesting case of an authoritarian regime, because it has established its own microcosm of social media for some time now, and tries to closely monitor and control it and censor problematic content, thereby limiting the influx of non-domestic social media communication (Rauchfleisch and Schafer 2015). The Chinese Party-state chose to live with the Internet inside its borders, not wanting to seal it off completely from the wider web of the world, or the broader segments of its own population (Lagerkvist 2010). When it first arrived in China in 1994, the Internet was a relatively free and unregulated space, widely regarded as a supporting tool for the 'socialist market economy', but government control over the Internet later increased (Endeshaw 2004).

When describing changes in a rapidly developing China, some refer to its media system as 'transitory' and 'mixed' (Curran and Park 2000). After all, social and media globalisation (e.g., increased travel, an elite youth often educated abroad, and foreign-produced television programming and popular culture) is today expected to impact heavily on non-free

---

[6] Numerous human rights groups have claimed that human rights issues in China have been mishandled, including the death penalty, the one-child policy, the dispute over the political and legal status of Tibet and the lack of freedom of the press in mainland China.

states like China. However, other observers (Price, Rozumilowicz, and Verhulst 2002) propose a series of 'stages of transition' for the democratisation process in transitional societies, which consist of legal-institutional and sociocultural factors: demonopolisation and professionalisation of the media, legal guarantees of its operation and a civil society in which these processes, ideas and openness are allowed to exist. In China, while excessive commercialisation has somewhat aided demonopolisation of the media system, Chinese Communist Party-led institutions still effectively control offline and online news production. The national public sphere is 'locked' or 'gated', as the party state is sufficiently strong to contain any dissemination of information that might destabilise its rule (Esarey 2005).

Internet Censorship

Take the example of Internet censorship. In 1998, the Communist Party of China feared that the China Democracy Party would engender a powerful new network that the political elite would not be able to control. Thus the 'Golden Shield' Project was launched, nicknamed the 'Great Firewall of China', in reference to the ancient Great Wall of China. This censorship and surveillance project, which was initiated in 1998 and began operations in 2003, is handled by the Ministry of Public Security of the Chinese government. The political and ideological background of the Golden Shield Project dates back to Deng Xiaoping's infamous declaration in the early 1980s: 'If you open the window for fresh air, you have to expect some flies to blow in.' The primary aim of the project is to block content by preventing IP addresses from being routed through the shield, and consists of standard firewalls and proxy servers. Rauchfleisch and Schafer (2015) investigated how the popular Chinese social platform Sina Weibo is actively censored under this project. They argue that, whereas apolitical life-world issues such as fashion or celebrities or even issues of common concern to political administrations at local, regional and national levels (e.g., environmental matters) are tolerated, posts doubting one-party rule, criticising corruption among political elites or discussing the protests of Tiananmen Square in 1989 or the Taiwan independence are prohibited and quickly censored (deleted from Weibo). For example, every year, users attempt to commemorate the Tiananmen protests, knowing that the censors are on high alert. In 2013, pictures of the 'tank man'—the famous portrayal of an unidentified man blocking the path of tanks in Tiananmen square in 1989—were posted on Weibo, but the tanks were replaced with big yellow ducks to camouflage the original picture. Similarly, other partially cartoonist versions of the pictures were published, using LEGO Angry Birds images in place of the tanks in attempts to evade censorship (Rauchfleisch and Schafer 2015).

In some instances, authorities tolerate the publications of incidents on Weibo that are of common concern at a local level but not at a national level, thereby allowing the existence of a 'local public sphere'. This is illustrated by the case of Yang Hui, a 16-year-old junior high school student who criticised how local authorities had handled the death of a karaoke parlour employee, and posted pictures taken at a demonstration afterwards, and who was eventually arrested by the local police for spreading rumours. Following online protests demanding the release of the teen, central government interfered at the local level, and Yang Hu was released after 7 days in custody. Another example is the protest against a chemical factory in Maoming involving uncensored circulation of pictures on Weibo for a certain time and encouraging an online discussion of the protest, whereas any online post representing and reinforcing social mobilisation is typically censored. Rauchfleisch and Schafer (2015:151) have discussed how these isolated cases demonstrate that 'even though Weibo communication is limited on many issues and in many ways, a set of issues, situations and conditions can be identified under which Weibo communication fulfils some criteria of a public sphere such as open debates about issues of common concern, continuous debates and a large number of participants'.

However, the evidence presented by these authors largely concerns local matters and is fragmentary at best and the cases discussed do not really contain any dissemination of information that might destabilise the party state's rule. In contrast, Chinese authorities appear to be quick to censor posts that might put the central government's rulings at risk. This was evidenced by the handling of the autumn 2014 student-led unrest in Hong Kong, which represented the first large-scale student protest for democracy in any part of China since the 1989 Tiananmen uprising. Hong Kong has retained a remarkable degree of freedom since the British handed it back to China in 1997, as it enjoys an arrangement of 'one country, two systems'. In this context, Hong Kong has a history of free expression and is semi-detached from the censorship by the mainland. Thus the authorities in Hong Kong are reined in by a legal system established by the British under which they cannot handle unrest in the same way as officials do in mainland China (i.e., with a combination of astute bargaining, tight control over media and the Internet and violence and ruthless treatment of protestors). Xi Jinping, China's president, is constrained by a desire to keep Hong Kong stable and prosperous, and to avoid the risk damaging one of the world's wealthiest economies (*The Economist* 4 October 2014:15, 69). As a result, Hong Kong's 'umbrella revolution', named after the means of protection that demonstrators carried against police pepper spray, was largely managed by Chinese authorities through censorship of pro-democracy protest posts on social media.

Another example of censorship was the banning of Instagram in mainland China. Many Chinese users of the service noticed that they could not access the service on particular days, while some posts showing support for the protests were removed from the Twitter-like service Weibo. Instead, only official news posts and criticism of the protests showed up on Weibo. According to the *South China Morning Post*, the number of Weibo posts that were inaccessible increased fivefold between Friday, 26 September, and Sunday, 28 September 2014. Comments still visible on the Weibo posts, however, showed a more diverse range of opinions, with some expressing scepticism and others support. 'How could they think that they can push back the bottom line simply by protesting? They are just too naïve', said one user. 'They are not against the central government's leadership. They just don't want the central government to interfere in their own politics', said another (BBC News: China 2014). Meanwhile, several pro-government Chinese media outlets criticised the protest, calling it an 'illegal assembly', although they also sought to play down the demonstrations, with newspapers refraining from publishing photographs and details.

By 2015, the protest seemed to have died down, but the dissatisfaction with the Chinese government was clearly on the rise. American writer and teacher Clay Shirky reminds us of the anti-corruption protests that broke out in the aftermath of the devastating May 2008 earthquake in Sichuan. The protesters were parents, particularly mothers, who had lost their only children in the collapse of badly built schools, the result of collusion between construction firms and the local government. Before the earthquake, corruption in the country's construction industry was an open secret, but after the collapse of the schools, citizens began sharing information on the damage and on their protests through social media tools. The consequences of government corruption were made broadly visible, and the corrupt practices went from being an open secret to a public truth. Shirky (2012) believes that in the case of such events, while the state may attempt to silence critics through censorship or propaganda, if it were to shut down Internet access or ban cell phones, it would risk radicalising otherwise pro-regime citizens or harming the economy. Repression, in Shirky's view, will prove to be counterproductive, and one day the Internet will transform the government. Currently, however, censors are still successful in protecting China's 'cyberspace sovereignty'.

Conclusion

Russia and China have witnessed explosive growth in the use of the Internet, with Russia representing the fastest-growing Internet and social media market in Europe, and China near the top worldwide. Although the Internet in its early days was relatively free in both Russia and China, their governments have since released a number of new laws, guidelines and regulations that have tightened control over online information. Russia had followed a relatively relaxed approach towards overt policing of the Internet, but on the eve of the December 2011 protests and in the 2013 and 2014 conflicts in Chechnya and Ukraine, the Russian administration decided to follow a pattern for Internet use similar to that of the traditional print and broadcast media, namely using it as an additional political tool for control and promotion of its own interests. A new set of Internet regulations, including the requirement for all online companies such as Facebook and Amazon to store user data in Russian territory, and the requirement for popular 'political' bloggers to register with the government, have raised concerns regarding increased political censorship. Meanwhile, the Internet continues to be heavily regulated in China, through two principal agencies—the MIIT and the General Administration of Press and Publication (GAPP) —but at least 20 other national-level bodies are also involved, in addition to countless provincial and local authorities. Alongside the overt government regulation, operators are required to engage in extensive and elaborate self-censorship and in the collection of data on users, which must be turned over to authorities on request. The Chinese government leads the world in the sophistication of its electronic monitoring of Internet activity, and it can and frequently does intervene to block communications considered offensive or dangerous and punish those involved (Shoesmith 2014). China's criteria for Internet censorship essentially apply the rules that have prevailed since the Tiananmen Square crackdown of 1989: 'do not jeopardize social stability, do not organize and do not threaten the party' (*The Economist* 21 April 2013).

Both repressive regimes provide clear examples of how to counter the explosive growth of the Internet and social media for consumers by limiting online use as a political tool for citizens. Chinese state power in the online sphere is more explicit, as it blocks social media platforms from the West such as Facebook, Twitter and YouTube. Furthermore, with the creation of the Great Firewall, a sophisticated and highly effective censorship and surveillance project, the Chinese leadership monitors online discussions, from the production of Internet content to routine searches for terms like 'democracy', 'freedom' and 'human rights' in the content. The Chinese state often uses the Internet to penetrate resistance organisations and to arrest cyber-dissidents. Whereas the Russian state has no system akin to the Great Chinese Firewall, it nevertheless constrains Internet openness and counters opposition voices by favouring less obvious, albeit equally effective, ways such as self-censorship and threats addressed to its netizens and bloggers. It also controls the online sphere by requiring Internet service providers to forward information to the state security services. There currently appears to be limited possibility to engage in a critical online discussion in a country defined by its Soviet past and the failure of democratic institutions in the young Russian state, characterised by 'ineffective political parties, a weak legislature, a dependent judiciary, and a media that does not function as a Fourth Estate' (Oates 2013). Self-censorship is particularly worrying when applied to journalists, with a minority of them actually willing to confront the Kremlin line on sensitive issues such as the conflict with Ukraine and the annexation of Crimea in 2014. The economic spillover of the Ukraine political crisis was evident in early 2015, as the West's sanctions led to a lack of access to financing, and to capital flight and a climate of uncertainty, locking Russia into a period of near-zero growth.

Globalisation and the social media do play a role in generating political change in repressive regimes, but it is subordinate to domestic political wars between the state and society (Lagerkvist 2010). The potential of online communication is limited in countries such as Russia that apply self-censorship and control, and where the democratic experience gives way to open propaganda, and it is similarly limited in countries such as China, where people rely on domestic platforms to stay informed and where netizens are sent to prison for what they post on the web. Both cases help us understand how the potential democratising power of the Internet and social media is limited in autocratic states, which manage to mute, constrain and control online debate and even use it to promote their own interests.

BIBLIOGRAPHY

BBC News: China. 2014. China Censors Hong Kong Protest Posts on Social Media, September 29. http://www.bbc.co.uk/news/world-asia-china-29411270 (accessed January 2, 2015)

Cicero Group. 2014. *Social Media in China*, May. http://www.cicero-group. com/wp-content/uploads/2014/05/Social-Media-in-China-V4.pdf (accessed December 29, 2014)

CNNIC (China Internet Network Information Centre). 2014. *Statistical Report on Internet Development in China*. January. http://www1.cnnic. cn/IDR/ReportDownloads/201404/U020140417607531610855.pdf (accessed December 29, 2014)

Curran J., and Myung-Jin Park. 2000. *De-Westernizing Media Studies*. London: Routledge.

Diebert R.J. et al. 2010. *Access Controlled: The Shaping of Power, Rights, and Rule in Cyberspace*. Cambridge: MIT Press.

Endeshaw A. 2004. "Internet Regulation in China: The Never-Ending Cat and Mouse Game". *Information & Communication Technology Law* 13(1): 41–57.

Eremenko, A. 2014. "Russia Speeds Up Law to Ban Most Foreign Web Services". *The Moscow Times*, September 25. www.themoscowtimes.com/news/article/ russia-speeds-up-law-to-ban-most-foreign-web-services/507820.html (accessed December 29, 2014).

Esarey A. 2005. "Cornering the Market: State Strategies for Controlling China's Commercial Media". *Asian Perspective* 29(4): 37–83.

Fossato F., J. Lloyd, and A. Verkhovsky. 2008. *The Web that Failed: How Opposition Politics and Independent Institutions are Failing on the Internet in Russia*. Oxford: Reuters Institute for the Study of Journalism.

Gibbs J. 1999. *Gorbachev's Glasnost: The Soviet Media in the First Phase of Perestroika*. College Station, TX: Texas A&M University Press.

Goodwin J. 1993. *Eisenstein, Cinema History*. Urbana, IL: University of Illinois.

Hallin D.C., and P. Mancini. 2004. *Comparing Media Systems: Three Models of Media and Politics*. Cambridge: Cambridge University Press.

Ho V., and A. Fung. 2015. "Cultural Policy, Chinese National Identity and Globalization". In *Global Media and National Policies: The Return of the State*, eds. T. Flew, P. Iosifidis, and J. Steemers. Basingstoke: Palgrave Macmillan.

Keane M. 2006. "From Made in China to Created in China". *International Journal of Cultural Studies* 9(3): 285–296.

Koshkin, P. 2014. The Kremlin Gives the Green Light to Shut Down the Internet. September 29. http://www.russia-direct.org/analysis/kremlin-gives-green-light-shut-down-internet (accessed December 29, 2014)

Lagerkvist J. 2010. *After the Internet, Before Democracy: Competing Norms in Chinese Media and Society*. Bern: Peter Lang AG.

Levitsky S., and L. Way. 2002. "The Rise of Competitive Authoritarianism". *Journal of Democracy* 13(2): 51–65.

Lonkila M. 2008. "The Internet and Anti-military Activism in Russia". *Europe-Asia Studies* 60(7): 1125–1149.

Michiewicz E. 1988. *Split Signals: Television and Politics in the Soviet Union.* New York, NY: Oxford University Press.

Michiewicz E. 1997. *Changing Channels: Television and the Struggle for Power in Russia.* New York: Oxford University Press.

Oates S. 2013. *Revolution Stalled: The Political Limits of the Internet in the Post-Soviet Sphere.* New York: Oxford University Press.

Paganini, P. 2011. 'The business of Censorship. Golden Shield Project, but not only …' 19 November. At http://securityaffairs.co/wordpress/204/cyber-crime/business-of-censorship-golden-shield-project-but-not-only.html (accessed 7 March 2016).

Partlett, W. 2012. Can Russia Keep Faking Democracy? *Brookings Institution,* May 22. http://www.brookings.edu/research/opinions/2012/05/22-russia-democracy-partlett (accessed December 22, 2014)

Price M., B. Rozumilowicz, and S.G. Verhulst. 2002. *Media Reform: Democratizing the Media, Democratizing the State.* London: Routledge.

Rauchfleisch A., and M.S. Schafer. 2015. "Multiple Public Spheres of Weibo: A Typology of Forms and Potentials of Online Public Spheres in China". *Information Communication & Society* 18(2): 139–155.

Ramo J.C. 2004. *The Beijing Consensus.* London: The Foreign Policy Centre.

Shambaugh D. 2007. "China's Propaganda System: Institutions, Processes and Efficacy". *China Journal* 57: 25–58.

Shirky, C. 2012. How the Internet Will (One Day) Transform the Government, June. www.chinaspeakersagency.com/2014/clay-shirky-internet-will-one-day-transform-government (accessed January 12, 2015).

Shoesmith, T.M. 2014. Internet Regulation in China, Data Privacy in China: Overview, January.

Social Media Fast Facts: China. 2014. http://www.emoderation.com/social-media-fast-facts-china (accessed December 30, 2014)

Sullivan J. 2013. "China's Weibo: Is Faster Different?". *New Media & Society* 16(1): 24–37.

The Economist (2013). 'How Does China Censors the Internet?' 21 April.

The Economist (2014a). 'Dreams about Russia, 15 February.

Voltmer K. 2000. "Constructing Political Reality in Russia: Izvestiya—Between Old and New Journalistic Practices". *European Journal of Communication* 15(4): 469–500.

Yu Hong. 2011. "Reading the Twelfth Five-Year Plan: China's Communication-Driven Mode of Economic Restructuring". *International Journal of Communication* 5: 1045–1057.

CHAPTER 9

India and South Africa; Post-colonial Power, Democratization and the Online Community

INTRODUCTION

In this chapter we explore the relationship between the processes of online mobilisation and political change in two states—India and South Africa—that operate within the so-called BRICS group of countries. The technological revolution provides opportunities to redress the long-standing imbalance between wealth and poverty and the spheres of political influence between states of the Global North and South. The post-colonial (British Empire) countries of India and South Africa have thus established information infrastructures to advance levels of Internet participation. The ability to communicate easily with one another may contribute to the processes of democratisation in the non-Western world.

The expansion of the social media has led to the decentralisation of traditional power structures, revealing changing notions of civil society. India and South Africa have thus incorporated the social media within their political communications processes. Political leaders have employed websites, blogs, Twitter and Facebook to effect a greater connection with their electorate. Alternatively, the 'buzz' associated with a tweet or a post has enabled grassroots social movements to mobilise public opinion over

© The Editor(s) (if applicable) and The Author(s) 2016   203
P. Iosifidis, M. Wheeler, *Public Spheres and Mediated
Social Networks in the Western Context and Beyond*,
DOI 10.1057/978-1-137-41030-6_9

issues-based campaigns. According to Shaili Chopra, the use of social media is able to realise this potential because it:

> connects people, gets them talking and sharing [to allow] campaigners to know the voters, target specific audience, splice demographics, mobilise support, and urge them to participate. When some of these people…get actively engaged in political debates, they become a great tool to spread the word and influence opinion. (Chopra 2014:2–3)

However, opposing arguments claim that these expectations have been confounded by long-standing economic and political interests, who have subverted the technology for their own ends. As such, have the post-colonial states utilised the information revolution to critically address the divisions of wealth and poverty? This chapter will consider whether the growth of social media within India and South Africa has enhanced or diminished the expectations of democratic reform.

First, we will explore in detail the technological, economic and political trajectories which have shaped the social media in India and South Africa. In this section, we discuss the levels of digital penetration and how the social networks were incorporated into these nations' communications sectors. ICTs have increased exponentially over the first and second decades of the twenty-first century, leading to the development of online communication strategies by political parties. However, social media take-up has been contingent on the electoral systems, the levels of democratisation and the nature of the political culture.

Second, we will provide a comparative analysis of the digital dividends relative to the 2014 general election campaigns in India and South Africa. We will discuss how the Indian political parties have embraced social media and the influence of the 2008 and 2012 US presidential campaigns. In contrast, we will consider how the South African parties employed online political communications in a more conventional way, and we will further discuss whether multimedia communications have contributed to electoral wins.

Finally, we will examine how social movements, protest groups and political reformers have used the social media to build issues-based campaigns, as we seek to understand whether these forms of electronic participation have advanced grassroots participation and freedom of speech. Both India and South Africa provide evidence of a system of regulations governing the dissemination of information across a burgeoning social media. While there are no laws that directly address social media practices in India, various forms of Internet censorship have been practiced by federal and state governments. In South Africa, social media have been protected by the 1994 constitution, which guaranteed the right of free speech, although controversies have emerged regarding the policing of the Internet (van der Westhuizen 2013). Therefore, we will discuss whether the new forms of e-democracy have been able to overcome the digital deficits in these states of the Global South.

INDIA AND SOUTH AFRICA: HISTORICAL AND POLITICAL CONTEXT

India and South Africa were both colonised by the British Empire during the nineteenth century. Within India there was a gradual imposition of imperial rule, and full powers were transferred from the East India Company to the British Raj in 1857 after the Indian Rebellion. In South Africa, the British won the battle for territorial supremacy against Dutch settlers (known as Boers or Afrikaners) in the Second Boer War (1898–1902). For these societies, independence was achieved only after a series of long and brutal struggles against the British rulers.

Yet democratic reforms were heavily compromised and marred by significant controversy. The 1947 partition of India based on Hindu–Muslim religious divisions led to the formation of India and West and East Pakistan (now Bangladesh), and was accompanied by massacres in the Punjab and the assassination of Mahatma Gandhi. Although India would preside over the world's largest democracy, its politics were dominated by the Gandhi family's dynastic power within the Indian National Congress (INC) and by the Hindu nationalism of the Bharatiya Janata Party (BJP). The use of authoritarian powers was also observed during the 'Emergency' period of the 1970s. The political scene has remained volatile, besieged by accusations of corruption and driven by caste-based sectarianism.

From 1948 to 1994, the prejudices of the National Party's Afrikaner leadership led to the promotion of apartheid, the system of racial segregation in South Africa. The subjugation of the African majority by post-colonial white rulers was brutally carried out by the repressive forces of the state, resulting in massacres in black townships such as Soweto, the death of activist Steve Biko in police custody and many other injustices. Beginning in the 1970s, various campaigns and political and sporting boycotts were put in place, designed to pressure the National Party to end apartheid. However, many countries maintained sanction-busting trade policies with the Afrikaner regime. For instance, Cold War ideological divisions and the availability of gold and diamonds led the USA and UK to trade openly with South Africa. Eventually, through the international campaign to free the imprisoned African National Congress (ANC) leader Nelson Mandela, apartheid was ended and universal suffrage achieved. Mandela was elected president of the newly convened nation in 1994.

Within these states, the difficulties associated with post-colonial power and questions of inequality remain problematic. India is still rife with national, regional, religious and caste divisions. Despite its 'rainbow nation' status, South Africa displays many of the economic and social disparities associated with the previous period of racial segregation. It is within this political and cultural context, therefore, that the digital revolution in India and South Africa has taken place. The respective levels of penetration of the communications services were further defined by the development opportunities in the countries of the Global South. Notably, as the BRICS nations became centres for financial growth, these societies became powerful forces within a reconfigured international political economy. Moreover, the various political constituencies and types of democratic practice have been key variables in shaping the nature of online forms of communication.

INDIA AND SOUTH AFRICA: ESCALATION OF THE INTERNET AND THE TAKE-UP OF THE SOCIAL MEDIA

As India has shifted from being a poor, mostly rural society, to a wealthier, modern urban culture, the penetration of new technologies has increased. Indeed, the concepts of 'Brand India' or 'new' India have hinged on the nation's knowledge economy (Bhaduri 2010:41). The wider distribution of ICTs emerged through the liberalisation of the telecommunications sector as part of the new economic policy introduced in July 1991. Subsequently, India has implemented other digital policies for economic and political advantage. For instance, the new Internet policy in 1998 and new telecom legislation in 1999 resulted in the establishment of Internet service providers (ISPs):

> The deregulation, liberalization, and privatization of the 1990s—and the end of what was derisively described as the 'licence-quota-permit Raj'— ushered in a rapid transformation in India's service industries, particularly in

information and communications technologies, signifying the transition of a large part of India's predominantly, agricultural economy into a knowledge-based, globalizing economy. (Thussu 2013:101)

Throughout the 1990s, the telecommunications industry was opened up to private sector investment in radio paging and mobile telephony. This led to the massive growth of Indian software industries, whose worth in 2012 was estimated to be more than US $1.2 trillion. This knowledge economy was composed of a highly skilled, technologically savvy English-speaking workforce, who allowed the nation to rise 'above...reductionist impressions...drawn from its essentially agrarian economy, abysmal poverty, social ills, rampant corruption and a teeming population'. (Bhaduri 2010:41)

Although India's Internet penetration remains at only 19 % of the total population, the country is nevertheless home to some 239 million users, which places it third, behind only China and the USA (Gopalakrishnan 2014). The vast majority of Internet users are in the 15–24 age group and live in the major cities. Forecasts estimate that there will be 330 million Internet users by 2016, and this figure will include a growing share of the rural population (Rajput 2014). A large number of users gain access to multimedia applications through mobile phones, given the availability of inexpensive rate plans and the roll-out of 3G services in 2011.

The Internet and Mobile Association of India (IAMAI) reported that, among 70 million active urban Internet users, 26.3 million achieved an online presence via their mobile devices (IAMAI 2013). Furthermore, at the end of 2011, the total Indian mobile phone subscriber base stood at 890 million, including about 300 million in rural areas, which represented an increase of 160 million subscribers from 2010 (Freedom House 2012). The number of mobile social network users was expected to grow to around 72 million by 2014. This growth has been driven by the reduced cost of smartphones and the launch of 4G services.

The increased use of mobile broadband access has gone hand in hand with the expansion of the social media. The March 2011 comScore Metrix commented that social networking sites have a penetration of 84 % of the Indian web audience, accounting for 21 % of users' time spent online (Rajput 2014). In 2010, the online audience measurement service ViviSense reported that Facebook had the highest reach among the social networks, accounting for 22.1 million users, followed by Google's Orkut system, with 18.5 million. Over the following 2 years, Twitter became extremely popular, accounting for 18 million users, placing India at the sixth highest global spot for microblogging sites. At the same time, the Indian blogosphere has remained vibrant and available across a wide variety of platforms. E-government programmes also exist in a variety of Indian states to encourage public participation and governmental accountability (Singh 2014).

In tandem, the South African government has enacted legislation to liberalise the communications sector to attract multimedia investment (Wasserman 2014). In 2006, the Electronic Communications Act restructured the information market by converting the previously vertically integrated telecommunications licences towards horizontal service layers. Consequently, the ICT economy has been divided between top-tier Internet access providers and downstream retail ISPs. According to the 2013 State of Broadband Report released by the UN Broadband Commission, 41 % of South Africans use the Internet, placing the country fifth in Africa and 44th among developing countries, and just above the 24 % average for the 128 Global South states (UN Broadband Commission 2013).

There have been distinct differences between the low rates of fixed broadband penetration and the wider roll-out of mobile broadband accessed through smartphones, tablets and Wi-Fi-connected laptop computers. As of 2012, there were 12.7 million wireless broadband subscribers, compared to 1.1 million fixed-line subscribers. Mobile broadband subscriptions have increased at a rate of 30 % per year, and at the end of 2013, there were three times as many mobile broadband as fixed connections. Moreover, the South African Social Media Landscape 2014 research study released by World Wide Worx and Fuseware noted that 87 % of social network users accessed these sites through their mobile phones. The study showed Facebook as the largest social network, with 9.4 million active users. Twitter had enjoyed 129 % growth, with a rise in the number of users from 2.4 million in 2013 to 5.5 million in 2014. As such, a significant proportion of Internet usage in South Africa has been given over to the social media.

Overall, social media usage is still limited by the levels of digital penetration in India and South Africa. However, in terms of online political communications, the growing engagement of Indian and South African social network users has allowed for new forms of connection and visibility. Mobile technology, the Internet and social networks can educate and empower young people, and have defined the concepts of identity among target audiences.

ONLINE POLITICAL COMMUNICATIONS WITHIN INDIA AND SOUTH AFRICA

Indian and South African political parties have taken advantage of social media to create new opportunities to communicate with the electorate. Essentially, party leaders have engaged in the 'Obamafication' (Kamat 2014) of political communications, to construct a public but highly personalised relationship with audiences:

> Personal communications via the social media brings politicians and parties closer to their potential voters. It allows politicians to communicate faster and reach citizens in a more targeted manner and vice versa, without the intermediate role of the mass media. Reactions, feedback, conversations and debates are generated online as well as support and participation for offline events. (Narasimhamurthy 2014:202)

Initially, Indian politicians who engaged in online forms of political communication were deemed individual oddities. For example, the early INC adopter Shashi Tharoor caused significant controversy with his 2009 'cattle class—out of solidarity with our holy cows!' tweet, in which he claimed that he would travel in economy class in accordance with the austerity measures being imposed by the government. Tharoor lost his post as minister of state for human resources development, and his recklessness showed how dangerous social media could be for politicians. However, the Indian political classes quickly learned how they could circumvent the 'negative sphere' of the traditional media. Tharoor's example demonstrated the political stir that social media could create and that such public attention might work to a politician's advantage.

Subsequently, the mainstream parties, BJP and INC, along with the newly formed anti-corruption Aam Aadmi Party (AAP) and the Samajwaid Party (representing the rural Yadav community), established Facebook and Twitter accounts. Both the BJP and INC conducted workshops designed to develop party members' social media skills so that they could cultivate an appropriate online 'voice' through which to speak to the electorate. INC Prime Minister (PM) Manmohan Singh and BJP opposition leader Narendra Modi employed social media to sustain a populist political discourse. Modi developed a 'first-mover advantage' (Chopra 2014) by employing India272.com (whose mission was to gain the 272-plus seats necessary for achieving a parliamentary majority), NitiCentral and his website NarendraModi.in. On 27 July 2013, Modi had 1,963,426

Twitter followers, while Singh had 680,782 followers. Moreover, Modi ensured that his speeches would be trended with Facebook and Twitter hashtags. The BJP leadership thus realised that Indian politics were being defined more by grassroots 'fans' and 'followers' than by top-down dialogues between the political elite and the electorate:

> [Indian] [p]olitical parties [were]…learning the nuances of the social media game. The hashtags are planned. The speeches are integrated into tweets. Politicians realize that suddenly thousands are speaking up; the general janta is now actively a part of the political mindshare or seeking it….Arvind Gupta of the BJP IT Cell believes it's definitely setting a narrative and influencing a lot of people. (Chopra 2014:17)

By employing the social media in this manner, Indian politicians have thus marketed themselves as brands to sustain their authenticity within their constituencies.

The BJP used cyber-campaigns to organise net-savvy party workers at a local level in order to establish a wide network of supporters. The party's India272 website utilised crowdsourcing techniques and encouraged volunteers to come up with slogans, poems and anthems. In addition, the BJP recruited local activists to register online supporters, such that it would have an army of volunteers to do its bidding (Kamat 2014). The AAP also employed digital media for recruitment drives and to collect revenue for political campaigns. The anti-corruption party, which was converted from a social movement, enjoyed electoral success in the Delhi regional assembly and state-level campaigns:

> What clearly came across in [the] AAP's use of the social media is how they used it as a means and not an end. As someone wittily put it, social media is an ingredient, not an entree. This ingredient most definitely changed the outcome for AAP, amplified its message, and swelled its fan base and loyalty. (Chopra 2014:143)

In comparison, South African politicians were less adept in absorbing social media into their party machinery. In a 2014 survey conducted by the social media research company Strategy Worx, it was discovered that the major parties (the ANC and the Democratic Alliance [DA]) and the two newly formed parties (the Economic Freedom Fighters [EFF] and the Agang SA) had achieved only a limited online presence. The ANC, rather than using interactive opportunities, continued to employ 'broadcasting' approaches to the use of the social media, achieving only 58,000 'likes' on its Facebook page (Alfreds 2014).

The DA enjoyed greater success, which was reflected by a surge in its Facebook likes to just over 57,000. The DA had also loaded video and image content on its websites and social networking platforms. Similarly, the Agang SA had understood that it could connect with its support base and brand its political leadership using social media. Strategy Worx concluded, however, that the new party's online communications techniques were hindered by problems associated with usability and content. The agency further commented that 'South African political parties have failed to understand that simple placement of events, speeches, manifestos, and offline information, does not constitute good online practice' (Strategy Worx 2014).

Both Indian and South African mainstream politics have evidenced changes in strategic thinking about online political communications. For the Indian parties, social media allowed leaders to be in constant contact with the electorate through cheaper modes of communications machinery. Subsequently, Facebook likes and Twitter hashtags have enabled Indian politicians to measure trends in public sentiment regarding party ideologies, platforms and policies. In contrast, South Africa has shown a reluctance to fully commit time, resources and energy to the online political resources. Despite the greater use of online resources in Indian politics, however, there remains the danger that the social media may misrepresent public opinion.

Consequently, there have been questions about the validity, credibility and trustworthiness of online political communications within the Indian and South African public spheres. For instance, many blogs, Facebook and Twitter posts have been subject to abusive commentaries littered with 'trolls' and 'flacks' (Chopra 2014:195). Thus, some have argued that there has been an 'over-democratisation', in which all voices declare the equitability of their worth. This in turn this will lead to polarisation of viewpoints, characterised by increased political volatility and the subsequent collapse of consensual behaviour. The leads to the question: Does a presence on the social media actually translate into votes to win election campaigns?

THE SOCIAL MEDIA AND ELECTION CAMPAIGNS IN INDIA AND SOUTH AFRICA

At the beginning of 2014, it was predicted that the social media would have a profound impact on the nature of the Indian and South African election campaigns. Online polling would enable the parties to trend their messages to their constituencies of support. Furthermore, despite the many caveats related to digital take-up, the complexities of the electoral processes, and the differences within the party systems, many contended that the social media could dictate electoral outcomes in India and South Africa.

THE 2014 INDIAN LOK SABHA PARLIAMENTARY GENERAL ELECTION AND THE SOCIAL MEDIA

In the 2014 Lok Sabha (lower house) parliament, 543 seats were contested among a total of 8251 candidates. On 16 May 2014, the BJP and its allies were declared to have won a sweeping victory, taking 336 seats. This win represented 31 % of the total vote and was the largest percentage claimed by any party in 40 years. This BJP landslide meant that for the first time since 1984, a single party had won enough seats (282) to govern independently rather than by forming a coalition.

As the campaign progressed, the Internet became a key information resource through which the public consumed political content. Search engines provided 'election hubs' that enabled Indian voters to receive updates regarding campaign-related news. Moreover, 29 million Indians engaged in 227 million Facebook interactions—posts, comments, shares and likes. In addition, politicians and journalists used social media platforms as newsfeeds to connect with one another in real time. As a result, the campaign was dubbed the 'first social media election in India's history'.

Although the BJP had included ICTs in its political communications strategies in 2009, Modi realised that the previously centralised techniques were out of sync with the interests of a younger generation of voters. Therefore, the party's strategists employed a 'shopping' approach, whereby they imported US online campaign techniques that they then modified and implemented, which 'suggest[ed] that they [had] been shopping quite a bit, and mostly from the Obama store' (Kamat 2014). The BJP established a 'social media war room' in which technologically literate youth workers formulated online campaign manoeuvres, collated information and analysed data. The party crowdsourced its manifesto, launched a point-ranking system to highlight the most effective local organisers on its India272.com website and sold Modi-inspired merchandise online. It also had 65,410 YouTube subscribers, which meant that the user-generated channel became a second screen for all its activities.

Modi participated in a Google+ hangout, which drew 20,000 questions and was viewed by nearly four million people on the web and TV. He employed separate Twitter accounts for the diverse non-Hindi-speaking Assamese, Kannada, Manipuri, Telugu, Malayalam, Oriya and Marathi communities. Subsequently, in rallies that occurred outside the Hindi-speaking belt, Modi used insights gathered from these tweets to design his speeches. By the time he had become the PM, Modi had received more than 16 million Facebook likes (ranking second only to Obama) and was the sixth most followed leader on Twitter worldwide. Upon winning the election, his victory tweet was the most re-tweeted post in Indian political history. At the same time, the BJP created a 'victory wall' upon which tweets and Facebook messages from supporters were displayed. In this way, the BJP engaged in a multi-platform approach for disseminating the party message in order to engage with the widest group of voters and to maximise Modi's appeal:

> [The] BJP is about the multiplicity of things that they are doing. For example, during Narendra Modi's Delhi speech, there were a large number of people present at the rally, but perhaps an equal measure were hearing the live speech from their mobile phones and if you opted in to his Twitter feed, you could receive his tweets on the go. And so [the] BJP—via Modi—has been able to scale up in massive way, leveraging different digital formats and reaching out to a larger audience using social media. Its effort is clearly in reaching the largest number of people, across strata, in the shortest possible time. (Lalawani quoted from Chopra 2014:96–97)

The BJP was not the only Indian political party to have learned its lessons from Obama. During the election, the AAP implemented a 'ground game' involving locally organised volunteers who targeted key 'battleground' constituencies such as Delhi. This virtual network of activists contacted over 20 voters per day to build a support base. The AAP's fundraising techniques also resembled those of the Obama campaign by the inclusion of small and large contributions gathered online.

With certain notable exceptions, such as the Bangalore South candidate Nandan Nilekani, who used Twitter for posts on how to improve the city, the INC leadership ignored the social media during the election campaign. Leaders of Congress, including the former president Sonia Gandhi and her son Rahul, who ultimately led the INC campaign, refused to establish an online presence. Only after they realised that this put them at a significant disadvantage did they set up Twitter accounts. This failure was a significant factor in the INC's collapse in support:

> Congress leaders considered the medium frivolous and dismissed it....Not getting onto the social media bandwagon was interpreted as arrogance, especially since Gandhi gave no interviews on the mainstream channels either. ... [Gandhi] also missed the bus on building a strategy and image as a youth icon, when it might have been in his reach, more than the other leaders he was expected to compete with. (Chopra 2014:122–123)

Conversely, Modi became a 'youth icon' and, as PM, has extended his social media appeal. He engaged in a round of Twitter diplomacy after the elections by responding to messages of congratulations from UK Prime Minister David Cameron and Russian President Vladimir Putin. He also connected with the vast Indian diaspora when he made well-received visits to the USA and Australia in the autumn of 2014. It was noted that his sold-out rally at Madison Square Garden was a testament to his online presence. Over the course of the tour, Modi garnered 163,724 US Facebook likes, and he announced his arrivals on his Twitter account with its own hashtag, '#ModiInAmerica' (Nair 2014). While India remains in the early phase of Internet adoption, the BJP's successful incorporation of ICTs has shown how future elections will be conducted. As Harini Calamur, the digital officer of Zee Media Corporation, asserted, 'If Mahatma Gandhi had been alive, he would have been on Twitter' (Chopra 2014:123).

THE SOUTH AFRICAN PERSPECTIVE: THE 2014 NATIONAL ASSEMBLY GENERAL ELECTION

On 7 May 2014, South Africa elected a new National Assembly. This was the fifth general election held under conditions of universal adult suffrage since the end of apartheid; it was the first election since Mandela's death and the first in which expatriates could vote. The incumbent ANC won the National Assembly election, with a reduced majority, from 65.9 % in 2009 to 62.1 % in 2014. The DA increased its share of the vote from 16.7 % to 22.2 %, while the newly formed EFF obtained 6.4 % of the vote.

As South Africa has over nine million Facebook users and five million Twitter users, the social media were predicted to play a significant role in the election process. Indeed, the electorate did use tweets, Facebook and online video material to air their views and provide commentary about the campaign. Additionally, South Africans celebrated their democratic rights by posting 'selfies' marked with thumbnails. Furthermore, public-led stories associated with 'mislaid' ballot boxes received traction when user-generated images were re-tweeted by politicians, including EFF leader Julius Malema, the DA's Helen Zille and Agang SA's Mamphela Ramphele, forcing authorities to investigate matters of electoral fraud with a greater sense of urgency.

The News24 website reported a record-breaking set of user-based statistics throughout the elections. On polling day, there were 1.7 million unique users and 22 million page views. This represented an unprecedented 220 % growth in unique users and a 484 % growth in page views. At 10 a.m. on voting day, the site peaked, with 102,000 concurrent views, breaking its previous record of 79,000 views, which were received for Oscar Pistorius' bail hearing on 19 February 2013. The site's interactive results map collected over a third of the total web and mobile traffic (Durrant 2014).

The mainstream parties utilised social media platforms to reach out to voters with varying degrees of success. The ANC recorded the largest Facebook growth, and its number of likes increased from 52,536 to 136,046 from 7 March to 2 May 2014. The ANC's Twitter audience also expanded by 1.79 %, to overtake the DA's Twitter supporter base, which had been the largest social network user group at the start of the campaign. The ANC developed an effective synergy between the digital services and campaign rallies, as the social media platforms were awash with images of packed stadia fronted by party supporters in t-shirts. During its Siyanqoba rally, which occurred over the weekend before the polling day, the party provided free Wi-Fi inside the FNB stadium, along with the #Siyanqoba post, and there was an associated spurt of interest within the ANC Facebook and Twitter accounts.

South African President Jacob Zuma gained 372,000 followers on Twitter and 48,000 likes on Facebook. However, due to the charges made by the DA, Agang SA and EFF concerning Zuma's misappropriation of funds during the refurbishment of his Nkandla residence, the ANC had to employ its Twitter accounts to defend the president. Therefore, to offset the negative publicity, the party's social media networks highlighted the ANC's ties to Mandela. It also made political capital out of Zuma's decision to withdraw from the European Union's African summit in protest of Egypt's invitation. The ANC youth wing's Twitter page was far more aggressive in combating Zuma's critics. For instance, a spoof tweet read,

'Malema has been arrested by the fashion police, they said "no amount of make-up could make him fashionable"'. And when Agang increased their criticism of the president, another tweet read, 'Secret Israeli special forces caught working in @AgangSA office'.

The DA achieved the highest level of engagement within Facebook and Twitter, using its accounts to make known the ANC's dirty tricks campaign of removing DA posters and replacing them with their own. The party delivered the most effectively integrated multimedia campaign with its #Ayisafani TV and YouTube political advertisements. Helen Zille, the DA leader and premier of the Western Cape province, gained 442,000 followers on Twitter and 289,000 likes on Facebook. In the third week of April 2014, Zille registered a total of 634 tweets, meaning she had posted 7.5 tweets an hour, or one tweet every 8 minutes per day. Similarly, the DA's National Assembly leader Mmusi Maimane had 42,000 followers on Twitter and received more than 11,000 likes on Facebook. He hosted a digital question-and-answer session with the hashtag #AskMmusi on Twitter and Facebook.

Yet, the negative focus of the DA's social media campaigning (#ImpeachZuma) was counterproductive. Moreover, Zille engaged in an ill-advised set of tweets concerning race-related political issues, and became involved in online spats with journalists. In 2012, she sparked public outcry when she quipped about 'educational refugees flooding the Western Cape from the Eastern Cape'. In February 2014, she accused the *City Press* reporter Carien du Plessis of political bias and factual inaccuracy (Burbage 2014). The personal nature of Zille's attack on the journalist received approbation:

> 'She is so terrified that she will be damned by her own complexion that she has to bend over to prove her political correctness', ran one of a string of attacks by Zille over two days, and: 'Carien is trying so desperately to hide the Missus class from which she comes'. (Pillay 2014)

Zille's online altercations thus reflected poorly on the DA, and demonstrated the dangers of social media's emphasis on personality-driven politics.

The new EFF and Agang SA parties made a few slight gains as a result of their social media presence. For instance, the EFF's leader Malema successfully built up a total of 478,000 followers on Twitter, having had 129,833 likes on Facebook in the year preceding the election. The party's use of the red beret as their colour and symbol (both online and offline) was heralded by commentators as 'a stroke of genius'. Alternatively, due to the extreme nature of the tweets it had posted about Zuma, the Agang party had to deny that its Twitter account had been hacked. One tweet read, 'We have not been hacked. The joke here is president Zuma's behaviour and the ANC ministers supporting him. Enough is enough.' (Burbage 2014)

However, for all the South African political parties, difficulties remained as to how well their social media presence could be translated into votes. Ultimately, the social networks in South Africa did not live up to the hype preceding the elections. The public used the Internet to become better informed about political issues, but engaged mainly in personal correspondence about campaign activities. In comparison to India, which evidenced the incorporation of US-style online electoral strategies, the South African parties used social media either to 'broadcast' their values or to attack their opponents. Thus, the chance for a more innovative use of social media had been wasted.

Social Movements, Protests and Censorship on the Internet in India and South Africa

Grassroots social movements and protest campaigns in both India and South Africa have utilised social media. Rajesh Lalwani, the founder of the Indian strategic social media consulting agency Blogworks, has noted that 'people are logging on to their social networks immediately after getting online [such that]...[t]he opportunities for participating in a conversation are more than ever before' (quoted from Rajput 2014:63). Similarly, South African social movements addressing the provision of affordable public services achieved national and international visibility through websites, online videos and mobile telephony. However, the opportunities for social movements were limited by online forms of censorship regarding the dissemination of free information.

India: Online Dialogues about Political Corruption, Protests and Social Reform

In 2011, the India Against Corruption (IAC) movement (which ultimately became the AAP under the leadership of Arvind Kejriwal) engaged in demonstrations against political malfeasance, achieving widespread attention when Anna Hazare began a hunger strike at the Jantar Mantar in New Delhi on 5 April 2011. Through the introduction of the Jan Lokpal Bill, the IAC sought legal redress against the fraudulent use of public monies by Indian governments. Consequently, the IAC was named by the US *Time* magazine as among its 'Top 10 World-News Stories' of 2011.

To mobilise the public's interest, 'netizens' trended anti-corruption messages on Facebook and Twitter. They submitted key words to ISPs, including terms such as 'Lokpal', along with video web streams of lectures provided by Kejriwal, and invited online contributors to interact with him. The filmmaker M.S. Chandramohan, one of the organisation's media strategists, commented that the webcast had received over 2300 questions from more than 20,000 unique viewers. In turn, a Mumbai-based start-up company, Juvenis Technologies, created a mobile phone application (app) for IAC members on the Android marketplace, which enabled them to leave messages of solidarity on a phone number held by the movement's core committee. Deepansh Jain, the founder of Juvenis, was an IAC volunteer who had introduced the app to solicit public support for Hazare's hunger strike. The IAC also benefitted financially by using its social media outlets to collect monies to popularise its message. As television producer and IAC member Abhinandan Sekhri commented:

> Initially we needed more people to join us and decided to use Facebook and Twitter to communicate with people who were becoming a part of... [t]he IAC connect with the social media in that sense happened more out of necessity, than as a well-thought out strategy...We [then] figured [out]...to open all channels for volunteers, funding and donations and communication via the fastest viral mode, which was the social media (Sekhri quoted from Chopra 2014:145).

The IAC's success led to other groups using social media; for example, the group 'Breakthrough' conducted its 'Bell Bajao' campaign against domestic violence through the social networks. Its blog, www.bellbajao. org, provided female victims the opportunity to share their experiences and tap into support networks. Indian attitudes regarding gender rights would be changed forever because of the public outrage engendered on social media in the wake of the infamous Nirbhaya case involving the gang rape, torture and death of a 23-year-old female medical student and the brutal assault of her male friend by five men on a private bus in Delhi on 16 December 2012.

Within days of the attack, the Facebook groups 'Gang Raped in Delhi' and 'Delhi for Women's Safety' were established, and received 5046 and 4263 'likes', respectively. In turn, other Facebook groups were formed, including 'Another girl gang raped in Delhi—Can we stop it?', 'Delhi Gang Rape–Please Don't Ignore "Must Read" For Damini', and 'Delhi Gang Rape–Protest'. Twitter posts such as 'Rashtrapati Bhavan', 'Delhi Gang rape' and 'Raisina Hill' became top-trending hashtags, while dedicated websites provided online petitions. Simultaneously, the Indian cyberspace became littered with blogs criticising the oppression of women and condemning the sexist views concerning rape. These platforms provided constant news flows, stimulated debate and led to public protests. This online revolt was fuelled by the anger of an emerging middle class of educated youth who were frustrated by the impotence of the Indian state in responding effectively to the rape case (Ahmed and Jaidka 2013:28–29).

These changes in social attitudes were further evident when lesbian, gay, bisexual and transgender (LGBT) activists took to social media to challenge prevailing prejudices. In 2009, the political authorities initiated legislation to allow homosexual relations to take place between consenting adults, under Section 377. However, the section was declared unconstitutional by the Delhi High Court on 2 July 2009. In 2013, the Supreme Court of India provoked further wrath by declaring its intention to reverse the law. A flurry of Twitter feeds and posts ensued, emphasising the regressive nature of the laws, in efforts to spread the debate for gay rights and to influence policymakers, judges and members of the public. Subsequently, the Supreme Court decided that any upholding or revocation of the section would be left to parliament and not to the judiciary.

The Indian political establishment had been unprepared for the storm of protest unleashed through social media. Online activists challenged power structures, social attitudes and unaccountable elites. The Indian social media thus informed and reflected a change in the younger generation's political attitudes. Accordingly:

> [i]t is evident that Twitter proved to be an effective tool during these protests at the disposal of a virtual army of activists acting as citizen journalists ready to tweet about every action from the ground. This army was not reporting but also freely expressing their opinion through their tweets, an advantage that had eluded the protest activists during pre-social media era. With the power to tweet your thought activists no longer have to unfurl huge banners [or] depend [on] the mercy of the traditional media to propagate their opinions. (Ahmed and Jaidka 2013:51)

SOUTH AFRICAN SOCIAL MOVEMENTS AND ELECTRONIC COMMUNICATIONS

Social movements in South Africa have mobilised against governmental failures to provide affordable water, electricity and sanitation services. These groups have included the Anti-Privatisation Forum (APF) in Johannesburg: the Anti-Eviction Campaign (AEC) in Cape Town and Abahlali baseMjondolo (AbM: shack dwellers in isiZulu) in Durban and Cape Town. They have challenged local government evictions, opposed utility cut-offs and mobilised resistance against the enforced installation of prepaid water and electricity meters. The groups have brought attention to the inequitable nature of top-down housing policies and the state's intimidation of the public:

> These movements have been very successful at putting issues on the national political agenda. They can operate as well in low-income areas of cities as in rural areas, and while they may make demands for rights, their approaches are often very realistic. Although they are sometimes ignored by the established national media…[they]…have [used] alternative media, often online, with which social movements have close relations. (Bebbington 2012)

The APF, AbM and AEC have used their websites to collate press articles, photographs and statements of solidarity in combination with leaflets and posters. These online communications have enhanced the organisations' national and international forms of visibility, while email distribution lists have enabled them to propagate marches and protest activities. Moreover, the websites have posted material concerning the arrest of activist arrests, so that journalists might report upon their court cases. The groups have also provided online videos detailing their successes (Willems 2011:492–493). In addition, these campaigners have employed Facebook, Twitter and YouTube, allowing members to follow events through the social networks.

Usage of social networking however, has remained limited. For example, the AEC's Facebook page has gained only 391 'friends' and 543 Twitter followers. Because of the lack of broadband and the expensive nature of fixed-line services, the South African campaigners have instead used mobile phones to communicate with one another. Mobile chat technologies like Mixit have not only drastically reduced costs, but have been used as tools of protest. For instance, the AbM backed up its complaints by asking activists to phone governmental officials to demand answers to its inquiries. At the same time, mobile phones have effected new forms of social capital. For instance, for families facing eviction, a short message service (SMS) text to an AEC community leader could prove to be vital. The AEC's campaign secretary noted that the use of mobile phones significantly reduced the many obstacles to organising collective action:

> I think mobile phones have changed the way we work because the mere fact is that nowadays we can SMS and call each other more frequently and also it assists in many dilemmas such as mobility. The way Cape Town is built it's very broad, it takes a lot of roads to get to one place and taking taxis sometimes is very difficult because you have to travel from A to B to C so with mobile phones we can frequently help each other. (Interview, 16 April 2010 quoted from Chiumbu 2012:199)

Yet despite the work of these groups, questions remain as to their success in effecting true reform of South African political values in the face of long-standing economic and political disparity. In particular, these social movements have had to resist a range of bureaucratic and extralegal restraints. Therefore, while the social media have drawn public attention to these inequities, they cannot be said to have provided the means to stem their effects.

ONLINE CENSORSHIP AND FREE SPEECH IN INDIA AND SOUTH AFRICA

There has been no definable Indian governmental policy to control Internet content beyond legislation that has dealt with matters of online security, obscenity and decency. The OpenNet Initiative, however, a project designed to monitor Internet censorship, contends that selective forms of multimedia censorship at federal and state levels have been practiced by the Indian political classes. In India, there have been covert controls in the dissemination of information across the social media.

In June 2000, India's parliament passed the Information Technology Act (ITA) to regulate Internet usage, which included recommendations to authorise digital signatures, ensure security controls and stop the hacking of online transactions. The ITA criminalised the publishing of obscene material and granted power to the police to arrest anyone who violated the legislation. Following the 2008 Mumbai terrorist attacks, in which 171 people were murdered, further amendments enabled the government to block or criminalise online content. In addition, in 2003, the Indian government established the Indian Computer Emergency Response Team (CERT-IN). This agency, which reviewed complaints against offensive content, was able to block public access to specific websites, and demanded that all licensed ISPs comply with its decisions. As it received its authority through executive order, judgments delivered by CERT-IN were not subject to legal redress or appeal.

Therefore, in accordance with their licensing agreements, Indian ISPs, search engines and cybercafe owners have been required to filter out websites identified as security risks. Furthermore, as no prior judicial approval for communications interception is necessary, central and state governments have intervened, and have monitored and decrypted online content. In 2009, the Supreme Court of India ruled that bloggers and moderators were subject to libel suits and criminal prosecution in for any derogatory comments posted on their websites.

The Internet has become an easy target for Indian politicians seeking to blame the social media for the nation's social ills. For example, when the Muzaffarnagar riots broke out in 2013 between Hindus and Muslims in Uttar Pradesh, authorities contended that they had been sparked by a YouTube video rather than a breakdown in community relations:

> The Prime Minister [Singh]…chose to focus on social media's role on fanning communal violence in his address at the National Integration Council. His views on hate speech on social media were echoed by many others, including Uttar Pradesh Chief Minister Akhilesh Yadav, Maharashtra Chief Minister Prithviraj Chavan, Assam Chief Minister Tarun Gogoi, Jharkhand Chief Minister Hemant Soren, Haryana Chief Minister Bhupinder Singh Hooda and Meghalaya Chief Minister Mukul Sangma. The majority of chief ministers, then, favour social media regulation. Ideas thrown forward included taking action within the current legal framework, setting up 'social media laboratories' to monitor posts under intelligence departments and even mobilizing NGOs and prominent citizens to counter social media rumours. (Kaul 2013)

With the proliferation of social media sites, however, civil society organisations have disputed the state's right to access user data. For instance, an Indian member of parliament (MP), Rajeev Chandrasekhar, commented that 'I am mystified by our government's approach both to the Internet and to the millions of Indians using it.…It does not adhere to the values of our republic and democracy' (Chandrasekhar 2012). In addition, despite Indian authorities' attempts to place controls on social media, technophiles argue that these rulings will become irrelevant as users find new ways to circumvent them.

Similarly, there has been debate within South Africa about the nature of free expression on the Internet. Freedom House has noted that political content has not been censored, and bloggers and online content creators have remained free from prosecution:

> The government does not restrict material on contentious topics such as corruption and human rights. Citizens are able to access a wide range of viewpoints, and there are no disproportionate government efforts to limit or manipulate online discussions. (Freedom House 2014)

Indeed, when the state tried to bring about greater restrictions, the proposed controls were rejected by the political leadership or overturned in the courts. In 2013, the controversial Protection of State Information (POSI) Bill was passed by both the upper and lower houses of the National Assembly to outlaw whistleblowing, publishing or accessing of restricted state information through the traditional and digital media. The legislation, which had taken 5 years to draft and had been subject to widespread debate, was accompanied by custodial sentences of up to 25 years for those 'divulging classified information'. However, in a surprising turn of events, Zuma refused to sign the 2013 bill into law, as it did not pass 'constitutional muster' (Smith 2013).

In 2010, the Christian advocacy group, the Justice Alliance of South Africa (JASA), compiled a document entitled 'Internet and Cell Phone Pornography Bill', which proposed outlawing the distribution of pornography by ISPs. This was presented to Deputy Home Affairs Minister Malusi Gigaba, who sought to fast-track a new regulation that would have compelled ISPs to filter out all pornographic content. The process was stymied in 2012 when the Constitutional Court upheld the ruling that any publication pre-screening (including Internet content) as required by the 2009 amendments to the 1996 Films and Publications Act was an unconstitutional impingement upon free expression.

Yet in no way can the South African Internet be described as an open terrain. For instance, under the terms of the 2002 Electronic Communications and Transactions Act (ECTA), ISPs have taken down notices regarding illegal content including child pornography, defamatory material and copyright violations. While members of the Internet Service Providers Association (ISPA) remain exempt from liability for third-party content, they can lose this protection if they do not respond to take-down requests. Thus self-censoring of content by ISPs has been necessary to avoid litigation. Moreover, South Africa participates in bi-lateral regional legal actions to combat cybercrime, and was successful in its demands for Google to remove defamatory content from its search engines.

In 2013, Internet freedom in South Africa was further threatened by the passage of the General Intelligence Laws Amendment Act, which legalised the bulk monitoring of mobile phone conversations, SMS and emails through the National Communications Centre (NCC). The law was justified on the basis of national security and the protection of citizens from terrorist attacks. However, many expressed fears that it would enable the NCC to monitor private conversations without a court-issued warrant. And despite Zuma's rejection of the POSI Bill in September 2013, many civil rights groups believe that the South African authorities will continue to seek to intercept online traffic:

> Nevertheless, concerns over the authorities' ability to illegally intercept private communications were further heightened...when research conducted by Citizen Lab revealed that two FinFisher command and control servers were discovered on the partially state-owned Telkom network in South Africa. Such servers are used to harvest data and user information such as 'screenshots, keylogger data, audio from Skype calls, passwords and more' collected by the spyware suite. (Freedom House 2014)

CONCLUSION

In this chapter we have considered the contemporary economic, political and social processes governing the practices of the information and communications sectors within India and South Africa. Both countries have seen limited but steady growth in digital penetration and take-up of broadband Internet services, which will continue with the further roll-out of online communications to rural populations. This has been accompanied by increasing political engagement among Indian and South African social media users.

The wider use of online resources has led the political parties to realise that they must refine their ways of communicating with the public. Within Indian politics, social media communications have allowed leaders to remain in constant connection with the world's largest electorate. Through Facebook likes and Twitter hashtags, politicians have measured public sentiment regarding trends, agendas and issues. For example, the BJP reformulated its online tactics in the run-up to and during the 2014 Lok Sabha election campaign. Subsequently, the party used social networks to propagate its political messages, define a strong image of leadership and engage with a ground force of political volunteers. The success of BJP's online communication activities was reflected in the party's electoral victory and the correspondingly dismal performance by the INC.

The response to online political discourse in South African politics has been less enthusiastic. While the public has employed social media to become informed about political issues, they have tended to engage in personal dialogue rather than political activism. This lack of political efficacy reflects on how the South African parties used the social networks to broadcast their values rather than engage in any form of reciprocity. Furthermore, the platforms were utilised to focus the parties' attacks on their political opponents, in particular with regard to Zuma's financial malfeasance.

Although the use of social media in mainstream Indian and South African politics has been mixed, social movements and protesters have indeed taken to the Internet to propagate their message. The digital platforms played a key role in the wider dissemination of the IAC's campaign strategies, and the social networks helped to engender public outrage at the Nirbhaya gang rape case. Social media have also enabled LGBT groups to protest against homophobic attitudes in Indian public life. Similarly, South Africa's social movements have employed websites, online videos and mobile telephony in their pursuit of equitable public services and economic justice.

Yet the opportunities for free expression have been hampered in both states by the repressive implications of laws, online forms of censorship and more covert types of self-censorship. Both Indian and South African authorities have exploited content regulation to intervene within the flow of Internet traffic. In India, politicians have achieved traction by portraying the multimedia sector as the purveyor of cybercrime. The South African government has also exercised regressive state control of private communications, bringing into question matters of free expression and democratic accountability. These concerns have led to extensive debate about whether the social media can provide the appropriate medium to overcome perceived democratic deficits within the states of the Global South.

Therefore, in India and South Africa, the democratic potential of the social media has been praised and damned in equal measure. Undoubtedly, the political parties and social movements have utilised the ICTs to broaden their popular appeal and to engage with the public. However, questions remain about how far the social networks can challenge the prevailing norms, values and prejudices which remain in these societies. Today, the ambivalent nature of social media may be best summed up as follows:

> Politics and social media will both face challenges going forward. As politicians learn to use the medium…there will be an effort to break formats, try new campaigns, and expose themselves to praise and criticism….Credibility of social media will remain a subject of debate for years to come but at the same time it will not stop the experiment of testing politics in the online world. (Chopra 2014:205)

BIBLIOGRAPHY

Ahmed, S., and K. Jaidka. 2013. "Protests Against #delhigangrape on Twitter: Analyzing India's Arab Spring". JeDEM 1(5): 28–58. http://www.jedem.org (accessed November 20, 2014).

Alfreds D. 2014. "SA Political Parties Stumble on Social Media—Analyst". *New24. com*, April 2. http://www.news24.com/Technology/News/SA-political-parties-stumble-on-social-media-analyst-20140205 (accessed November 20, 2014).

Bebbington T. 2012. "Social Movements can Change the Developing World", *Economic and Social Research Council Shaping Society*, October 10. http://www.esrc.ac.uk/news-and-events/press-releases/23583/social-movements-can-change-the-developing-world.aspx (accessed November 20, 2014).

Bhaduri A. 2010. "India Unwired—Why New Media is Not (yet) the Message for Political Communication". In *Social Media and Politics: Online Social Networking and Political Communication in Asia*, ed. P. Behnke. Singapore: Konrad-Adenauer-Stiftung Media Programme Asia.

Burbage F. 2014. "Twitpolitik: Parties Tweet Furiously as Election Campaigns Intensify", *The South African,* April 3. http://www.thesouthafrican.com/twitpolitik-parties-tweet-furiously-as-election-campaigns-intensify/ (accessed November 20, 2014).

Chandrasekhar R. 2012. "Don't Kill Freedom of Speech", *Times of India*, November 30. http://rajeev.in/News/Dont_Kill_Freedom/Times_of_India.html (accessed November 20, 2014).

Chiumbu S. 2012. "Exploring Mobile Phone Practices in Social Movements in South Africa—the Western Cape Anti-Eviction Campaign". *African Identities* 10(2): 193–206.

Chopra S. 2014. *The Big Connect: Politics in the Age of the Social Media.* Noida: Random House India.

Durrant N. 2014. South Africa: The Role of Social Media in Political Campaigns. *All Africa.Com,* June 5. http://allafrica.com/stories/201406091382. html?page=2 (accessed November 20, 2014).

Freedom House. 2012. *India Country Report,* Freedom on the Net, Freedom House.

Freedom House. 2014. *South Africa Country Report,* Freedom on the Net, Freedom House. https://freedomhouse.org/report/freedom-net/2014/ south-africa#.VIGFYMk7Fdg (accessed November 20, 2014).

Gopalakrishnan G. 2014. "How the Digital Media Galvanized the Indian Elections", *Lewis PR 360: PR Blog Covering Communication Trends, Social Media and More,* June 17. http://blog.lewispr.com/2014/06/how-digital-media-dominated-the--elections.html (accessed November 20, 2014).

Kamat P. 2014. "The Obamafication Of Indian Political Campaigns", *India at the LSE: LSE's engagement with India,* April 11. http://blogs.lse.ac.uk/indi-aatlse/2014/03/17/the-obamafication-of-indian-political-campaigns/ (accessed November 20, 2014).

Kaul M. 2013. "Social Media Becomes the Scapegoat in India the Regulation of Social Media in India has been a Subject of Great Controversy", *Index on Censorship,* October 7. http://www.indexoncensorship.org/2013/10/india-social-media/ (accessed November 20, 2014).

Nair N. 2014. Narendra Modi in US: Indian Media Happy, Chinese Media Calls it Ludicrous, *India.com,* September 29. http://www.india.com/news/india/ narendra-modi-in-us-indian-media-happy-chinese-media-calls-it-ludicrous-160817/ .

Narasimhamurthy N. 2014. "Use and Rise of Social Media as Election Campaign Medium in India". *International Journal of Interdisciplinary Studies* 1(8): 202–209.

Pillay V. 2014. The DA's Growing Zille Headache. *Mail and Guardian.* February 28. http://mg.co.za/article/2014-02-27-zilles-tweets-rile-the-da (accessed November 20, 2014).

Rajput H. 2014. "Social Media and Politics in India: A Study on Twitter Usage among Indian Political Leaders". *Asian Journal of Multidisciplinary Studies* 2(1): 63–69.

Singh J.P. 2014. "E-government as a Means of Development in India". In *Bits and Atoms: Information and Communication Technology in Areas of Limited Statehood,* eds. S. Livingston, andG. Walter-Drop. Oxford: Oxford University Press.

Smith D. 2013. South Africa Secrecy Law Surprise as Zuma Rejects Controversial Bill: Campaigners Celebrate after President Sends Protection of State Information Bill Back to Parliament. *The Guardian,* September 12.

Strategy Worx. 2014. How SA Political Parties Fare Online—Not so Well, Actually. *The Media Online*, February 8. http://themediaonline.co.za/2014/02/how-sa-political-parties-fare-online-not-so-well-actually/ (accessed November 20, 2014).

Thussu D.K. 2013. *Communicating India's Soft Power: Buddha to Bollywood*. Basingstoke: Palgrave Macmillan.

United Nations Broadband Commission. 2013. The State of Broadband 2013: Universalizing Broadband. September. http://www.broadbandcommission.org/Documents/bb-annualreport2013.pdf (accessed November 20, 2014).

van der Westhuizen C. 2013. South Africa: Confronting Choices About Free Expression: As the G20 Nations Prepare to Meet in St Petersburg, Russia in Early September, Index on Censorship is Exploring the nations' Records on Free Expression. *Index on Censorship*, August 7. http://www.indexoncensorship.org/2013/08/south-africa-a-bric-confronting-choices-about-free-expression/ (accessed November 20, 2014).

Wasserman H. 2014. "The Ramifications of Media Globalization in the Global South for the Study of Media Industries". *Media Industries* 1(2).

Willems W. 2011. "Social Movement Media, Post-apartheid (South Africa)". In *Encyclopaedia of Social Movement Media*, ed. John D.H. Downing, 492–495. London: Sage.

CHAPTER 10

Japan, South Korea, Brazil: Post-industrial Societies; Hard and Software

INTRODUCTION

In this chapter, we present an inter-regional comparison of East Asian and Latin American societies to highlight the nexus of sociocultural, political and economic change as it unfolded in selected post-industrial countries of the two areas, namely Japan, South Korea and Brazil. From a sociological point of view, post-industrialist or 'knowledge' society refers to the state of societal development when the service sector generates more wealth than the manufacturing sector (Bell 1974). In addition to their status as post-industrialist societies and engines of regional economic development, these countries were selected because of their multiculturalism and heavy use of social media. Japan and Korea are obviously a natural fit in terms of geography, culture and political practice. Both societies are fascinating economic and business powers, with rich culture and technical wizardry. Both received fundamental Western aid after their respective wartime eras, and have become leaders in hardware and software technologies. Tokyo, Japan's capital city, for example, is the world's largest metropolitan area, with a population exceeding 30 million. Brazil, on the other hand, with its diverse cultural background, is a leading emerging-market economy, helping to drive both regional and global growth. Focusing on these post-industrial nations, our analysis illustrates the ways in which different development strategies and different 'politics' involved in the processes of regulation and governance and the use of social media have yielded either widely divergent results or unexpected similarities. Whereas East Asian

© The Editor(s) (if applicable) and The Author(s) 2016
P. Iosifidis, M. Wheeler, *Public Spheres and Mediated
Social Networks in the Western Context and Beyond*,
DOI 10.1057/978-1-137-41030-6_10

economies have often been dubbed 'tigers' or 'dragons', Latin American economies have typically been cast in negative terms, producing paradigmatic poles on 'dependency', 'populist democracy' and 'bureaucratic authoritarianism'. Yet the stabilisation and, in most cases, acceleration of the Latin American economies by successive governments has led to 'economic miracle' countries such as Brazil.

In terms of technological developments and social media usage, Japan and South Korea are two of the most technologically advanced nations. Japan has the world's second highest number of social media users, after the USA, and users have enthusiastically embraced trends such as blogging and social gaming. But serious events such as the 2011 earthquake and tsunami have also evidenced the impact of social media. During the chaotic days following these devastating events, with hundreds of thousands in shelters with no phone service, many turned to services like Facebook and Twitter to post personal news or keep in touch with the world. In the other Asian country, South Korea, while many people are using social media for pleasure, they are using social networking for political reasons as well—for example, to voice their worry about the threat of war on the Korean Peninsula, or their desire for their government to cultivate a better relationship with the Pyongyang government. Meanwhile, Brazil, with 67 million active users on Facebook (making it the second largest market outside the USA), can be viewed as the 'social media capital of the world'. With saturation being reached in advanced Asian nations as well as in the USA and Europe, this Latin American country holds the potential for massive growth.

In this chapter, we explore issues surrounding the use of the Internet and social media in the post-industrial societies of Japan and South Korea, and in the fast-developing and social media-obsessed Brazil. More specifically, we begin the chapter by exploring the historical and political context in the East Asian and Latin American regions, as well as outlining the technological, economic and political factors that have shaped online communication within Japan, Korea and Brazil. We offer statistics related to the levels of digital penetration and the adoption of social media as sources of information in the countries under scrutiny. Second, we present the regulatory framework surrounding online communications as well as the use of social media platforms during election campaigns. It is striking that politicians in Korea and Brazil have fully embraced the use of social media for the promotion of their policies, whereas until very recently, Japanese law forbade candidates from using the Internet during election campaigns. Furthermore, the monitoring and censoring of Internet content by the Korea Communication Standards Commission (KSC) has provided obstacles to foreign companies such as Google trying to enter the Korean market. Third, we critically discuss the contribution of social networking tools to the mobilisation and empowerment of people and to the process of democratisation. In this context, we assess whether social networks have provided an alternative space and conduit for information otherwise not available, as well as an alternative trajectory of social action such as demonstrations.

EAST ASIA AND LATIN AMERICA: THE HISTORICAL, ECONOMIC AND POLITICAL CONTEXT

In the post-World War II era, certain East Asian economies including Japan and South Korea emerged as perhaps the most successful in terms of economic development. This remarkable regional economic growth began in Japan after the devastation of World War II in the 1940s, and by the 1960s it was the regional leader. This expansion was swiftly followed by the rise of South Korea and Taiwan in the 1970s and 1980s. These societies grew relatively rapidly from an agricultural base into light industries such as textiles and clothing, and even more rapidly into heavy industries including steel, shipbuilding, automobile manufacturing and, more recently, consumer electronics. These economies moved to so-called primary export-oriented industrialisation (EOI), where export-led growth speeds up the industrialisation process of a country through the exportation of goods and services, opening domestic markets to competition (Gereffi and Wyman 1990). A World Bank overview (1993) noted that East Asia's rapid growth and industrialisation in the period from 1960 to 1990 was associated with equity, public policy, macroeconomic stability and institutional and human capital development (such as education). However, the 1997 Asian financial crisis and accompanying recession slowed the economies in the region. Japan's rapid post-war expansion—propelled by the automobile and consumer electronics industries—suffered the effects of a recession in the 1990s under a growing debt burden that successive governments had failed to address. The crisis began in Thailand and spread to South Korea.

However, the 1997 Asian crisis did not result in the type of situation that Latin American nations experienced in the 1980s (this period is commonly known as Latin America's 'lost decade'[1]), and in any case, Taiwan was scarcely affected, while South Korea returned to a growth phase in just 2 short years. Japan has lost its status as the world's second largest economy, having ceded the position to China in 2010, although it continues to claim superiority in the automobile industry (Toyota) and family entertainment products (Nintendo Wii).

While East Asian economies moved to EOI, Latin American countries adopted secondary import substituting industrialisation (ISI), in which infant industries lacking international competitiveness are helped by their respective governments in developing a domestic market. International financial institutions, notably the World Bank and International Monetary Fund, claimed that East Asian economic success was achieved because of the adoption of free market mechanisms, whereas the Latin American slowdown was attributable to excessive government interference in the economy. But this neo-liberal stance fails to acknowledge that governmental involvement was (and still is) an essential component of East Asian economic development. Arguing against the neo-liberal paradigms that marked East Asia's economic development to the emergence of a free market in the region, Johnson (1982) noted that in Japan, the state was instrumental in sponsoring economic growth; following a long tradition of government involvement in economic management during the pre-war period, strong bureaucratic and government-guided industrial policy were key to Japan's post-war industrial advancement. In Korea, government-sponsored schemes encouraged the growth of family-owned industrial conglomerates such as Hyundai and Samsung, which helped transform Korea into one of the world's major economies and a leading exporter of automobiles and electronic goods. Brazil, on the other hand, has traditionally been characterised by a high degree of state connection with the wider business community[2] and President Dilma Rousseff's belief that a strong

---

[1] In the 1960s and 1970s many Latin American countries like Brazil, Argentina and Mexico borrowed huge sums of money from international creditors, notably the World Bank, for industrialization and infrastructure programmes. While these countries had soaring economies at the time, and thus the creditors were happy to continue to provide loans, the world economy went into recession in the late 1970s and 1980s and oil prices skyrocketed, creating a breaking point for most countries in the region.

[2] During the dictatorship years, the state in Brazil, as well as many of the other countries of the region, was traditionally assigned a role of political control and censorship. State intervention in Latin America was further aimed at reinforcing governmental powers rather than promoting democratic communications. As Fox and Waisbord (2002:xxii) noted, the whole Latin American region has had a culture of promiscuous relationships between governments and the media, thereby undermining aspirations for democratic media change.

state role remains necessary in strategic areas, including the banking, energy and oil industries. Thanks to government-backed development of offshore fields, Brazil has become self-sufficient in natural resources such as oil, ending decades of dependence on foreign producers. Yet allegations of government corruption remain on the political agenda. Rousseff's approval ratings have fallen to an all-time low amid a large corruption scandal at the state-owned energy giant Petrobras, as well as elevated inflation and a deteriorating economy.

In Brazil, as well as the rest of Latin America, the period known as the national development and industrialisation phase (1930–1960) witnessed the passage of embryonic media legislation defining the principles of the radio–electromagnetic spectrum as a public space and the implementation of antitrust rules to combat concentration of ownership. The Brazilian economy had been stabilised under Fernando Henrique Cardoso in the mid-1990s, and accelerated under Luiz Inacio Lula da Silva in the early 2000s, which resulted in economic and social advantages such as the adoption of anti-poverty programmes, greater equality and upgraded public services. However, after almost two decades of growth, reaching 7.5 % in 2010, economic growth slowed to a mere 0.9 % in 2012, leading to government cutbacks and wide-scale protests. Social conditions remain harsh in the large cities of Rio de Janeiro and São Paulo, where a third of the population lives in favelas, or slums. Brazil's diverse and colourful cultural background, a product of ethnic and cultural mixing during the period of Portuguese colonisation, is manifest in the many celebrations and festivals, such as the Rio Carnival that attracts numerous tourists each year.

In contrast, Japan remains a traditional society, stressing the values of harmony, consensus decision-making and social conformity, with strong social and employment hierarchies, where workers typically remain with the same employer throughout their working lives. However, this tendency has begun to fade as the young generation is increasingly influenced by Western culture and ideas. In direct contrast to the predominantly young Brazilian population (62 % of Brazilians are under 29 years of age), Japan's population has been ageing at an alarming rate, due to a combination of minimal net immigration and low fertility rate of roughly 1.2 children born for every Japanese woman. Japan's relations with its neighbours (especially South Korea and China) are still heavily influenced by the legacy of Japanese actions before and during World War II. Koreans, on the other hand, are warm and generous people, although they rarely smile or laugh. Relations with its northern neighbour remain a major concern in Seoul, particularly regarding North Korea's fragile economy and its nuclear ambitions.

With regard to the development of the Internet and social media, the different historical, sociocultural and economic paths followed by these societies have resulted in different usage patterns and regulatory approaches. Internet security restrictions in Korea emanate from the Korean War. For example, map data cannot be exported, as they may fall into the hands of the North Koreans. Yet, unlike the Internet freedom enjoyed by both businesses and consumers in Brazil, these regulations provide obstacles to foreign companies trying to enter the Korean market. In addition, Japan has very specific visions of 'conformity' and 'privacy' guided by the cultural, ethical and ideological values enshrined within society. This also contrasts with the governmental and political system in Brazil, where embedded values and practices have called for an open and unregulated web. New media laws, replacing those in place since the military dictatorships of the 1970s, have helped overcome obstacles that have historically undermined democratic journalism in Brazil and the rest of Latin America, while increasing usage of the Internet and social media have raised awareness of the roots of Brazil's structural inequalities and provided opportunities for civic expression and engagement. While local politics and globalisation have impacted on the development of the Internet and social media in both regions, the use of social media for protests in Brazil is evident, whereas it is less common in Japan and Korea, where there may be less volatile or open forms of political culture. Brazilians enjoy Internet freedom, and local civil society actors have used social networks to promote their policies, but the Japanese and Korean governments have attempted to regulate and censor the Internet, including Japan's very strict laws governing election campaigning.

While all three societies can be characterised as post-industrial, with Japan and Korea labelled as ferocious 'tigers' and Brazil having become one of the leading BRICS nations and the economic driver of Latin American economies, the levels of development have differed, as Brazil, unlike the two Asian countries, has emerged from a mixture of post-colonialism and political dictatorship. By examining East Asian and Latin American development from a comparative perspective, this chapter provides a comprehensive view of three post-industrial societies that have become leaders in their respective regions, and explores the ostensible 'politics' involved in the process of regulation, governance and use of social media within these states.

JAPAN

The Digital Media Environment

Data provided by the International Guide to Social Media (2014) reveal that the Japanese spend the greatest amount of time online (2.9 hours a day) among countries worldwide. Japan has the fourth largest population of Internet users globally, as noted in a study conducted by Singapore Management University (http://www.translatemedia.com/translation-services/social-media/guide-to-international-social-media, accessed 7 April 2015), and the Japanese have been described in the US media as 'blog-wild', given their dominance of the blogosphere (close to 32 million people in Japan blog, representing one in four in a country of about 127 million). As much as 40 % of Japanese blogging is conducted on mobile phones, although Internet use and blog content are typically entertainment-oriented and have little to do with politics. Unlike many of their Western counterparts, bloggers in Japan generally shy away from politics, controversy and barbed language (Abjorensen 2013:22). Online gaming is hugely popular, suggesting that distraction and entertainment take priority over political discussion. An academic study revealed little taste for political engagement or discussion in the use of social media; instead, the five top reasons given for adopting social media were killing time, having fun, getting information about areas of interest, contact with friends and ease of communication with friends (cited in Abjorensen 2013:38).

In terms of regulation, the Japanese government has made substantial effort to regulate and censor the Internet. The major players involved in telecommunications and Internet legislation are politicians, Ministry of Internal Affairs and Communications (MIC) bureaucrats, communications companies and broadcasters such as Nippon Telegraph and Telephone Corp. (NTT), KDDI Corp. and Softbank Corp. Over time, the MIC has developed online policies and laws in a setting where bureaucrats, rather than politicians, usually prepare bills (Nishioka and Sugaya 2014:121–122). Regarding the Internet specifically, officials promote the use of filtering software against what they judge to be harmful information on the web. Key areas of concern are group suicides, the production of explosives, and child prostitution and rape. Internet filtering initiatives against group suicide include requiring Internet service providers (ISPs) to disclose information to the police on senders of messages regarding planned suicides, educating the public about the dangers of 'harmful online information' and providing enhanced availability of related consulting services, increasing the monitoring of suspicious sites and encouraging the installation of Internet-filtering software by schools and public offices. Meanwhile, Internet-filtering initiatives against child prostitution and rape have concentrated on dating sites, since it is estimated that there are about 5000 competing dating sites within the country, and Japan's National Police Agency has reported that 85 % of all crimes related to online dating involve minors (see https://wiki.smu.edu.sg/digitalmedi-aasia/Digital_Media_in_Japan#Regulations, accessed 7 April 2015).

Japan's Social Media Landscape

The social media landscape in Japan, one of the world's largest economies, is diverse and well developed, with many players competing for market share. International social networking platforms such as Facebook and Twitter are battling for dominance alongside large domestic networks such as Mixi and GREE. Similar to the situation in China, the domestic social networks in Japan have remained more popular than Facebook, but unlike China, the growth and popularity of local social networking sites has not been achieved through governmental Internet constraints and blocking of foreign sites. People on this island in the Pacific Ocean are extremely mobile-centric, which has led local brands to focus their energy on engaging consumers through social media on mobile devices (Spackman 2014). As the country was an early adopter of mobile Internet (Internet penetration in Japan was over 86 % in 2014), most local Japanese social networks have been developed for mobile use. In addition, the Japanese tend to remain closed and restrained in expressing themselves on social media. Between 2006 and 2011, the local network Mixi, founded in 2004, was the number-one choice among media platforms, largely because it ensured privacy and anonymity by allowing online pseudonyms. However, the network was rather late in adopting smartphone-compatible technology, which eventually resulted in a loss of users. Meanwhile, Facebook and Twitter have been gaining ground, especially among college students and the younger generation in general, who are more open-minded and ready to display aspects of their private lives in online forums, and local-language competitors have gradually lost popularity (Spackman 2014).

Table 10.1 shows that the microblogging site Twitter, which launched its Japanese version in 2008, is highly popular, with 30 million active users,

Table 10.1 Top five social networks in Japan (May 2014)

Social network	Active users (millions)
Twitter	30
GREE	29
Mixi	25
Facebook	17
LINE	36

Source: Simcott 2014; also http://www.digitalstrategyconsulting.com/intelligence/2013/02/top_6_social_networks_in_japan.php (accessed 5 April 2015)

largely because it allows its users to retain their anonymity online. The Japanese place a high value on this element of privacy, as it allows them to be less inhibited in voicing their opinions. Japanese Twitter users regularly break tweeting records. At one point during the 2010 FIFA World Cup in South Africa, Japanese users were tweeting 3283 times per second, and within an hour of the 2011 earthquake, more than 1200 tweets per minute were being sent from Tokyo. Meanwhile, the number of active users on Facebook has grown to almost 17 million (a 300 % increase over 2012). While the Japanese had been hesitant to subscribe to the network due to the real-name policy,–this situation changed dramatically after the 2011 tsunami and earthquake. Because Japanese society is characterised by high levels of social conformity, social networks generally take some time to gain popularity, but the destructive events of 2011 triggered a wave of new subscribers. The growing embrace of westernisation in general among Japanese youth has also contributed to the increased take-up. Today, the platform tends to be used more as a business network, with some business persons adopting it to market themselves and promote their accomplishments. In addition, it is used more heavily by graduates for job-hunting than people mid-career.

The local network GREE, founded in 2004 and launched on mobile a year later, has around 190 million users worldwide, with 15 % of its users (29 million) based in Japan. After its mobile launch, GREE shifted its focus away from social networking, and towards mobile gaming. Mixi, also founded in 2004, accepts members by invitation only and is restricted to those over 18 years of age. It provides users with their own page, where they can blog, share photos and form communities. Mixi was once the largest social network in the country, but with the growing popularity of other platforms—Twitter, primarily, but also Facebook—its role has been diminished, with just over 25 million users. Launched in 2011, LINE, with about 36 million users, is more an instant-messaging application, similar to China's WeChat, than a traditional social network. The basic functionality allows users to send text messages and make free calls to other users who have the app installed on their smartphones. Finally, Mobage, with around 40 million users, is a social mobile gaming platform on which developers can deploy their games so that they can be discovered and shared by mobile gamers.

Social Networking Through a Crisis: The Role of Social Media in the 2011 Japan Earthquake and Tsunami

The disasters of 2011—the earthquake, tsunami and nuclear accident—profoundly affected both the extent and type of social media usage in Japan. According to Wallop (2011), websites powered by broadband connections became a lifeline for many when mobile phone networks and some telephone landlines collapsed in the hours following the 8.9-magnitude earthquake. With hundreds of thousands of customers trying to call or text at the same time, many mobile phone networks and landline operators were unable to cope in the immediate aftermath of the crisis. International networks Twitter, Facebook and Skype, alongside local popular network Mixi, became the easiest, quickest and most reliable way to keep in touch with relatives, as well as to provide emergency numbers and information to those in stricken areas. Twitter and Facebook are still not as popular in Japan as in other countries, but the number of Facebook accounts alone has increased approximately tenfold since before the earthquake. In fact, the surge in use drove sites such as Twitter and Facebook into the mainstream, where they have remained since. Japanese users who had long been unwilling to use their real names online, sticking to local anonymous networks like Mixi, were suddenly revealing the names of dead relatives and posting pictures of their destroyed homes (Alabaster 2013). Technology helped in other ways, for the NHK, the Japanese state television broadcaster, was streaming footage via iPhone applications to viewers on the other side of the world, allowing the international community to watch live pictures.

The results of a survey carried out by Peary, Shaw and Takeuchi (2012) suggest that social media demonstrated a very high level of reliability during the disaster, regardless of their role, location or level of affectedness.

For individuals who were directly affected, the convenience and the capability for mass communication were the most important reasons for utilising social media during the disaster. These networks were subsequently used for vital relief functions such as safety identification, location of displaced persons, sources of damage information, support for disabled individuals, volunteer organising, fundraising and moral support systems. In the same vein, Tseng, Chen and Chi (2011) showed that the use of social media could benefit government bodies and NGOs in disaster preparedness and disaster relief actions. Public figures can use social media to aid survival in the face of crisis and to generate resources through donations and volunteer efforts. Indeed, this was exactly the action taken a couple of weeks into the crisis by Katsunobu Sakurai, the mayor of Minami-Souma, who uploaded a video on YouTube in an appeal for volunteers, food and supplies to save his town (Tseng, Chen, and Chi 2011).

The social media have provided a source of information flow independent of those dominated by the state and mass media, often challenging the official versions of events. To some extent, social networks have offered individuals new ways to associate and collaborate, and have occasionally provided individuals a route through which to mobilise and form larger collectives capable of mounting coordinated actions. In the months since the disaster unfolded, Japan has witnessed a very powerful example of the potential of social media as a tool for social and political action (Slater, Keiko, and Kindstrand 2012). As is now well known, a massive explosion wracked a nuclear power station in north-eastern Japan, which had been badly damaged in the devastating earthquake and tsunami. The government sought to play down fears of a meltdown at the Fukushima 1 plant, although officials later announced that the cooling system of a second reactor at the plant had failed, sparking fears of further explosions or leakage of radioactive material. In the decade prior to the earthquake and tsunami, Japan's anti-nuclear power movement was peripheral at best, but as the deeply ingrained illusion of nuclear power as 'safe' began to unravel, the fear of—and opposition to—nuclear energy increased exponentially. The sense of urgency provoked spontaneous mobilisation in new and constantly changing network configurations, culminating in thousands marching against nuclear power in Tokyo on 10 April, 7 May and 11 June 2011 (Slater, Keiko, and Kindstrand 2012).

As Abjorensen (2013:35–36) noted, in a crisis situation, with communications and power disruptions, social media became a 'go-to' point for information. Twitter use, for instance, increased from one in 20 Japanese in 2009, to one in 2 or one in 3 by the end of 2012. The author went on to argue that take-up of online activity has extended beyond the immediate crisis, to fierce discussions in its wake, as leftist activists and pundits have joined their right-leaning rivals in a robust online debate about the role of nuclear power in Japan following the Fukushima disaster, the world's worst in a quarter-century. A perceived lack of timely and credible information from officials and media about radiation risk generated a post-disaster Twitter clamour, which saw the number of its computer users spike by some five million, to 17.5 million, in March 2011 (Abjorensen 2013). It is clear, then, that social media were instrumental in enabling connections among disparate groups for a common cause. Social networks thus acted as a facilitator, revealing that it is through the deployment of technology, rather than simply its availability, that social activism may be achieved.

Social Media and Political Campaigning

Japan is a mature democracy, having held elections for over a century, and providing its citizens political freedom including the right to vote and freedom of expression. It has a national system of government in which the Japanese parliament, or diet (the 'Diet'), functions as the highest organ of state power. The Diet is composed of the House of Representatives (lower house) and the House of Councillors (upper house). The Liberal Democratic Party (LDP) has been in power since 1955, except for a brief 11-month period between 1993 and 1994, and from 2009 to 2012, when the Democratic Party of Japan (DPJ) formed a government. In the 2012 election, the LDP regained government control, and it currently holds 295 seats in the lower house and 115 seats in the upper house. But unlike those of other developed democratic countries, the laws governing election campaigning in Japan have not kept pace with the far-reaching changes in political and public communication. Until as recently as 2013, Japanese law forbade candidates from using the Internet during election campaigns, which extended to simple things such as updating their websites, appearing online or even tweeting their names. In effect, Japan's Public Offices Election Law (POEL), passed in 1950 (Act no. 100 of 1950), precluded candidates for public office and political parties from using communication, information or political advocacy tools available on the Internet during the official election period. As Wilson (2011:3) opined, POEL undermined political freedom and directly clashed with the desire of political actors to freely promote their ideals, disseminate policies, engage in political discussion and gauge political currents via Internet tools. It also hampered voters' rights, citizens' participation in the political process and the actions of grass-roots activists. With time, Japan's election and campaign law came to contrast sharply with the country's widespread Internet diffusion and the popularity of Web 2.0.

A rewriting of the rigid election law, however, occurred in 2013, bringing about a sea change in electioneering practices. Two bills have been submitted to the Diet: one by the LDP–New Komeito Party ruling coalition and the other sponsored by Your Party and the DPJ. Both bills would enable candidates, for the first time in the country's history, to use the Internet in campaigns, including blogs and social networking services such as Facebook and Twitter. The governing conservative LDP, historically known more for its good old handshakes-on-the-street campaigns, has emerged as an unlikely leader on the social media front. Led by Prime Minister Abe—who in 2013 had 145,000 followers on Twitter and 373,000 'likes' on his Facebook page— the LDP has unleashed a social media war, training its candidates to use iPad minis and urging them to subscribe to Facebook, Twitter and YouTube. The political party even developed a smartphone game—called Abe Pyon, or 'Abe Jump'—that features a cartoon version of Shinzo Abe being vaulted into the sky. As he jumps higher, players are able to unlock facts about the party, eventually earning a superhero cape (Tabuchi 2013). It may be that Japanese candidates are coming late to the social media party, but the change in the law has already engendered innovative campaign strategies. Political commentators expect this to result in greater transparency in Japanese politics and more robust political discussion by giving voters direct access to lawmakers, and to reverse chronically low youth voter turnout (in the last two parliamentary elections in 2010 and 2012, turnout among voters in their 20s was less than 40 % [Tabuchi 2013]).

Indeed, social media sites provide political parties and candidates the opportunity to promote and revise their policies based on feedback received from a wide range of the electorate. The introduction of Internet campaigns is also expected to spark debate between voters on policy issues and to encourage typically apolitical young people to participate in the democratic political process. With the Internet, voters can push for issues that are important to them and challenge television news stories that have tended to focus on particular issues and to set the election agenda. Politicians and citizens in Japan, however, are well aware that in countries that have already legalised online election campaigns, the Internet has dramatically changed the face of the electoral process, for better or for worse. The greatest concern in Japan, a nation known for its social conformity, resistance to change and caution in matters of privacy, is how to prevent the occurrence of libel through identity theft. Japanese voters recall that during presidential elections in neighbouring South Korea, as well as in other developed democracies such as the USA, malicious slander was frequently circulated on the Internet as part of smear campaigns against certain candidates. In South Korea, for example, in September 2014, the National Police Agency announced measures to prevent the spread of malicious online postings regarding President Park Geun-Hye, whose personal life has been a topic of socially divisive and destructive online comments. The new bill empowers Internet service providers to address privacy issues and to delete malicious comments where appropriate. It also provides for punishment of identity fraud (falsifying identity and posting damaging messages) with large fines or even imprisonment for up to 2 years. It remains to be seen whether these privacy concerns will be addressed promptly, and if transparency will be enhanced, as Japan at last begins to embrace the Internet phenomenon and revises its electoral laws.

SOUTH KOREA

The Northeast Asian country of South Korea (officially the Republic of Korea) consistently tops the UN ICT Development Index, a tool that benchmarks societies' use of global information technologies. With 41 million Internet users, Korea is among the countries with the highest online penetration in the Asia-Pacific region, and is the world leader in Internet connectivity, with 84 % Internet penetration and an average download speed in the capital city of Seoul of 47 Mbps—five times as fast as the average cable modem in the USA. In terms of mobile user demographics, more than 78 % of Koreans use smartphones, with the heaviest use in the 18–24 age bracket. The country is a pioneer in innovation, and in January 2014, the Korean government announced plans to roll out a 5G mobile network by 2020, with an investment commitment of US $1.5 billion. Korea hosts top mobile telecommunications and technology firms including Samsung and LG, and the government plans to implement new features such as ultra-HD, hologram transmission and top-of-the-line social networking services. As Steimle (2015) notes, all this may paint a picture of Korea as the ideal place in which to launch a social media start-up. However, despite its ideal environment for technological innovation, Korea's strict regulation of the Internet has stifled, rather than nurtured, its social media potential (Steimle 2015).

Korea's Social Media Landscape

Similar to Japan, Korea's most popular network and messaging platform, KakaoTalk, is not foreign-based, but home-grown. Since the time of its launch in 2010, Korean-headquartered KakaoTalk has been the country's most popular social network, and today boasts approximately 48 million active users per month, with 39 % penetration (*see* Table 10.2). The multifaceted messaging platform allows free calls, multimedia messaging and event scheduling, as well as in-application shopping. In its latest Technology Fast 500 Asia Pacific survey, Deloitte named KakaoTalk the number-one technology company in the Asia–Pacific region (*see* Steimle 2015). However, in October 2014, the site encountered issues with user privacy, as fears of state surveillance caused a large number of users to defect to foreign messaging applications. KakaoTalk responded by introducing security features like message encryption and publicly announcing that it would not allow authorities to monitor user messages. The co-chief executive of the company, Lee Sirgoo, publicly apologised to users and assured them that the site would make privacy a top priority in cases of a clash between privacy and state regulations. It is clear, then, that Korean social media users value privacy as much as their Japanese counterparts, and it was not clear whether the company's decision to deny prosecutors' access requests would force the company into a legal confrontation with the government. Despite these privacy concerns, however, KakaoTalk still has wide a reach in the domestic market, and brands can use the messaging platform for marketing purposes.

Table 10.2 Top four social networks in Korea (end of 2014)

Social network	Active users (millions)	% Penetration
KakaoTalk	48	39
Facebook	29	26
Twitter	19	13
LINE	14 million	9

Source: Steimle 2015; *see also* http://www.statista.com/statistics/284473/south-korea-social-network-penetration (accessed 5 April 2015)

Foreign-based social network platforms Facebook and Twitter are also popular, with 29 million and 19 million active users, respectively (*see* Table 10.2). The messaging platform LINE is a subsidiary of Korea's Naver Corporation, and has about 14 million users in its home country. As shown above, however, it has proven most popular in other parts of Asia, especially Japan, where it has 36 million active users (*see* Table 10.1) but also Taiwan, Thailand and Indonesia. It should be noted that Cyworld was Korea's largest social network (in its prime in 2011 it boasted a user base of 24.7 million), but following two unsuccessful attempts to enter international markets, the platform announced the shutdown of its global service in 2012, eventually giving way to Facebook (Steimle 2015).

Internet Regulation

The KCSC is the administrative body that monitors and censors the Internet content in this country of 50 million people. KCSC's Internet censorship is rigorous. In 2013, it blocked or deleted 104,400 websites or pages, mainly based overseas, up from the blocking of about 40,000 foreign websites and the deletion of about 18,000 domestic server-based websites or pages in 2012. Despite the high rates of connectivity, Korea has some odd Internet regulations for a nation that is among the most digitally advanced. For instance, the KCSC blocks 'objectionable' content, including pornography, prostitution and gambling, all of which are illegal in the country, and school children cannot play online games in the evening. Adults who wish to play online games at night are required to provide their resident registration numbers, and until 2014, commentators were required to use their legal names when posting comments. In addition, Google Maps can provide directions only via public transit, not by car, bike or on foot; and maps and other navigation data cannot be exported outside the country. Many of the security restrictions stem from the Korean War—map data, for instance, cannot be exported, as they may fall into the hands of the North Koreans. These regulations, however, provide obstacles to foreign companies trying to enter the Korean market. Google, for example, finds it difficult to offer competitive mapping services because of the map data export restriction. Consequently, Korea is one of the few places where Google is not the number-one search engine. Instead, Naver, a Korean-language search engine, is the top search site in the country (*see* http://venturebeat.com/2013/10/14/korea-internet-regulation).

Virtual child pornography is at the centre of concerns, and it is strictly regulated both domestically and internationally. Korea joined the global regulatory trend by amending the definition of child pornography in paragraph 5 of Article 2 of the Act on the Protection of Children and Juveniles from Sexual Abuse in September 2011. The original definition stated that 'the term "child or juvenile pornography" means the depiction of children or juveniles doing an act specified in subparagraph 4...', whereas the amended definition states that 'the term "child or juvenile pornography" means the depiction of children or juveniles, or of persons or expressions that can be recognised as children or juveniles...' Since the adoption of the amendment, there has been a sharp increase in the arrest and prosecution of alleged perpetrators of the distribution, consumption/use or simple possession of virtual child pornography (Yoo and Lee 2014:149). In addition, under the 2005 Act on Promotion of Information and Communication Network Utilization and Information Protection, the distribution of the following types of information through the ICTs is prohibited: any information related to the distribution, sale, lease or public exhibition of obscene content; repeated delivery of content that causes fear or anxiety; any information that damages, destroys, deletes, modifies or forges ICT system data; information that discloses national secrets; information related to speculative activities prohibited by law; and information that attempts, aids or abets the commission of a crime (for additional detail, see http://unpan1.un.org/intradoc/groups/public/documents/APCITY/UNPAN025694.pdf).

As reported in *The Economist* (2014), critics have suspected Korean state political interference. In 2004, Internet users were required to include their names and ID numbers on political comments in the run-up to an election. In 2009, those posting any comments on websites with over 100,000 daily visitors had to do the same. That law has since been rescinded, and although the government is easing some restrictions, it is stepping up its monitoring of social media. For instance, in 2011, the KCSC established a special subcommittee on social media, and the following year asked for the removal of 4500 comments on networking sites including Facebook and Twitter—13 times as many as in 2010. The number of comments deleted increased to 6400 in 2013, reinforcing the impression that the KCSC essentially operates as a censorship body (*The Economist* 2014).

The most common form of censorship currently involves ordering ISPs to block the IP address of anti-government websites. Precisely because of South Korea's Internet censorship, website restrictions and extremely detailed anti-government laws, there is no strong anti-government group in the country. Since the freedom to criticise government leaders and their policies is limited to the extent that it 'endangers national security' or is considered by censors to be 'cyber-defamation', freedom of speech and democratisation suffer. In this way, this otherwise futuristic country is stuck in the 'dark ages'.

Election Campaigns and Social Media

Unlike Japan, where the use of the Internet and social media for political campaigns remained officially banned until very recently, in Korea, election campaigns using social networking services such as KakaoTalk, Twitter and Facebook have intensified (Takeda 2012). Korea, like Japan, had effectively restricted the support or criticism of certain candidates on the Internet following the Constitutional Court's ruling in 2011, although it has since been widely accepted that campaigns using social media enhance voters' freedom of political expression (*see* Kim Eun-jung 2011).

Recent Korean elections have underscored the emergence of social networking services as a crucial tool in the political arena. Twitter, Facebook and home-grown networks such as KakaoTalk were widely used to mobilise voters in party campaigns and public debates. In 2012, one in five Koreans used at least one social network platform for communication of political messages. Those in their 20s showed the highest social media take-up rate, at 61 %, followed by 30-somethings at 35.5 %. The rates for those in their teens and 40s were 35.3 % and 16.9 %, correspondingly. A survey showed that Koreans spent an average of 73 minutes, 12 seconds per day on social networking sites, longer than they spent on text messages or phone calls (Park Han-na and Yoon Min-sik 2013:45).

Moon Jae-in, the former chief of staff to the late President Roh Moo-hyun, was first to announce his bid for the presidency in July 2012, followed one month later by Park Geun-hye, the daughter of late authoritarian President Park Chung-hee and long-time presidential hopeful (Park, Han-na, and Min-sik Yoon 2013:53). As the above-mentioned ruling has made it officially possible to use social media during the presidential election period, social networking platforms were used heavily in the last two presidential campaigns, which involved President Park Chung-hee and her major contender, Moon. Kim Chul-kyun, head of the Park camp social networking headquarters, described the social media 'as the most appropriate ones to show a candidate's human aspects and nurture a sense of affinity' (Takeda 2012). In fact, Park's party grabbed the attention of voters after it posted rare pictures of Park's private life on KakaoTalk, including the candidate making coffee in her kitchen and playing with her dog. Likewise, Moon, a former close aide to late President Roh Moon-hyun, who won the presidential election supported by 'netizens' in 2001, has been aggressively posting messages on Twitter and Facebook. Cho Han-ki, Moon's social media chief, declared that 'Twitter can multiply many times the original tweet through retweeting [so] its influence is unfathomable' (Takeda 2012).

Opinions posted on social networking sites can affect the political scene. In a country where more than 30 million people carry smart-phones, the use of social media to interact with the public is now essential. It is likely that future political campaigns will revolve around social media, and it is worth watching how the political role of the younger generation, who has grown up using the Internet, will develop. But developments should be treated with caution. Park Han-na and Yoon Min-sik (2013:59) ask: Will social media platforms maximise their advantage and become the new leaders of South Korea's political landscape, or will they retreat into minority status after their moment of glory? Some commentators (Takeda 2012) are also cautious about linking liberalised Internet use to the enhancement of democracy, for although voters can post messages freely, political camps have strengthened efforts to monitor postings so that they can promptly counter or halt the propagation of any unfavourable comments.

While the social media environment in both Asian societies of Korea and Japan is well advanced, with social network sites used as a tool of social and political action, the respective governments have attempted to regulate and censor the Internet and social media by blocking specific sites. Conversely, the largely unregulated web in the leading Latin American economy of Brazil has enabled social movements and grass-roots organisations to have a say. Social media-driven protests in Brazil have proliferated, and the social media are now viewed as an alternative virtual space within which to react to government propaganda and the traditional media's typically government-friendly coverage. We now turn to Latin America's largest digital democracy.

BRAZIL

Online and Social Media

According to comScore (2014), Brazil is among the world leaders in online engagement, with users spending about 30 hours per month online on their PCs and/or laptops, 7 hours more than the global average. Latin America as a whole is one of the world's fastest-growing Internet markets, and as will be shown below, various authors have described the web's positive economic, social and political implications, with the potential to create a more democratic and participatory society (*see* Matos 2014; Waisbord 2015). In fact, 40 % of Latin America's 169 million Internet users are in Brazil. From February 2013 to February 2014, the number of unique visitors grew by 11 %, reaching 80,000 at the end of February 2014, compared to 72,000 at the end of February 2013. In terms of online audience profile, it is not surprising that 65 % of the total Internet audience comprises people aged 35 years or younger. From February 2013 to February 2014, the large states of São Paulo and Rio de Janeiro had the highest increase in Internet usage, with growth of about 25,000 and 10,000 unique visitors, respectively.

In terms of the average number of daily visitors to social media websites, Brazil ranks highest among Latin American countries, and the average minutes per visit is greater than the average for each of the five major global regions (North America, Europe, Latin America, Asia Pacific and Middle East–Africa). Accounting for up to 10 % of the total minutes spent on social media globally, Brazil ranks second in total time spent on social media sites (comScore 2014). Facebook is by far the most popular social network in the country, followed by other social sites such as LinkedIn and Twitter. The social media site Orkut was the most popular in Brazil, but after 10 years of operation, it closed down in September 2014 after 10 years of operation, and most of its users have now migrated to Facebook. As such, Facebook is by some distance the top social networking site in the country, with Brazilians in 2014 spending more time on Facebook than the spent online by the populations of Mexico and Argentina combined. The social networking landscape is growing rapidly, as evidenced by the number of users on Facebook, which increased 179 % between January 2013 and June 2014.

Table 10.3 shows the most popular social networks in Brazil as of mid-2014, based on their numbers of unique visitors. Facebook led the group,

Table 10.3 Top five social networks in Brazil (mid-2014)

Social network	Unique visitors (in millions)
Facebook	66.98
ShareThis	38.24
Google+	13.56
LinkedIn	13.09
Twitter	11.49

Source: comScore (2014); also http://www.statista.com/statistics/254734/most-popular-social-networking-sites-in-brazil (accessed 8 April 2015)

with almost 67 million, followed at some distance by ShareThis at about 38 million, and Google+ (14 million), LinkedIn (13 million) and Twitter (11.5 million).

In terms of regulation, there are no government restrictions on access to the Internet, and there have been no citizen complaints of government monitoring of e-mail or Internet chat rooms. Individuals and groups can thus use the Internet, including email, to express their views. In fact, in April 2014, Brazil's president signed into law a wide-ranging civil rights bill for Internet users and ISPs (the 'Marco Civil da Internet', or 'Marco Civil'). The law (12,965/2014) was foreseen as early as 2009, but was only recently made a priority by the Brazilian government in the wake of Edward Snowden's revelations about US National Security Agency (NSA) espionage activities targeting Brazilian communications data. Briefly, the Marco Civil da Internet introduces protections of a number of rights for Internet users and ISPs, encompassing freedom of expression, interoperability, the use of open standards and technology, protection of personal data, accessibility, multi-stakeholder governance and open government data. Privacy will be dealt with by a general data protection bill still making its way through the Brazilian legislative process (*see* Cooper 2014).

The Changing Social and Political Landscape

Since the 1980s, Latin America's social and political institutions have witnessed various changes, ranging from the collapse of military dictatorships in the mid-1980s, to the adoption of economic neo-liberal reforms, calls for social and economic inclusion and equality and the alignment of media regulatory policies with the public interest. In fact, since the early 2000s, the region has experienced one of the most active periods of media reform, with public mobilisation, openness to global flows, emergence of the Internet and online citizen debate, changes in judicial processes and the passage of dozens of new bills and policies, and litigation related to new media legislation. Media systems in countries that have been under leftist rule over the past decade (Argentina, Bolivia, Ecuador, Uruguay, Venezuela and, to a lesser extent, Brazil and Nicaragua) are significantly different today, as they have introduced reforms covering wide ground, including legislation around freedom of information, content and media ownership regulation, the legal status of community media and the management of public funding. Virtually every country in the region has seen civic mobilisation around matters of media and information, although Brazil stands out as a traditionally closed country, where the web is beginning to play a crucial role in public life, changing the government's relationship with citizens, mobilising citizen protest against government actions and effecting government policies that are more open and transparent (*see* Matos 2014; Waisbord 2015).

Brazil's economy grew by 7.5 % in 2010, its strongest performance in a quarter-century, and scarcely affected by the global economic crisis and the Lehman collapse in 2008. However, this economic spurt proved to be short-lived, and growth rates in more recent years have stalled, with a mere 0.9 % rate of economic growth in 2012 (*The Economist* 2013). According to Moseley and Layton (2013), despite Brazil's substantial economic and social gains over the past decade, Brazilians rank as some of Latin America's most dissatisfied citizens regarding government social services. The authors specifically refer to Brazilians' low approval of three areas of public services—the quality of roads, public schools and public health services—eventually resulting in demonstrations triggered by Internet and social media activism. A second common complaint among protestors has been the fundamentally greedy and corrupt political system in Brazil. In 2012, around 65 % of Brazilians believed that the political system was corrupt—a figure that is not necessarily high by regional standards, but which merits further attention as an individual-level indicator of likely participation in political protests. Third, most Brazilians do not have a high regard for system support. Despite its recent economic boom, in 2012 Brazil still ranked 22nd among 26 countries in the Americas in terms of support for national political institutions. This type of disenchantment can motivate individuals to adopt more aggressive forms of political participation in an effort to make their voices heard. Fourth, political efficacy and widespread dissatisfaction with Brazil's system of democratic representation is another source of frustration potentially fuelling protests. In 2012, less than 35 % of Brazilians thought that politicians were interested in their opinions, an indication of how disconnected most citizens feel from their political system (Moseley and Layton 2013).

Social media-driven protests in Brazil have recently gained momentum, and the social networks have begun consolidating their forces into an alternative virtual space, reacting to the partisanship and typically government-friendly coverage of traditional media such as *TV Globo* and mainstream newspapers like *Folha de São Paulo* and *Estado*. The web has enabled social movements and NGOs to increase their visibility and influence. This was the case with *Viva Rio*, an NGO designed with the goal of enhancing citizen access to the web as well as information technology literacy, especially among poor neighbourhoods throughout the state of Rio. At the same time, disadvantaged and marginalised groups have seen the Internet and social media as a means of organising protests to pressure political elites to engage with their electorate and honour their promises. The 2011 and 2012 March Against Corruption protests in the aftermath of the 2005 Mensalão scandal (a case of vote-buying corruption involving senior advisors to Luiz Inacio Lula da Silva that threatened to bring down the Lula government) were very much a social media-driven action. The 2013 protests known as the Confederations Cup riots (as the FIFA Confederations Cup was taking place at the time) were public demonstrations in several Brazilian cities, initiated by the 'Movimento Passe Livre' (Free Fare Movement), a local charity that advocates free public transportation. The demonstrations were initially organised to protest increases in bus, train and metro ticket prices, but grew to include other issues such as government corruption and police brutality against demonstrators. By June 2013, the movement had grown to become Brazil's largest since the 1992 protests against former President Fernando Collor de Mello (1990–1992). Social media's role was pivotal in organising demonstrations of public outcry, and helped keep protesters in touch with one another.

But, most strikingly, it was the events during the FIFA World Cup in the summer of 2014 that saw protesters and police clashing in almost every city hosting the games of the World Cup (Rio, the capital Brasilia, and two other World Cup host cities, Belo Horizonte and Porto Alegre). Protesters were angry at the huge sums of money[3] the government spent

---

[3] Brazil paid a high cost for hosting the World Cup. The stadiums alone cost Brazil $4 billion (£2.4 billion), plus a further $7 billion for associated infrastructure. At $11 billion, this

on preparations for the World Cup, as well as for the Olympics, which Rio will host in 2016. But the battles were not just being fought in the street. As many were angered by what they saw as a misrepresentation of the issues by traditional media outlets, new independent media collectives and networks emerged. These were empowered by smartphones, digital cameras and apps such as TwitCasting and TwitCam that allowed them to broadcast live online, presenting their own version of events. Some of them reached a huge domestic audience, and looked to expand their reach internationally as well. One such group was the Midia Ninja, a self-styled loose collective of citizen journalists that first emerged during the summer 2013 Confederations Cup protests. Their main objective was to present an alternative narrative to the mainstream media by reporting live from the frontline (*see* http://www.theguardian.com/world/2014/apr/27/social-media-gives-new-voice-to-brazil-protests, accessed 10 April 2015). Together, the social media networks gave voice to civil society and grass-roots players and contributed to the democratisation of the country's social and political institutions. At the same time, social network platforms challenged the partisan character of the traditional media and fostered the perception that organisations like *TV Globo* and newspapers like *Folha de São Paulo* and *Estado* play a crucial role in maintaining the status quo.

The Use of Social Media in Brazilian Elections

The expansion of digital democracy in Brazil is clearly evident in the political arena. Since the early 2000s, the Internet has been actively used for political campaigning. During the 2010 presidential elections, female politicians Dilma Rousseff (Worker's Party; PT) and Marina de Silva (Green Party) saw the Internet as a means to promote their policies and to mobilise voters. One month prior to the October 2010 elections, Marina de Silva appeared to be the most popular candidate on social network sites, primarily due to her appeal to youth. She boasted the largest number of users in her online profiles on social networking sites such as Facebook (41,977) and the now-defunct Orkut (46,584), while Dilma Rousseff concentrated on Twitter (235,519 followers). In fact, young voters were an important target, as nearly 80 % of Brazilians aged 16 (the legal voting age) to

was the most expensive World Cup in history. Many Brazilians believe that they are the ones who will ultimately pay the bill, and have dismissed the argument that the tournament's legacy will mean it was money well spent.

25 use the Internet at least once a week, well above the national average of 47 %. If the 2010 campaign highlighted the importance of social media networks, the most recent (26 October 2014) general elections in which Rousseff was narrowly re-elected were indeed seen as a crucial battleground for the election, even before the campaign period officially started. According to *The Economist* (2014), in 2010, Facebook was used at least once a month by only six million Brazilians, but as the country geared up for the October 2014 presidential poll, an overwhelming 83 million Brazilians used the site, leaving only the USA and India with larger Facebook populations. Furthermore, one Brazilian in ten tweeted and one in five used WhatsApp. In terms of the political agenda, the 143 million voters witnessed a campaign characterised once again by accusations of corruption, nepotism and incompetence, suspicious delays in the release of government data on deforestation and poverty, and rumour-mongering on social networks (*see* http://www.theguardian.com/world/2014/oct/26/dilma-rousseff-favourite-brazil-presidential-election-aecio-neves, accessed 11 April 2015).

It may come as a surprise that women leaders came to the fore in conservative regimes traditionally characterised by gender inequality, but as Matos (2014) has noted, since the impeachment of former President Fernando Collor de Mello in 1989 and the publication by the press of corruption practices by members of the Lula government in 2005, there has been a rise in political cynicism and an increase in corruption scandals. Such a volatile political scene created fertile ground for the emergence of strong women candidates, many of whom were perceived by the public as more trustworthy. Both the 2006 and 2010 presidential elections were thus marked by the presence of strong women figures, from Heloisa Helena to Marina de Silva and Dilma Rousseff.[4] Prior to the 2010 elections, the web's role in political campaigns was marginal at best, but things have changed dramatically since then, with the proliferation of political websites like Observatorio da Imprensa, as well as the creation of politicians' own websites, to inform or engage citizens. Sites such as TVoto, Repolitica, Eleitor 2010, Transparencia Brasil and VotenaWeb have begun to occupy a prominent place in the Brazilian political blogosphere, stimulating public debate and civic engagement, and providing people with information regarding the political process. The purpose of

[4] Women political leaders in Latin America also include Christina Kirchner in Argentina and Laura Chinchilla in Costa Rica.

the VotenaWeb site (www.votenaweb.com.br), for example, is to allow citizens to closely follow the work of Brazilian MPs, including viewing proposals that are sent to congress and monitoring votes on specific issues (Matos 2014).

Commentators have also pointed to the importance of blogs during the last two presidential elections, in 2010 and 2014, in allowing citizens to obtain information beyond the views of mainstream media. This is evident in a report by the Internet analytics company comScore, as published in an article in March 2011 by the *Folha de São Paulo*:

> One of the reasons for the popularity of blogs in Brazil in October 2010… was the presidential election. The months of October and November showed record numbers of people accessing blogs (39.3 million in November). These users visited 2.25 billion blog sites during that period. The number of people using blogs increased in 2010 also when looking at the trend; 71 % of the Brazilian online users accepted blogs, while the global average was 50 %. (cited in Bailey and Marques 2012:397)

In the case of Brazil, it appears that the changes occurring in journalism practices related to ICTs is a process similar to that observed in many countries:

> New components are absorbed in the process of news production, new forms of relationship are established between the different social actors involved in the process, while major media conglomerates develop a steady process of colonization of new media platforms, leaving most alternative voices talking among themselves outside the mainstream news spaces and only occasionally engaging with the wider public sphere. (Bailey and Marques 2012:408)

The Internet, social media and blogging may offer the possibility of a more participatory democracy. The exclusion of citizens from the web, however, has important sociocultural and economic implications. The phenomenon of digitally excluded citizens violates the fundamental right to be informed and to engage in public and political life, and at the same time it affects emerging post-industrial economies like Brazil in terms of employment and investment. The number of Internet hosts in Latin America, and in Brazil in particular, has grown recently at a rate of more than 100 % (*see* Internet World Stats), but the region still lags behind East Asia, North America and Europe. Regional access inequality is still visible and can be attributed to the lack of proper infrastructure, eventually resulting in higher broadband costs. Governmental steps towards digital inclusion within the region include the Computers for All (Computador para Todos) programme, which has allowed low-income families to purchase PCs, and the GESAC project (Governo Electronico Servico de Atendimentoao Cidadao), which aims to include citizens from remote Brazilian areas. In terms of the adoption of ICTs to communicate more efficiently with the public and stimulate their participation, the e-government programme responds to civil society's demands for greater transparency in the administration of public funds. However, roughly 17 million people in Brazil are fully illiterate, and another ten million are dubbed 'functional illiterates'. A PC cannot serve as an engine of economic growth and educational inclusion for persons living without electricity, or who do not have the proper technical skills (Matos 2014). Addressing these limits in access and connectivity requires more strenuous efforts on the part of the government, as well as encouragement of the corporate sector to invest in infrastructure projects.

Conclusion

This chapter has explored the sociocultural, political and economic factors which have affected the development of ICTs in the post-industrial societies of Japan and South Korea, and in fast-developing Brazil. Tremendous growth has been observed in all three countries in digital technologies, online communication and the use of social media platforms. Japan and Korea are among the top countries worldwide in Internet users, while Brazil is rapidly developing in terms of Internet use, social media and blogging. The use of home-grown social media has expanded in these countries, although foreign-based platforms like Facebook and Twitter are popular as well. Citizen journalism such as blogging has developed across all three countries. In Brazil and Korea, blogging is especially popular during election campaigns, but in Japan, the Internet and blogs are accessed on mobile phones, and are mainly entertainment-oriented, having little to do with politics. Privacy is highly valued by Japanese users, who prefer networks that guarantee their anonymity. The potential of social media for democratic reform within these societies is in evidence. During the disasters of 2011 in Japan—the earthquake, tsunami and nuclear accident—social media provided a source of information flow independent of those dominated by the state and mass media, often challenging official versions of events. In a similar vein, recent social media-driven protests in

Brazil represented an alternative virtual space in reaction to the partisanship and government-friendly coverage of the traditional media. In Korea, the world leader in Internet connectivity and among Asia-Pacific countries with the highest online penetration, while campaigns using social media can enhance voters' freedom of political expression, Internet regulations in this highly digitally advanced nation represent barriers to foreign companies trying to enter the Korean market.

Without doubt, social networking sites have contributed to the mobilisation and empowerment of citizens in all three post-industrial countries. In the months since the earthquake, tsunami and nuclear disaster events in 2011 began to unfold, Japan has witnessed the potential of social media for organising social and political action, challenging official government views about the safety of the nuclear programme, and bringing Japan's anti-nuclear movement into the mainstream. Social media platforms in Korea have maximised their potential, becoming the new leaders across the political landscape, allowing users to freely post messages. Some observers, however, remain cautious, as political elites have strengthened efforts to monitor postings in order to identify and block unfavourable comments. In Brazil, the Internet and social media have been actively used for political campaigning, leading to the expansion of digital democracy. Yet Brazil has had to tackle issues regarding the exclusion of certain citizens from the web, which has important implications for the democratisation process. In sum, online and social networks in these countries have provided an alternative space and a conduit for information that would otherwise be unavailable, as well as an alternative trajectory for social action such as protests and demonstrations.

CHAPTER 11

The Social Media and the Middle East

INTRODUCTION

Throughout the countries of the Middle East and North Africa (MENA), there has been an influx of social media outlets over the last few years. Within the region, the large numbers of satellite television channels and radio stations, and the hundreds of newspapers and magazines, have been accompanied by the exponential growth of the digital media. Therefore, some contend that grass-roots political movements have represented a force to counter the decades of censorship associated with autocratic Arab governments. This has been welcomed as a healthy sign of an emerging democracy, shaped by the power of these 'independent' information resources. Conversely, concerns have been expressed that the social media outlets have provided the means through which anti-democratic terrorist forces have spearheaded a brutal counter-revolutionary upsurge.

This chapter addresses the complexity of the changes on the social media scene within the Middle East. The consequences of political reform associated with the use of the Internet and the rise of the social movements related to the 'Arab Spring' (*see* Chap. 5) have been a double-edged sword. On the one hand, social media have facilitated greater opportunities for alternative values and social formations to challenge the long-standing autocratic rule in the region. A greater degree of online political engagement has been observed in countries such as Saudi Arabia, Egypt, the UAE, Jordan, Kuwait, Turkey and Iran, although these states have

© The Editor(s) (if applicable) and The Author(s) 2016   257
P. Iosifidis, M. Wheeler, *Public Spheres and Mediated
Social Networks in the Western Context and Beyond*,
DOI 10.1057/978-1-137-41030-6_11

remained vigilant in their attempts to control the social media. On the other hand, the Internet has been a contributory factor in the regional tensions associated with the Israeli–Palestinian dispute, the war in Syria and the rise of the Islamic State of Iraq and the Levant (ISIS):

> The most sinister change in the way war is perceived through the media springs from what just a few years ago seemed to be a wholly positive development...as the course of the uprising in Syria has shown...[that]...the Internet can also be used to spread propaganda and hate. 'Half of Jihad is media' is one slogan posted on a jihadist website which, taken broadly, is wholly correct. (Cockburn 2014:127)

To provide a comprehensive analysis of these changes, in this chapter we will consider the development of the social media throughout the MENA region. We will begin by outlining the technological, economic and political trajectories which have shaped online communications within the Middle Eastern countries, with detailed analysis of the levels of digital penetration, the drivers of online economic growth and the ways in which the social networks have been employed as sources of information across the MENA countries.

Second, we will discuss the extent to which the social media have contributed to regional political and democratic reforms. The 'Green Revolution' in Iran in 2009 marked the origins of the Arab Spring and the unleashing of democratising forces elsewhere in the region, such as Turkey in 2013. With regard to the Israeli–Palestinian dispute, the Internet has contributed to a more complex discourse about Zionist and Arab nationalist positions, and online activists have thus challenged the dominant political or military communications. This in turn may facilitate opportunities for political consensus, while simultaneously exacerbating divisions in the war for 'virtual supremacy'.

Third, the negative effects of social media have been crystallised in the actions of terrorist groups, who have used the Internet 'to expand their reach, create virtual communities of like-minded extremists, and capture a larger universe of more diverse talents and skills' (Jenkins 2011). The online communications of ISIS in particular have shocked local and international audiences while encouraging the recruitment of like-minded Jihadists. Its brutal yet sophisticated use of YouTube, Facebook and Twitter has enabled ISIS to propagate its message of a worldwide caliphate and to enlist international support. We thus conclude the chapter by

considering the implications of such disparate use of social media throughout the MENA region.

The Middle East: Historical and Political Context

Historically, the Middle East has been subjected to a variety of forms
of colonial and post-colonial rule. The defeat of the Turkish forces in
World War I led to the division of the Ottoman Empire between France
and Britain across Palestine, Mesopotamia and Arabia. In addition, the
French and British empires held colonial control over North African states
including Algeria, Morocco and Egypt. After World War II, the region
saw the rise of post-colonial forms of Jewish Zionism and Arab nationalism. Because of its rich oil resources, the MENA region was the target of
Western investment, and became a focus of tensions between the USA
and the Soviet Union (USSR) in the bipolar world of the Cold War era.
Consequently, oil-producing nations such as Saudi Arabia and the Gulf
States such as the UAE, along with the geopolitically important Egypt,
Syria, Iraq and Iran, emerged as regional powers. This resulted in an array
of autocratic rulers, often backed by the USA or USSR, who employed
them as regional strongmen to protect their respective interests.

The other local superpower in the region is Israel. In 1917, the British
government issued the Balfour Declaration, which recognised the rights
of diasporic Jews to form a homeland within the Holy Land of Palestine.
From 1921 to 1948, the UK operated the British mandate of Palestine,
which saw the migration of European Jews during the interwar years. This
influx of Jewish migrants significantly expanded after World War II as a
consequence of the Holocaust. Zionist leaders such as David Ben-Gurion
argued that a moral incentive existed for the establishment of the secular
State of Israel, which led to a short insurgent war to remove British forces.
The Jewish state was subsequently recognised by the USA and the UN in
1948. Moreover, due to US geopolitical interests and the power of Jewish
lobbying groups such as the American Israel Political Action Committee
(AIPAC), Israel has enjoyed a filial relationship with the USA, from which
it has received economic and military support.

The displacement of the many thousands of Palestinians that accompanied the Milkhemet Ha'atzma'ut (War of Independence) or the al-Nakba
(the Catastrophe) hardened the lines between Israel and the Arab states.
The Israeli–Palestinian dispute was further polarised by the 1967 Six-Day
War, the 1972 Munich Olympics hostage killings, the 1973 Arab–Israeli

War and oil crisis, the settlements on the West Bank, the incursion into Lebanon, the growth of religious Jewry and the intifadas of the 1980s and the 1990s. Importantly, the Arab nationalist Palestinian Liberation Organisation (PLO), which had opposed Israel through a campaign of violence and terrorism, ceded control to the theocratic Islamic-led Hamas in Gaza and Hezbollah in Lebanon.

Elsewhere, the incorporation of Arab nationalism with theocratic power came to be associated with the rise of Islamic fundamentalism. The 1979 Iranian Revolution marked a sea change in attitudes towards the West, and crystallised harsher anti-Western sentiment. There was also a rise of Saudi terrorist forces such as al-Qaeda, led by Osama Bin Laden. Although these forces had fought the USSR as part of the US-funded Mujahedeen in Afghanistan during the 1980s, they felt betrayed by the USA, and such hostility resulted in the devastating 9/11 attacks on New York City and Washington, D.C. in 2001. The 'War on Terror', led by US and UK forces, resulted in the conflict in Afghanistan to remove the Taliban and the rekindling of the 1990–1991 Gulf War hostilities with Iraq's Ba'athist Party dictator Saddam Hussein. Despite the initial justification for the response as necessary to protect international security, the imperialist US foreign policy and military presence resulted in the growth of anti-American sentiment throughout the Middle East.

The end of the Bush administration with the election of Barack Obama raised initial optimism that this would lead to a change in US foreign policy, which would be more favourably received. However, America's regional unpopularity has been perpetuated by its continuing occupation of Afghanistan, its failure to effect democratic reforms in Iraq and the collapse of Obama-led multilateral efforts to intervene in Syria. These difficulties, combined with the unforeseen consequences of the reassertion of military rule in Egypt and insurgent anarchy in Libya after the Arab Spring, have resulted in a mixed picture with regard to processes of democratisation within the region (Haynes 2015).

Moreover, as the Arab Spring descended into the 'Summer of Reckoning', ISIS emerged from the remnants of al-Qaeda in 2012–2013. This fundamentalist Sunni organisation has grown in size to account for approximately 30,000 fighters across Syria and Iraq. The strength of ISIS is a product of the long-standing enmities due to state repression, its link to former Ba'athist Iraqi military leaders and the failed Shiite leadership of the US-backed Nouri al-Maliki, and has been further sustained by US involvement in the insurgent-led civil war against the Syrian dictator

Bashar al-Assad since 2012. ISIS captured a stockpile of US-made weaponry and has achieved military success by taking control of major Iraqi cities including Mosul and Tikrit.

Furthermore, ISIS-affiliated groups have fed upon the chaos that has characterised the bloody insurgencies existing within Libya. It has made its presence felt internationally, claiming responsibility or support for individualistic brutal incursions within western Europe, such as the Charlie Hebdo killings in Paris or the murder of a freedom speech activist in Copenhagen in 2015. It is within the complexities of these political, religious and cultural divisions that the use of blogs, Facebook pages, likes, tweets and hashtags has continued to grow apace. Moreover, the various political constituencies and democratic practices that exist across the region have shaped the online forms of political communication. These variables have led to both foreseen and unforeseen consequences of the employment of the social media within the MENA region. Needless to say, these events continue to evolve, and the picture is rapidly changing.

THE MIDDLE EAST SOCIAL MEDIA PENETRATION, ECONOMIC OPPORTUNITY AND ONLINE NEWS PROVISION

The Middle East is characterised by a diverse range of nationalities, ethnicities, religions and cultures. This has resulted in significant differences in the take-up of online services within the region, with the Gulf States enjoying the greatest levels of digital penetration. The Internet has been widely distributed within the Middle East's most populous states, including Egypt (82.5 million), Iran (80 million) and Saudi Arabia (28 million), whose 39 million, 45 million and 18.3 million Internet users, respectively, have outstripped the combined total for Syria, Jordan, Kuwait, Lebanon and Oman. Despite these digital divides, at 30 June 2014, there were 111,809,510 Middle Eastern Internet users, which accounted for 48.3 % of the total regional population. Taken as a whole, Arab citizens within the MENA region have access to a wide range of domestic technologies on a level in line with—and on several occasions above—the world average (Northwestern University 2014) (Table 11.1).

Over 82 million Arabs use social media, of which 88 % are daily networkers. In terms of gender and age, 65 % are men and 35 % are women, while 36 % of users are aged 18 to 24 years. A survey by Northwestern University in Qatar of users in Qatar, Saudi Arabia, Lebanon, Egypt, Tunisia and the UAE demonstrated that participants spent on average

Table 11.1   Internet usage and penetration in MENA countries, June 2014

Country	Population (Est. 2014)	Internet usage	Penetration percentage
Egypt	82,500,000	39,000,000	47.3
Iran	80,840,713	45,000,000	55.7
Iraq	32,585,692	2997,884	9.2
Palestine (West Bank)	2,731,052	1,687,739	61.8
Jordan	6,528,061	5,700,000	87.3
Kuwait	3,268,431	3,022,010	92.5
Qatar	2,123,160	2,016,400	95.0
Saudi Arabia	27,345,986	18,300,000	66.9
Syria	22,597,531	5,920,553	26.2
United Arab Emirates	9,206,000	8,807,226	95.7

Source: Internet World Stats 2014: http://www.internetworldstats.com/stats5.htm (accessed 21 April 2015)

3.2 hours per day on social networks. Tunisian and Bahraini Internet users were found to be the most voracious social networkers, each devoting 4.1 hours daily (Northwestern University 2014). Facebook remains the most popular social network, with 56 million or 90 % of users, of which half log in on a daily basis. The network has a regional penetration rate of just less than 50 %, so there is considerable opportunity for further growth. For instance, there are already over 16 million Egyptian Facebook users, and take-up continues to grow at a steady pace. It was only in Qatar that Facebook was used by less than 75 % of Internet users.

The next most popular network is Twitter, with 5,797,500 users, with Arabs producing ten million tweets per day (Arab Social Media Report 2014). Twitter enjoys relatively large user numbers in Egypt (the second highest in the region at 519,000), but this represents only 0.6 % of the population. The most extensive national use of Twitter occurs within Saudi Arabia, with 1.9 million subscribers. Saudi users of the microblog are responsible for almost half the tweets produced across the region on a daily basis, with 90 % of these communications in Arabic. Instagram, which is owned by Facebook, has also emerged as a popular platform for electronic commerce (e-commerce), while more Arab professionals utilise LinkedIn to develop business relationships and new connections. Although LinkedIn usage has remained relatively small, accounting for only ten million network users, at the end of 2013, this represented an increase of 5.8 million per annum in take-up.

Due to an unprecedented 200 % rise in Saudi mobile phone usage, a vast number of users within the kingdom access their social media networks through cell phones or mobile technology such as iPads. For instance, over half of the YouTube views in Saudi Arabia are via mobile devices, as are 40 % in the UAE. Consequently, uploaded content on YouTube has become available to a large online audience. For instance, EyshElly, a YouTube programme created by UTURN Entertainment, has achieved a subscription level of 2.2 million viewers and has received more than 245 million views. Overall, with 90 million YouTube views per day, the Arab region is second only to the USA in number of views (Khan 2014).

Alongside this growth in personal use, MENA countries have witnessed greater social media use by businesses. Digitalisation has been estimated to have created over 400,000 new jobs throughout the Middle East region, accounting for a total GDP increase of $16.5 billion (Elzeini 2015). According to a 2012 report by the Dubai School of Government, 89 % of the sampled new businesses in Egypt agreed that social media was a key tool for start-ups (Arab Social Media Report 2012). The founders of these new companies, who were invariably below the age of 30, used social media to market their products, present initiatives, make connections and recruit staff, resulting in significantly reduced entry costs. In addition, the social media have spread regional awareness of technical advances to a wide array of industrial actors:

> Several years ago, Mahmoud Ahmed, a 25-year-old university graduate, was frustrated with having to travel for seven to twelve hours from his city of Qena to attend technological expos in Cairo or Alexandria. He envisioned a time when these expos could be hosted in Upper Egypt, so he posted his idea on Twitter and soon found supporters. Such was the beginning of S3Geeks. Today, the group has representatives in ten governorates, an established organisational structure, and is well positioned to pioneer the integration of ICT in Upper Egypt. (El-Gendi 2014)

This facilitation of business opportunities has occurred hand in hand with the privatisation of telecommunication operators and the deregulation of information technology markets. In turn, through the use of social media, a range of actors have realised that they can broker personal (friends and families) and public forms of interactive communication. The networks have thus become key modes for the distribution of newsfeeds. Young Arabs in particular trust the social media over the rigid, state-sanctioned television news media (Radcliffe 2015). These developments have led to calls for greater freedoms of expression:

> This energetically charged younger generation should have the ability to think boundlessly without being criticised and prevented to. Promoting freedom of conscience is not solely a task left to the government; rather, it's a responsibility all citizens in whose interest it is to allow the youth to prosper...When we know very well that freedom of thought void of societal and governmental pressures will give rise to new ideas for more a sustainable and secure future, it would be irresponsible to allow such barriers to entry and pressures on free expression to persist. (Elzeini 2015)

Yet, while there have been some national policies for economic and political liberalisation, there remain strong controls over the provision of online information services. Deborah Wheeler (2009) noted that Arab states have maintained autocratic power over the flow of information resources, while seeking to attract inward and outward investment for e-commerce. Consequently, Arab states have persisted in 'attempts to police cyberspace, to publicly punish cyber dissidents...and to filter the web' (Wheeler 2009:19). Therefore, one must consider the interplay between the social media and regional politics to gauge the extent to which the World Wide Web has both promoted state power and acted as a countervailing challenge to the dominant elites.

THE SOCIAL MEDIA AND POLITICAL MOVEMENTS: OPPORTUNITIES AND REPRESSION IN IRAN AND TURKEY

As the networked population has gained greater access to information, social movements have spread across the Arab world and have often been confronted with violent repression. For instance, the protests associated with the Iranian 'Green Revolution' against the disputed outcome of the 2009 general election and the controversial victory of President Mahmoud Ahmadinejad were facilitated through Facebook and Twitter. According to Annabelle Sreberny and Gholam Khiabany:

> Many Iranians on Facebook changed their profile picture to a green square that included the text 'where is my vote', while many non-Iranians tweaked the icon to 'where is their vote'. Facebook turned green. It became a space for posting video...articles...photographs that had been sent by mobile or

> e-mail attachment from people in Iran. Facebook became an enormous distribution site of new or recycled materials. (Sreberny and Khiabany 2010:173)

At the same time, Iranian activists used Twitter to provide real-time updates of the events. An iconic video of a group of protesters marching down Tehran's Valiasr Street, shouting, 'Mousavi, take back my vote!' went viral when attached to the microblogging site (Mason 2012:34). Another YouTube video showed what followed, as the baton-wielding Iraqi riot police charged the unarmed crowd. This frightening footage was attached to blogs and Facebook and Twitter sites to demonstrate the terror and chaos accompanying the brutal subjugation of the political demonstrators. In addition, the protesters employed a range of online 'mashups' to achieve a range of expression. These social media representations reflected a new form of political creativity which expressed an underlying solidarity to the cause. They demonstrated the politics of attraction, as protestors could articulate their sympathy to one another and engage in further activities to propagate their message.

In response, the Iranian government censored the social media by filtering the websites and taking them down as a result of the protests. However, Freegate, an anti-censorship software developed by the Global Internet Freedom Consortium, was employed to a limited degree to offset the state controls. At an international level, hackers from the West kept the online channels open despite the Iranian regime's attempts to close them down. Furthermore, as the Iranian authorities cracked down on traditional media outlets, international news agencies employed user-generated content, and the 'momentum of the protests fed off this cycle of guerrilla newsgathering, media amplification, censorship and renewed protest' (Mason 2012:35). Although the Iranian protest would ultimately be lost, it was nonetheless a powerful force:

> All the ingredients were present of the uprisings that would, eighteen months later, galvanise the Middle East and beyond: radicalized, secular-leaning youth: a repressed workers' movement with considerable social power; uncontrollable social media; the restive urban poor. (Mason 2012:37)

Similar claims were made regarding the online mobilisation of the Turkish protesters who demonstrated in Istanbul's Taksim Square during the summer of 2013 (Mason 2013). The civil unrest began on 28 May

2013 in response to the violent eviction of peaceful protesters who were engaging in a sit-in against the urban re-development of Taksim Gezi Park. Video footage showing the excessive violence of the riot police was posted online, which sparked greater unrest across Turkey. Demonstrations and strikes were called for on a range of issues involving freedom of the press, the rights of expression and assembly, and Islamic Prime Minister Recep Tayyip Erdogan's encroachment upon Turkey's secularist traditions.

On 1 June 2013, the police withdrew from Taksim Square, and the sit-in was taken up again, during which the protesters lived in tents, organised a library and medical centre, set up food banks and established their own media centre. As Turkish broadcasters imposed a news blackout, the camp organisers used Twitter and Facebook to provide updates from the occupied Gezi Park, distributed photos on Flickr and Tumblr and uploaded videos to YouTube. The Twitter hashtag #direnGeziPark was tweeted over 1.8 million times in 3 days. The protesters typically used smartphone handsets to live-stream video images of the protests (Social Media and Participation Lab 2013). Messages of support for the demonstrations poured in from around the world. These included tweets from the Dutch footballer Wesley Sneijder, who was playing for the Istanbul football club Galatasaray (Hutchinson 2013). However, the Gezi Park demonstration was cleared by riot police on 15 June 2013. Videos and photos subsequently uploaded to social media sites showed the brutal deployment of tear gas and water cannons to disperse the protesters.

Throughout the crisis, Erdogan declared that the rioters were mere 'looters', who were using the social networks to undermine the legitimate government. He claimed, 'There is now a menace which is called Twitter....The best examples of lies can be found there....To me, the social media is the worst menace to society' (Letsch 2013). After the 'Turkish Spring', Erdogan's antipathy towards Twitter, Facebook and YouTube hardened even more. In 2014, he was angered by the leak of damaging information gleaned from wiretaps of Twitter, just in time for the local spring elections. This led Turkish authorities to temporarily shut down the microblogging site on 20 March 2014. While the closure was later declared unconstitutional, Erdogan's government also tried to find ways to close YouTube and Facebook. A former pro-government columnist, Nazli Ilicak, described the restrictions as akin to 'a civil coup':

> The disruption sparked a virtual uproar with many comparing Turkey to Iran and North Korea, where social media platforms are tightly controlled. There

were also calls to take to the street to protest, although some users equally called for calm. Turkish internet users were quick to come up with their own ways to circumvent the block. The hashtag #TwitterisblockedinTurkey quickly moved among the top trending globally. (Rawlinson 2014)

Such repression has not been confined to Turkey. The social media have provided the dictatorial Syrian government with the means to propagate its messages and to hack into opponent sites. Throughout 2014, there were several high-profile stand-offs between Middle Eastern governments and social media activists. In Egypt, after the 2013 military coup which saw the removal of the Muslim Brotherhood, the state authorities imposed a crackdown on social media (Cockburn 2014:117). The military government announced it would use See Egypt (a sister company to the US cybersecurity firm Blue Coat) to implement unprecedented surveillance measures for Facebook, Twitter and Skype users.

This was the first time that the Egyptian government had used Deep Packet Inspection technology, which facilitates the geolocation, tracking and extensive monitoring of Internet traffic. These technologies were employed to enhance the state's repressive powers, to track dissenting groups and to target atheists and lesbian, gay, bisexual and transgender (LGBT) groups. When tendering for Internet surveillance companies, the Egyptian Ministry of the Interior made conspicuous the types of online communications it was seeking to outlaw:

> Blasphemy and scepticism in religions; regional, religious, racial, and class divisions; spreading of rumours and intentional twisting of facts; throwing accusations; libel; sarcasm; using inappropriate words; calling for the departure of societal pillars; encouraging extremism, violence and dissent; inviting demonstrations, sit-ins and illegal strikes; pornography, looseness, and lack of morality; educating methods of making explosives and assault, chaos and riot tactics; calling for normalising relations with enemies and circumventing the state's strategy in this regard; fishing for honest mistakes, hunting flesh; taking statements out of context; and spreading hoaxes and claims of miracles. (Frenkel and Atef 2014)

At the same time, in May 2014, during an appeals case for the blogger Raif Badawi, the Saudi Arabian courts increased his sentence from 600 lashings and 7 years in prison to 1000 lashings and 10 years of imprisonment. He was fined one million riyals, equivalent to 200,000 euros, for 'violating Islamic values and propagating liberal thought'. In October

2014, when three lawyers were jailed for 5–8 years, they were also banned from tweeting messages critical of the judiciary. Saudi Arabian authorities have considered changing the Anti-Cybercrime Law to target social networking sites that they have deemed to promote content at odds with their dominant Islamic values (Radcliffe 2015).

However, as Paul Mason commented, these autocratic controls have come at a cost to authorities, as they have realised that the Internet 'is a network of networks, containing non-hierarchical pathways that simply do not allow you to switch part of it off...[and so] this is a signal moment [where]...once-respected [statesmen have turned] into...Canute-like [clowns]' (Mason 2014a). Therefore, the dichotomy which exists between the imposition of state controls to censor and to propagandise their values, against the tide of alternative positions associated with grass-roots activism, has become evident in one of the Middle East's most intractable conflicts—the Israeli–Palestinian dispute.

THE 2014 GAZA DISPUTE AND THE SOCIAL MEDIA: ISRAEL DEFENSE FORCES VERSUS HAMAS

The Internet has played a crucial role in the asymmetric 'information war' between Israel and Palestine. Both sides have a long-standing tradition of using the media to sway international opinion. This was apparent during the Israeli military incursion against the Hamas-controlled Gaza Strip territory in the summer of 2014. The Israelis developed public relations machinery to propagate their view of Hamas as an illegitimate terrorist organisation. However, as Hamas received positive coverage from news organisations such as Al Jazeera, both sides took to social media:

> The propaganda war between Israel and the Palestinians is not new, but this battle-round is being fought with unprecedented ferocity. And like the asymmetry in the military conflict, the strength and resources of the Israel social media troops outweigh those of Hamas and other Palestinian organisations. (Sherwood 2014)

The Israel Defense Forces (IDF) and the Foreign Ministry realised that they needed to engage in a form of 'perception management'. The IDF social media tsar Avital Leibovich described an effective social media campaign as one that created a 'buzz' through a plethora of posts and blogs such that 'the message was very clear, and it also went to the audience we aimed at' (Kerr 2014). This understanding can be traced back to the 2008–2009 Gaza War, when the army launched its own YouTube channel, which showcased grainy, handheld-filmed battlefield footage from young recruits depicting the Israeli assault. Despite the international condemnation of 'Operation Cast Lead', the military claimed it had won a decisive public relations victory, as its YouTube videos were viewed over two million times.

Subsequently, the IDF increased its social media budget and investment in manpower. On 14 August 2011, it launched its first official Facebook page in English, quickly boasting 90,000 followers. The IDF's software engineers made major changes to the platform's protocols to serve their priorities. They retooled the Facebook template's 'like' button so that it read 'Click "like" if you support the IDF's right to defend the State of Israel from those who attempt to harm Israelis' (Stein 2014). Similarly, they reconfigured Twitter by drafting a boilerplate that could deliver real-time responses to counteract detractors, creating a variety of pro-Israeli hashtags to tag their tweets. The IDF Twitter account subsequently grew rapidly, to more than 327,000 followers, while its Facebook site surpassed 380,000 likes (Stein 2014).

By the time of the 2014 Gaza conflict, or 'Operation Protective Edge', the IDF was employing social networks to argue that the airstrikes were being made in retaliation to the Palestinian rocket attacks aimed against Israeli civilians. To this end, it posted numerous daily updates and published dozens of YouTube videos highlighting the nature of the Hamas security threats. These included night-time videos showing rocket fire coming from the Gaza Strip into Israel's residential areas. In addition, a video was uploaded that was entitled 'What Is It Like to Be Attacked by Rocks?' This video included scenes of teenage boys lobbing stones at people and breaking the windows of passing cars. Towards the end of the video, a caption was shown which read, 'The media consider rock-throwing a harmless provocation'. This was followed by a recording from inside a vehicle as the windshield was being smashed, accompanied by the question, 'Do you still agree?'

The IDF also created an application ('app') on its blog to ask international audiences to 'imagine' how they would react if Hamas were in their country and firing rockets at their cities. The Israeli social media sites offered users a set of maps that they could use to superimpose the Gaza Strip on other countries, such as the USA and Britain, to indicate the security threat. The IDF social networks also used the familiar agenda-setting tactic of creating 'talking points', including Hamas' use of innocent Palestinians as 'human shields', and declaring that Gaza had been extensively leafleted with warnings about Israeli retaliation to the continuous rocket attacks. Captain Eytan Buchman, an IDF Spokesman's Unit operative who worked extensively with American media, described the tactics:

> We're operating on almost every single account we can to make sure that we can get out our message as fast as possible to as many different audiences as possible. This is to both increase our legitimacy, to be transparent, and almost as importantly, to combat misinformation that's being flooded out from inside Gaza. (Ungerleider 2012)

It appeared, then, that the IDF maintained the balance of power with regard to the deployment of the social media. Throughout the 2014 Gaza conflict, however, Hamas employed Facebook, YouTube and particularly Twitter as countervailing newsfeeds to propagate its own position on the devastating nature of the air attacks. While it had access to fewer online resources and gained only 58,000 Twitter followers, Hamas' military arm, al-Qassam, increased its activities by posting and tagging messages in Arabic, English and Hebrew.

These tweets trended to international users, who then widely disseminated the accompanying distressing pictures of civilian casualties, injured children and the destruction of homes. In this way, Hamas provided a minute-by-minute account of the unfolding battle, posting a deluge of viral images of the Palestinian dead or wounded, as it sought to 'humanise' the effects of the battle. As a government spokesman, Ihab al-Ghussein, commented, 'It's not just about taking pictures of dead people....We're now telling [the story of] this family, and how they were eating breakfast when they were killed' (Hirshauge et.al. 2014).

The Hamas Interior Ministry website issued detailed guidelines entitled 'Be Aware—Social Media Activist Awareness Campaign' to instruct Palestinians on how to hone their messages. The images were accompanied by emotive terms such as 'genocidal aggression', 'resistance' and 'martyrs' to intensify the daily discourse. The site included a video that could be uploaded so that activists could 'play their part in strengthening the home front and in properly conveying [the] information worldwide' (MEMRI 2014). In addition, it advised Palestinians who were linked with Western users on ways to conduct their conversations:

When speaking to the West, you must use political, rational, and persuasive discourse, and avoid emotional discourse aimed at begging for sympathy. There are elements with a conscience in the world; you must maintain contact with them and activate them for the benefit of Palestine. Their role is to shame the occupation and expose its violations. (Hamas Interior Ministry taken from MEMRI 2014)

This approach to the use of social media suggests that Hamas understood that it had to tailor its message to a range of target audiences. It could create an online presence which related to both Palestinian and Western users who, in turn, could inclusively 'feel' that they were participating in an online community. Hamas also clearly understood the necessity of establishing a dialogue with Israeli social media users to realise a successful online campaign. In a well-publicised example, an Israeli woman responded to a Hamas tweet in Hebrew by correcting its grammar. Hamas replied by explaining how the mistake had occurred and thanked her for the correction. At the same time, it tried to turn Israelis against their government by releasing a song, 'Shake Israel's Security', which was sung in Hebrew and Arabic, and showed militants firing rockets. This grass-roots approach on the part of Hamas led some to question the effectiveness of the IDF:

Is Israel losing the media war? In the last few days...this question has consumed the global media. And most have agreed: in the age of social media, with abundant mobile technologies in the hands of Gaza Palestinians and their global supporters, the Israeli state-sponsored media strategy has failed. From the @IDFSpokesman, we get didactic infographics. From Palestinians in Gaza, viral jpegs from the ground. The Israeli military does not understand the nature of the social media playing field, pundits have implied, and their message is failing. (Stein 2014)

At the very least, this shows that the official Israeli discourse was being disputed, and it further demonstrates a reversal of the previously asymmetric nature of the conflict. Pro-Palestinian tweets and Facebook likes appealed to millions of Muslims across the Global South. Therefore, for some, the social media have created a public space where civil society actors could establish a more truthful and nuanced version of the Gaza dispute (Mason 2014b).

Conversely, the online communications of the IDF and Hamas may have facilitated an echo chamber in which the predefined prejudices of the two antagonistic societies were reinforced (Lloyd 2014). For instance, in a memorable Twittersphere graphic, an ideological void was shown to exist between the 'blue' Internet, which comprised the Israelis, the Jewish diaspora and the US Tea Party, and the 'green' Internet, which included Muslims and anti-war movements. Therefore, viewed from this perspective, the ability of social media 'to dissolve spin and propaganda becomes relative' (Lloyd 2014). Indeed, one may contend that the online networks have polarised opinion rather than achieving harmony, thereby exacerbating the rise of international terrorism in the wake of the 'clash of civilisations' (Huntington 1996; Goldman 2014).

TERRORISTS AND SOCIAL MEDIA: ISIS, HOLY WAR AND A WORLDWIDE CALIPHATE

As Eric Louw (2005) commented, the terrorists occupy the communications business as much as any state actor. The 9/11 terrorist attacks demonstrated that al-Qaeda understood that carrying out a heightened political assault against the USA was a means by which they could command the unqualified attention of the global news media (Kellner 2011). The dangers to security inherent in the new technologies became evident in November 2012, when Pakistan's entire mobile phone network was switched off during a week of Shia celebrations. This action was taken even as fears were expressed that Sunni insurgents would target the festivities by using cell phones to remotely detonate bombs:

> Technological change and resulting revolution in communications and information storage and retrieval has allowed a wide variety of groups to exploit a remarkable range of new approaches to enhance visibility. It is not unusual for terrorist groups to film their activities, distributing propaganda by CD, DVD and the Internet. (Moran 2015:158)

Subsequently, other groups have become more effective in mobilising public fear through the social media. Beginning in May 2011, the Taliban tweeted under the handle @alemarahweb, gaining more than 7000 followers. Elsewhere, the Somalian cell al-Shabab amassed Twitter followers, while the Nigerian Boko Haram defended its 2011 Christmas attacks in Kono with a YouTube video. In Beirut, teenage boys played computer war games which were adapted by Hezbollah so that the enemy aggressors became Israeli soldiers. These examples all illustrate the effective use of the

Internet by these groups to spread terror, disseminate their ideology and radicalise their membership.

While internal Iraqi Sunni and Shiite divisions and the insurgencies associated with the Syrian War have contributed to the expansion of ISIS, it is its use of the social media that has built its momentum. Its media wing, al-Furqan, has propagated its fundamentalist Sunni ideologies through Facebook, YouTube, Twitter (#SykesPicotOver, which referred to the 1916 deal between Britain and France to carve up the Middle East region), Instagram, Tumblr, Internet memes (#CatsOfJihad), and other networks. Through its Facebook presence, ISIS has promoted a holy war in Syria, Iraq and Yemen. In the Gulf States, it has employed Twitter as its principle source of communication.

ISIS' postings have placed an emphasis on 'martyred' Sunni suicide bombers and have praised its soldiers' brutality in Syria and Iraq. It has uploaded YouTube videos of Shiite Iraqi army prisoners in Tikrit being hog-tied and forced face-down into shallow graves before being shot. The shocking images of the blood-covered bodies of the soldiers were accompanied by captions declaring that the massacre had avenged the death of ISIS commander Abdul-Rahman al-Beilawy:

> ISIS is making effective use of startling images depicting their operations, notably including mass executions of Iraqi soldiers…Their fearsome reputation, bolstered by such images, has translated into success on the battlefield, with Iraqi security forces fleeing strategic towns and cities rather than engage the militants directly. (Jordan Perry quoted from McElroy 2014)

In 2015, the group released online video of the slaughter of 21 Egyptian Coptic Christians and the burning alive of the captured Jordanian air force pilot Moaz al-Kasasbeh.

ISIS YouTube clips have included what it had claimed to be Alawites chain-sawing Syrian Sunnis to death, when in reality, it had uploaded videos of Mexican drug lords humiliating their rivals. Similarly, ISIS has used the social media to mislead militiamen into thinking that they were fighting Iraqi soldiers who had been ordered to rape and torture their wives and daughters (Cockburn 2014:132). These messages have been accompanied by online hate preachers who have incited YouTube followers to take up arms against Shiites, Christians, Sufis and Jews. For example, an Egyptian video logger ('vlogger'), Sheikh Mohammed al-Zoghbi, called on God to protect Sunnis from 'the criminal traitors and the criminal Shia' (Cockburn 2014:130).

Moreover, ISIS has uploaded horrific videos to promote its caliphate against the international community. These have included the beheadings of Western hostages, including journalists James Foley and Steven Sotloff and aid workers David Haines, Alan Henning and Peter Kassig. With the exception of the murder of the former US Army Ranger Kassig (which occurred off-screen), the gruesome acts were shown in their entirety, with the hostages speaking a few words before they were executed. The videos were available to any Internet users internationally, and were taken up by mainstream news organisations. The US Fox News network was castigated after it released on its website the al-Furqan video of the death of Moaz al-Kasasbeh as he was burned alive. The decision by Fox received criticism not only with regard to matters of taste and decency, but in providing ISIS with yet another platform from which to spread hatred. Indeed, ISIS bloggers boasted, 'Whoever is looking for the al-Furqan version [of the video], here it is and it cannot be deleted because it is on an American network' (Woolf 2015).

For ISIS, posting the executions online served a dual purpose: to cause havoc within the local population and to instil horror throughout the West. Of particular concern, the masked executioner of the hostages in the YouTube videos was a UK national, who spoke to the camera with a strong London accent. The notorious terrorist was dubbed 'Jihadi John' (in reference to the late John Lennon of the Beatles) by the hostages, and became an iconic figure across the social media. In this manner, Jihadi John played a key role in ISIS' dramatic use of online propaganda and its recruitment of Western nationals. His real name was revealed as Mohammed Emwazi, the 26-year-old son of Iraqi parents living in West London. He had graduated with a degree in computer programming from the University of Westminster, and taken up a post in Kuwait as a salesman in 2011, and was placed under surveillance by UK security agencies.

ISIS has thus used social media to draw foreign governments back into the conflict in the MENA region, and it has magnified its own sense of importance in the Middle East and across the international community. While ISIS has often fabricated the extent of its military victories, many of the murderous posts have proven to be all too real. The wide distribution of these extreme images 'explains the ferocity of the conflict in Syria and the difficulty the participants have in negotiating an end to their civil war' (Cockburn 2014:132). As such, the Internet has contributed to a period of uncertainty characterised by theocratic intolerance, brutal subjugation and ideological prejudice.

The Online Marketing of Brand ISIS: The 'One Billion Campaign', 'Cool Jihad' Twitter Trending and International Recruitment

ISIS has employed slick videos, Instagram content and podcasts to recruit like-minded Muslims (the 'one billion campaign') in foreign countries. For instance, the group uploaded speeches of its leader, Abu Bakr al-Baghdadi, calling upon Sunni youth to join its international jihad, proclaiming: 'Be prepared in arms and keep your finger on the trigger and be ready for the zero moment for the decisive battle which is now upon us' (Channel Four News 2014). Interestingly, the group has used the West's branding techniques against it by adopting media tools associated with rolling news channels, Hollywood movies, reality shows and music videos. Thus, in contrast to Osama bin Laden's fuzzy, monotonous camcorder sermons of the early 2000s, Islamist extremists have developed a sophisticated marketing strategy. As Patrick Cockburn commented:

> Looking at a selection of such online postings, what is striking is not only their violence and sectarianism but also their professionalism with which they are produced. The jihadists may yearn for a return to the norms of early Islam, but their skills in using modern communications and the Internet are well ahead of most political movements in the world. By producing a visual record of everything it does, ISIS has greatly amplified its political impact. Its militants dominate social media and produce well-made and terrifying films to illustrate the commitment of their fighters as they identify and kill their enemies. (Channel Four News 2014:127–128)

ISIS has provided online material in Arabic, French and English to target international youth. The al-Hayat Media Centre, for example, produced a music video of the song 'Let's Go for Jihad', which provided English translations to encourage jihadists to 'rush to the battlefield' to 'claim your victory' and to 'slaughter until the day of judgement'. The video included slow-motion clips of gunfire and explosions which had a computer game appearance. Another recruitment video consisted of edited footage drawn from the *Grand Theft Auto* video game, pronouncing that 'your games which are producing from you, we do the same actions in the battlefields!!' Such a 'cool' version of Jihad was echoed by a British fighter Abu Sumayyah al-Britani who, in a podcast, maintained that fighting for ISIS in Syria was better than playing *Call of Duty*.

The sophisticated use of information technology became further apparent in April 2014 when ISIS established a free-download app on Twitter on the web and on Google Play for Android mobile phones—'The Dawn of Glad Tidings'. This was ostensibly designed to update users with the latest news from the battlefronts of Northern Iraq, and it received 40,000 posts a day. However, 'Dawn' had a more pernicious purpose, as its software had been calibrated with keywords, links and hashtags to trend automatically to other Twitter accounts, while avoiding spam detectors. In effect, the app hijacked the user's mobile phone by transforming it into a transmitter for ISIS tweets across the Twittersphere.

In addition, ISIS orchestrated several hashtag campaigns during which thousands of activists repeatedly tweeted hashtags so that they would trend on Twitter. This skewed the results of the top-trending tags on the popular Arabic Twitter account @ActiveHashtags, enabling ISIS to receive an average of 72 re-tweets per tweet. Thus, the group's viral messaging gained further traction, allowing it to attract greater international interest. According to the Brookings Institution, in 2014, there were up to 90,000 active Twitter accounts spreading ISIS propaganda (Berger and Morgan 2015).

While most terrorist organisations have tended to keep their internal media, information and communication highly controlled, ISIS realised that the social networks could bring together previously disparate groups of like-minded followers. In an ironic replication of Barack Obama's grassroots deployment of the social media in his presidential campaigns (*see* Chap. 4), the terrorists have used the online platforms to self-organise as members of a virtual community. Therefore, ISIS has cultivated the social networks such that fellow 'brothers' and 'sisters' may act as surrogate family members to radicalise and recruit new supporters:

> Thus…the online space becomes an echo chamber, facilitating radicalisation as well as encouraging and assisting individuals to join ISIS. Foreigners joining ISIS utilize the Internet to assist their crossing. Many already in Syria provide practical advice and encouragement. They post on blogs, engage on public response sites, and invite interested individuals to engage on more private message streams when it comes time to plan the actualities of travel. (Saltman 2014)

Consequently, ISIS has recruited several thousand Western-based Islamic fighters. For instance, in March 2015, three British Muslim teenage girls, Kadiza Sultana, Amira Abase and Shamima Begum, were groomed by ISIS through the social networks and subsequently fled to Syria. Such incidents have intensified government calls for Google, Facebook, YouTube and Twitter to take down ISIS-related uploads or posts from their sites. These demands have placed the social media organisations in a problematic position. On the one hand, they do not want to be purveyors of online terrorist content. However, such self-censorship undermines their credibility with the users who have valued them as 'free media' platforms upon which they can post, upload or disseminate their private communications.

THE ONLINE BATTLEGROUND: THE REMOVAL OF ISIS' SOCIAL NETWORK ACCOUNTS AND ITS RESPONSE

With these events, both Facebook and Twitter have developed stronger guidelines concerning the nature of violent material put on their platforms. In December 2014, Facebook linked warnings to the ISIS videos posted to its site, stating that their content might 'shock, offend and upset'. These alerts prevented the videos from being automatically played on its uploaded feeds. One of the first ISIS posts affected involved the shooting of the French policeman Ahmed Merabet during the January 2015 Charlie Hebdo attacks. Thus, Facebook has attempted to tread a fine line between protecting its users from accessing offensive content while retaining their rights of free expression.

Twitter's terms of service have banned 'direct, specific threats of violence against others', and it followed YouTube by closing down several ISIS-related accounts. In July 2014, one of the company's UK executives, Sinead McSweeney, informed a House of Lords committee that the microblogging site had employed over 100 people on a 24/7 basis to examine posts associated with ISIS. And in September 2014, Twitter removed the replacement account run by a UK-based ISIS supporter, Rayat al-Tawheed, within minutes of its relaunch (Hern 2015).

On 10 February 2015, in the wake of the Charlie Hebdo killings, the infamous hacktivist group 'Anonymous' announced on its public repository website Pastebin that it had declared war on ISIS (Saul 2015), and that it was conducting 'Operation ISIS' to treat the terrorist posts and uploads like a virus. It subsequently maintained that it had 'exposed or destroyed' 800 Twitter accounts, 12 Facebook pages and over 50 e-mail addresses that it believed were linked to ISIS. In turn, on 18 March 2015, Anonymous announced it had delivered to Twitter a list of accounts which 'named and shamed' approximately 9200 ISIS members. (Hamill 2015)

However, it was later reported that the US security agencies had argued that the actions of Anonymous had hampered its war against the terrorists. In particular, the 'spooks' contended that ISIS' social media profiles provided the best way to gather intelligence, and that they had hoped to gain a greater amount of data. They declared, 'All Anonymous has done is make ISIS more tech-savvy and cut off the information supply' (Hamill 2015). It was also suggested that Anonymous' attempts to remove ISIS from the Internet would only serve to drive it further underground. Several subsequent reports commented that ISIS either had developed its own version of Facebook—'5elafabook'—or had retreated into the 'dark web', the area of the Internet where content cannot be retrieved through search engines. By using untraceable networks, the deep web conceals its users' locations from the policing agencies who conduct network traffic analysis. This has led to fears that the dark web has become the perfect place for undetected terrorists to coordinate with one another. Moreover, in response to the attempts to remove it from the social media, ISIS issued its online opponents the following vitriolic riposte:

> You started this failed war....We told you from the beginning it's not your war, but you didn't get it and kept closing our accounts on Twitter, but we always come back. But when our lions come and take your breath, you will never come back to life. (Hern 2015)

CONCLUSION

This chapter has considered the economic, political and cultural factors which have shaped the development of the information and communications sectors within the Middle East. Throughout the MENA region, there has been significant growth in digital penetration. In particular, a major take-up of broadband Internet and mobile telephony services has occurred within the Gulf States, Saudi Arabia and Egypt, which is reflected in the region's expansion in its usage of Facebook, Twitter and YouTube, and the demands to use these social media platforms for commercial exploitation. This has been accompanied by a greater degree of political engagement among social network users in Iran, Turkey, Israel and

Palestine, along with the countries (Tunisia, Egypt, Libya and Syria) involved in the Arab Spring.

Yet the opportunities for free forms of online expression have been limited in these states by retrogressive laws and censorship. In response to grass-roots protest movements, both Iranian and Turkish authorities have employed repressive measures to stem the flow of Internet traffic, temporarily shutting down the social networks. Such concerns have led to major debate about whether social media can indeed overcome the perceived democratic deficits within these societies. The social networks have also been accused of perpetuating the propaganda war that has dominated the Israeli–Palestinian dispute. The 2014 Israeli military incursion into Gaza was accompanied by extensive use of tweets, hashtags, re-tweets, Facebook likes and blog posts by both the IDF and Hamas. Where once the social networks held the promise for building consensus to achieve conflict resolution, in reality they have contributed to the formation of echo chambers of prejudiced opinion, exacerbating the division between the diametrically opposed sides.

Moreover, the social networks have been instrumental in the transformation of ISIS from a fractured and disintegrating group of renegades into a populist movement. This extremist organisation has effectively used these new information resources to amplify its impact by husbanding its fundamentalist ideologies to spread fear throughout the region and to attract international support. ISIS' software engineers have demonstrated a comprehensive understanding of the viral capacity of social media. Through their use of online applications, they have trended messages across the Twittersphere to gain further traction. In turn, ISIS' online presence has led the social networks to remove a large number of ISIS-related Twitter and Facebook accounts, and has prompted the hacktivist group Anonymous to declare an information war on the terrorists. However, some have suggested that the development of the dark net will enable ISIS' information-savvy leaders to find potentially untraceable ways to circumvent the legal and institutional controls of the past.[1]

Therefore, the potential of social media to aid democratic reform within the MENA countries has been extolled and castigated in equal measure. For many, the optimism associated with the 2011 Arab Spring

---

[1] On 22 June 2015, it was announced that a Europe-wide policing initiative (Europol) would be formed to track and close down social media accounts associated with ISIS, as another 5000 European citizens had been recruited online.

has evaporated, as expectations have devolved into the far more unpredictable outcomes of the 'Summer of Reckoning'. Consequently, it remains to be seen whether the influence of social networking sites will ultimately prove to be beneficial or detrimental in extending the democratic rights of Middle Eastern citizens throughout the region.

BIBLIOGRAPHY

Arab Social Media Report. 2012. "Social Media in the Arab World: Influencing Societal and Cultural Change?" Dubai School of Government's Governance and Innovation Program. http://www.arabsocialmediareport.com/UserManagement/PDF/ASMR%204%20updated%2029%2008%2012.pdf (accessed March 21, 2015).

Arab Social Media Report. 2014. "Arab Social Media Report." Dubai School of Government's Governance and Innovation Program. http://www.arabsocialmediareport.com/home/index.aspx> (accessed March 21, 2015).

Berger, J.M., and J. Morgan. 2015. "The ISIS Twitter Census Defining and Describing the Population of ISIS Supporters on Twitter." *Centre for Middle East Policy at the Brooking Institute.* The Brookings Project on US Relations with the Islamic World Analysis Paper No. 20, March 2015. http://www.brookings.edu/~/media/research/files/papers/2015/03/isis-twitter-census-berger-morgan/isis_twitter_census_berger_morgan.pdf (accessed March 21, 2015).

Channel Four News. 2014. "#Jihad: How Isis is Using Social Media to Win Support." *Channel Four News.* June 17. http://www.channel4.com/news/isis-iraq-social-media-jihad-billion-campaign-recruit-video (accessed March 21, 2015).

Cockburn, P. 2015. *The Rise of Islamic State: ISIS and the New Sunni Revolution.* London: Verso.

El-Gendi, Y. 2014. "Social Media and Economic Development in Egypt." *Middle East Institute.* http://www.mei.edu/content/article/social-media-and-economic-development-egypt (accessed March 21, 2015).

Elzeini, S. 2015. "Social Media's Economic Revolution in the Gulf." *Foreign Policy Association.* http://foreignpolicyblogs.com/2015/02/09/social-medias-economic-revolution-in-the-gulf/ (accessed March 21, 2015).

Frenkel, S., and M. Atef. 2014. "Exclusive: Egypt Beings Surveillance of Facebook, Twitter, and Skype on Unprecedented Scale.' *BuzzFeed.* September 17. http://www.buzzfeed.com/sheerafrenkel/egypt-begins-surveillance-of-facebook-twitter-and-skype-on-u#2apm87r. (accessed March 21, 2015).

Goldman, L. 2014. "The Gaza War has Done Terrible Things to Israeli Society." *The Globe and the Mail.* July 24. http://www.theglobeandmail.com/globe-debate/the-gaza-war-has-done-terrible-things-to-israeli-society/article19737911/ (accessed March 21, 2015).

Hamill, J. 2015. "Spooks Left 'furious' After Anonymous Hacktivists Name and Shame 9,200 ISIS Supporters, Sources Claim." *The Daily Mirror.* March 18. http://www.mirror.co.uk/news/technology-science/technology/spooks-left-furious-after-anonymous-5355738 (accessed March 21, 2015).

Haynes, J. 2015. "Religion and International Conflict". In *International Security Studies in Theory and Practice,* ed. P. Hough, S. Malik, A. Moran, and B. Pilbeam. London: Routledge.

Hern, A. 2015. "Isis Threatens Twitter Employees Over Blocked Accounts: Terror Group Supporters Threaten Social Network, As Well as Co-founder Jack Dorsey Specifically." *The Guardian.* March 2. http://www.theguardian.com/technology/2015/mar/02/isis-threatens-twitter-employees-over-blocked-accounts-jack-dorsey (accessed March 21, 2015).

Hirschauge, O., N. Casey and L. Fleisher. 2014. "Israel and Hamas Take Fight to Social Media." *Wall Street Journal.* July 23. http://www.wsj.com/articles/israel-and-hamas-take-fight-to-social-media-1406130179 (accessed March 21, 2015).

Huntington, S.P. 1996. *The Clash of Civilizations and the Remaking of World Order.* New York: Simon & Schuster.

Hutchinson, D. 2007. "The EU and the Press: Policy or Non-policy?" In *Media and Cultural Policy in the European Union,* ed. K. Sarikakis, 24 European Media studies.

Hutchinson, S. 2013. "Social Media Plays Major Role in Turkey Protests." *BBC News.* June 4. http://www.bbc.co.uk/news/world-europe-22772352 (accessed March 21, 2015).

Jenkins, B.M. 2011. *Stray Dogs and Virtual Armies Radicalization and Recruitment to Jihadist Terrorism in the United States Since 9/11.* Santa Monica: Rand Corporation.

Kellner, D. 2011. *Media Spectacle and Insurrection 2011: From Arab Uprisings to Occupy Everywhere.* London: Bloomsbury.

Kerr, D. 2014. "How Israel and Hamas Weaponized Social Media: More Militaries and Armed Groups are Using Social Media as a Weapon of War—But When Ground Skirmishes are Mirrored by Cyber-social Battles, Managing the Message Can Get Messy." *C/Net.* January 13. http://www.cnet.com/uk/news/how-israel-and-hamas-weaponized-social-media/ (accessed March 21, 2015).

Khan, F. 2014. "90 Million Videos Viewed Daily on YouTube in KSA." *Arab News.* March 7. http://www.arabnews.com/news/536196 (accessed March 21, 2015).

Letsch, C. 2013. "Social Media and Opposition to Blame for Protests, says Turkish PM", *The Guardian.* June 3. http://www.theguardian.com/world/2013/jun/02/turkish-protesters-control-istanbul-square (accessed March 21, 2015).

Lloyd, J. 2014. "Media and the Middle East." *BBC Radio 4.* September 18. http://www.bbc.co.uk/programmes/b04gnhnv (accessed March 21, 2015).

Louw, P.E. 2005. *The Media and Political Process*. London: Sage Publications.

Mason P. 2012. *Why It's Kicking Off Everywhere: The New Global Revolutions*. London: Verso Press.

Mason, P. 2013. "Analysis: The Hopes that Blaze in Istanbul". *BBC News,* June 3. http://www.bbc.co.uk/news/world-europe-22752121 (accessed March 21, 2015).

Mason, P. 2014a. "Seven Reasons Why Turkey's Twitter Ban Matters to the World." *Channel Four News*. March 21.http://blogs.channel4.com/paul-mason-blog/reasons-turkeys-twitter-ban-matters-world/587 (accessed March 21, 2015).

Mason, P. 2014b. "Gaza Conflict: An Israeli Soldier's Question." *Channel Four News*. July 27. http://blogs.channel4.com/paul-mason-blog/gaza-conflict-israeli-soldiers-question/1364 (accessed March 21, 2015).

McElroy, D. 2014. "Iraq Crisis: Isis Cracks a Savvy Social Media Advance", *The Daily Telegraph*. June 17. http://www.faceiraq.com/inews.php?id=2812101 (accessed March 21, 2015).

The Middle East Media Research Institute (MEMRI). 2014. "Hamas Interior Ministry To Social Media Activists: Always Call The Dead 'Innocent Civilians'; Don't Post Photos Of Rockets Being Fired From Civilian Population Centers' MEMRI Special Dispatch No. 5799. July 17. http://www.memri.org/report/en/print8076.htm#_edn1 (accessed March 21, 2015).

Moran, A. 2015. "Terrorism". In *International Security Studies in Theory and Practice*, ed. P. Hough, S. Malik, A. Moran, and B. Pilbeam. London: Routledge.

Northwestern University in Qatar. 2014. *Entertainment Media use in the Middle East A Six-Nation Survey by Northwestern University in Qatar in Partnership with Doha Film Institute*. http://mideastmedia.org (accessed March 21, 2015).

Radcliffe, D. 2015. *Social Media in the Middle East: The Story of 2014*. Cardiff School of Journalism, Media and Cultural Studies. https://www.academia.edu/10113094/Social_Media_in_the_Middle_East_The_Story_of_2014 (accessed March 21, 2015).

Rawlinson, D. 2014. "Turkey Blocks Use of Twitter After Prime Minister Attacks Social Media Site." *The Guardian*. March 21. http://www.theguardian.com/world/2014/mar/21/turkey-blocks-twitter-prime-minister (accessed March 21, 2015).

Saltman, E. 2014. "ISIS Have Used Social Media to Wreak Havoc in Iraq and Syria, But We Can Stop Them: The Group's Expert Use of Facebook and Twitter has Helped Fuel Their Support." *The Independent*. June 17. http://www.independent.co.uk/voices/comment/isis-have-used-social-media-to-wreak-havoc-in-iraq-and-syria-but-we-can-stop-them-9542838.html (accessed March 21, 2015).

Saul, H. 2015. "Operation Isis: Anonymous Vows to Take Down Accounts Associated with Extremist Group." *The Independent.* February 10. http://timesofindia.indiatimes.com/world/middle-east/Operation-Isis-Anonymous-vows-to-take-down-accounts-associated-with-extremist-group/article-show/46190594.cms (accessed March 21, 2015).

Sherwood, H. 2014. "Israel and Hamas Clash on Social Media." *The Guardian.* July 16. http://www.theguardian.com/world/2014/jul/16/israel-hamas-clash-social-media (accessed March 21, 2015).

Social Media and Political Participation Lab. 2013. *SMaPPDATAREPORT: A Breakout Role for Twitter? The Role of Social Media in the Turkish Protests.* New York University. http://smapp.nyu.edu/reports/turkey_data_report.pdf (accessed March 21, 2015).

Sreberny, A., and G. Khiabany. 2010. *Blogistan: The Internet and Politics in Iran.* London: I.B. Tauris.

Stein, R. 2014. "How Israel Militarized the Social Media." *Mondoweiss: The War of Ideas in the Middle East.* July 24. http://mondoweiss.net/2014/07/israel-militarized-social (accessed March 21, 2015).

Ungerleider, N. 2012. "Inside the Israeli Military's Social Media Squad." *Fast Company.* November 19. http://www.fastcompany.com/3003305/inside-israeli-militarys-social-media-squad (accessed March 21, 2015).

Wheeler, D.L. 2009. "Working Around the State: Internet Use and Political Identity in the Arab world. In *The Routledge Handbook of Internet Politics,* ed. A. Chadwick and P.N. Howard. London: Routledge.

Woolf, N. 2015. "Fox News Site Embeds Unedited Isis Video Showing Brutal Murder of Jordanian Pilot." *The Guardian.* February 4. http://www.theguardian.com/media/2015/feb/04/fox-news-shows-isis-video-jordan-pilot (accessed March 21, 2015).

CHAPTER 12

Conclusion

Throughout the past two decades, the social media have been used by a wide range of global actors, including the international public, activists, governments, NGOs and the ICT industries. The networked community has grown at unprecedented levels, from millions in the early 1990s to billions, by the second decade of the twenty-first century, leading to a denser communications landscape, and one that is more accessible and more participatory and engaging, allowing for enhanced public speech and greater ability to undertake collective action. Over 60 % of people worldwide use social networks, with Brazil, Russia, India, Hong Kong, Japan, the USA and China among the most engaged countries. Online media tools such as text messaging, social networking and photo-sharing have given the public the means to coordinate rapid and massive political responses to governmental actions, thereby enhancing democracy and the public sphere. Social media have been instrumental in effecting regime change (such as the massive text message-led demonstrations against Philippine President Joseph Estrada in 2001), enabling individuals to freely access information (e.g., the ability to use Wikipedia and Google during the June 2009 uprising of the Iranian Green Movement) and in organising protests (including the 2011 Greek and Spanish demonstrations against anti-austerity measures). Online platforms have been widely used in countries such as South Korea to mobilise voters in party campaigns and public debates, and they became a lifeline for many people in Japan following the earthquake, tsunami

© The Editor(s) (if applicable) and The Author(s) 2016   285
P. Iosifidis, M. Wheeler, *Public Spheres and Mediated
Social Networks in the Western Context and Beyond*,
DOI 10.1057/978-1-137-41030-6_12

and nuclear disasters of 2011. Social media-driven protests in Brazil during the FIFA World Cup in the summer of 2014 challenged the pro-government bias of the traditional media and allowed citizens to present their own version of events.

Yet despite these victories, in equally many cases, the social media have had little effect in advancing public dialogue and shifting national politics. The demise of the Arab uprisings and the ongoing censorship employed by autocratic Arab governments proved that these states remained vigilant in their efforts to control online forums. Some have expressed concerns that the social media outlets have enabled a brutal counter-revolutionary upsurge spearheaded by anti-democratic terrorist forces. The recent revelations of US government surveillance of both its own citizens and those abroad have cast doubt on arguments of enhanced electronic agoras within the public. In some cases, social media tools have enabled authoritarian states to effect increasingly sophisticated means of monitoring citizen behaviour. The repressive regimes of China and Russia provide clear examples of government measures to counter the explosive growth of the social media among consumers by limiting citizens' use of online activity as a political tool for. With Russia, we have shown that much of the democratising potential of social media has been limited by the government's almost complete control of the national information sphere. At the same time, in China, projects such as the Great Firewall, designed to keep out 'undesirable' foreign websites like Facebook, Twitter and YouTube, and the Golden Shield have demonstrated the explicit exercise of state power within the online sphere by Chinese authorities. In effect, then, the democratising potential of the social media must be assessed within the constraints of national political systems.

With this in mind, the present study supports Evgeny Morozov's contention that the social networks are resources that both revolutionaries and authoritarian governments can deploy for their own purposes (Morozov 2012). In a progressive sense, the social media no longer merely provide conduits for the exchange of personal messages with friends or loved ones, for these messages are now shared among the global public and are often journalistic in nature, providing a conduit for news-sharing and news-gathering. However, these networks may also be used to the detriment of society, for entrenching dictators and threatening dissidents, making the promotion of democracy more difficult. Actions on social networks can also be enormously damaging, and generally speaking, once the genie is out of the bottle, it is impossible to put it back in.

In this volume, we have addressed policy and regulatory issues associated with the social media and identified key policy variables within national governments. We contend that the articulation of a public interest framework in a regime of social media governance must consider both traditional concerns (such as access, media plurality and freedom of expression) and emerging concerns. These new concerns include privacy and intellectual property rights, transparency around data processing and the protection of users from harmful content (violence, sexually explicit content, hate speech and harassment). While some of these are not new, specific points of focus in the social media era include issues regarding the accessing and utilisation of user data by social media platforms, typically for advertising and marketing purposes and/or insurance companies. Content ownership, especially the application of copyright laws to the practices by which social media facilitate the production and dissemination of user-generated content, may also involve the integration of copyright material. The protection of minors has gained renewed interest within the online world, as attempts are made to define enhanced safeguards for user data, the vulnerability of minors to sexual predators, and their exposure to hate speech and online bullying.

The core issue discussed in the book is whether the social media do, in fact, provide new forms of participatory democracy, and result in an enhanced public sphere. It is often assumed that social media applications such as Facebook, Twitter and YouTube are empowering people and rendering political processes more democratic. However, we have shown that such optimistic claims of democratisation and empowerment made possible by social media should be treated with caution, for they can be viewed as idealistic and representative of technological determinism. The introductory chapter thus intentionally took a more circumspect and open-ended approach, offering a balanced view of both sceptics and optimists. The following two sections tested these concepts against empirical material drawn from the Global North and South. The former explored the relationship between online mobilisation and policy change among mature, liberal democracies, while the latter shifted the focus from the Western world to non-Western, developing countries and authoritarian regimes. It is our firm belief that the focus on both mature and emerging markets allows for comparative analysis and strengthens the international scope of the project. In this sense, it contributes to the burgeoning literature on social media, democracy and the public sphere.

BIBLIOGRAPHY

Morozov E. 2012. The Net Delusion: The Dark Side of Internet Freedom. *Public Affairs.*

INDEX

© The Editor(s) (if applicable) and The Author(s) 2016   289
P. Iosifidis, M. Wheeler, *Public Spheres and Mediated*
Social Networks in the Western Context and Beyond,
DOI 10.1057/978-1-137-41030-6